# Patriots and Propaganda

# CHINA AND THE WEST IN THE MODERN WORLD

## William Christie and Sophie Loy-Wilson, Series Editors

China and the West in the Modern World publishes original, peer-reviewed research on relations between China and the West from the accession of the Manchu Qing dynasty in 1644 to the present. The series brings into play different national and disciplinary perspectives to achieve a more thorough and cross-culturally nuanced understanding of the political, economic, and cultural background to the negotiations and realignments currently underway between China and Western nations.

*The Poison of Polygamy*
Wong Shee Ping, translated by Ely Finch

*South Flows the Pearl: Chinese Australian Voices*
Mavis Gock Yen, edited by Siaoman Yen and Richard Horsburgh

*Tribute and Trade: China and Global Modernity, 1784–1935*
Edited by William Christie, Angela Dunstan and Q.S. Tong

*Made in Chinatown: Chinese Australian Furniture Factories, 1880–1930*
Peter Charles Gibson

*The Flip Side: Old China Hands and the American Popular Imagination, 1935–1985*
Stuart Christie

*In the Face of Diversity: A History of Chinese Australian Community Organisations, 1970s–2020s*
Nathan D. Gardner Molina

*Patriots and Propaganda: Chinese Australians and the Politics of Loyalty, 1930s–1940s*
Bolin Hu

# Patriots and Propaganda

## Chinese Australians and the Politics of Loyalty, 1930s–1940s

Bolin Hu

SYDNEY UNIVERSITY PRESS

**Reproduction and communication for other purposes**
Except as permitted under Australia's *Copyright Act 1968*, no part of this edition may be reproduced, stored in a retrieval system, or communicated in any form or by any means without prior written permission. All requests for reproduction or communication should be made to Sydney University Press at the address below:

Sydney University Press
Gadigal Country
Fisher Library F03
University of Sydney NSW 2006
Australia
sup.info@sydney.edu.au
sydneyuniversitypress.com

A catalogue record for this book is available from the National Library of Australia.

ISBN 9781761540233 paperback
ISBN 9781761540424 hardback

ISBN 9781761540240 epub
ISBN 9781761540226 pdf

Cover image: Chinese Ministry of Information, Australian Office, Sydney (1946). *A China Pictorial.* http://nla.gov.au/nla.obj-3089050109.

We acknowledge the traditional owners of the lands on which Sydney University Press is located, the Gadigal people of the Eora Nation, and we pay our respects to the knowledge embedded forever within the Aboriginal Custodianship of Country.

For my parents, Hu Yanchu and Lin Bin, with love

# Contents

# Author note

The anglicisation of the Chinese language across the 20th century has been used where possible in this book, including names and cities. These spellings were in common usage and thus mirror the context of the time. When such anglicisation has so far not been identified, pinyin based on their Mandarin pronunciation is employed. For personal names rendered in pinyin, the customary Chinese sequence of surname preceding given name is observed. In both anglicised and pinyin forms, the corresponding traditional Chinese characters are supplied where they have been identified. To ensure consistency, traditional Chinese characters are used throughout the book for all Chinese-language primary and secondary sources, including those originally published in simplified Chinese.

# Acknowledgements

Thinking is a pleasure, but writing is suffering. A PhD, as the joke goes, is short for Permanent Head Damage – and this book is the by-product of such an affliction. Born from a doctoral thesis hammered out in the wake of that cerebral ordeal, its arrival in published form owes everything to the unwavering support, generosity, and belief of many individuals and institutions, to whom I am more indebted than words can repay.

I would like to express my heartfelt thanks to Malcolm Campbell and Paul Clark, whose patient mentorship and generous engagement provided strength and clarity in moments of doubt. They offered thoughtful guidance throughout the many iterations of my thesis and believed in its potential, even when I struggled to see it myself. David Walker's deep insights into the history of Australia–Asia relations, coupled with his unwavering encouragement, gave me the confidence to keep moving forward. I am equally grateful to Hu Dekun and Xu Youzhen for their firm support, which served as an anchor during my most uncertain stages. The scholarship of Wei Shuge, particularly on Chinese propaganda, was a great source of inspiration, and I remain indebted to her and Brian Moloughney for their incisive and thoughtful feedback. Portions of this book were previously published in the *Journal of Chinese Overseas* and *Australian Historical Studies* – I thank the editors, especially Tim Rowse, and the anonymous reviewers whose feedback helped shape these chapters into their present form.

This book has also grown within a rich and generous community of scholars and peers. Their reflections, critical questions, and generous encouragement have helped shape both the content and the voice of this work. I extend my warmest thanks to Michael Williams, Kate Bagnall, Shan Windscript, Jon Piccini, Gwyn McClelland, and Duncan Campbell, all of whom left meaningful traces in different chapters. I also wish to thank the publisher's anonymous reviewers, as well as the editors and proofreaders – Naomi van Groll, Susan Keogh, Rebecca Hamilton, and William Christie – for their valuable suggestions and meticulous attention to detail. I am grateful to Mei-fen Kuo for her guidance in navigating the archival landscape surrounding the Australian Kuomintang. Alan Baumler generously shared his insights into Chinese propaganda in the Americas. My sincere thanks also go to Julia Martínez, who helped connect me with Glenn Mar and Gordon Mar, whose support was truly indispensable. Peter Gibson kindly shared his thoughts on my book proposal with Sydney University Press. I would also like to acknowledge Jennifer Frost, Paul Taillon, Rosalind Henshaw, Josanne Blyth, and the other staff of the History Department at the University of Auckland for providing an intellectually stimulating and nurturing academic environment.

Institutional support played a foundational role in making this book possible. The University of Auckland provided not only an academic home but also a refuge during a formative and demanding period in my life. I am grateful to the China Scholarship Council, whose support relieved the financial burdens of my PhD study. I am also thankful to the National Archives of Australia for awarding a scholarship that allowed me to continue archival research during the isolating days of the COVID-19 pandemic. I benefited immensely from the exchange of ideas within academic communities, including the Australian Historical Association, Dragon Tails Committee, New Zealand Asian Studies Society, International Australian Studies Association, Chinese Studies Association of Australia, New Zealand Historical Association, and the International History of East Asia Seminar Committee at Oxford.

As a study grounded in the histories of China and Australia, this book would not exist without the dedicated work of archivists, librarians, and staff across many institutions. I would like to express sincere thanks to the National Archives of Australia, National Library of Australia, Second Historical Archives of China, Academia Historica, State Library of New South Wales, State Archives and Records of New South Wales, State Library of Victoria, Noel Butlin Archives Centre at the Australian National University, Sir Louis Matheson Library at Monash University, and the University of Melbourne Archives. I am also grateful to the Australian Department of Foreign Affairs and Trade Library for their generous contribution to my research.

The process of rewriting this book began during my time working in Wellington, New Zealand. I am especially thankful to Nandini Jagdeesh Kannan for her thoughtful leadership and to my colleagues, who created a workplace that was both supportive and collegial. The final stages of revision took place at the Research Institute of Global Chinese and Area Studies at Huaqiao University, where I was given the time and resources to focus fully on completing the manuscript. My sincere thanks to Wu Xiaoan, Li Zuojie, and Zheng Wenbiao for their steadfast support. I also deeply appreciated the academic exchange with colleagues from varied research backgrounds, particularly Pang Koon Kein, Zhu Yali, Huang Ming-Hui, Lee Pui Tak, Liu Juntao, and Li Meng. Financial support from the Huaqiao University Early Career Researcher Grant (23SKBS021) and the 2024 Australian Studies in China Programme from the Foundation for Australian Studies in China removed the anxiety that often shadows academic labour.

Some debts stretch far back. I am forever thankful to my high school teachers who nurtured my love for history at a time when the subject was being sidelined in China's examination-driven system. Their quiet encouragement gave me the confidence to pursue a path that was neither easy nor obvious. I would like to especially thank Dong Xiuying, Xiong Hai, Li Ping, Yu Ping, and Wu Yanli for their early and enduring support.

Friendship has been a guiding light throughout this journey. Special thanks to Tong Xiangwei, a loyal companion and welcoming host in both Wuhan and Sydney for over seventeen years. His wife, Xing Mengxi, deserves culinary accolades – her mastery of both Chinese and

Western cuisines has turned many meals into edible poetry. Though on different life paths, Lian Zhenzhen has remained a true friend, and I was honoured to help name his son, Lian Yicheng, and become his godfather. Chen Jian, Wang Yang, Zhang Jiachi, Yu Zhimiao and Lu Kai have provided lasting friendship and support. I fondly remember Zhao Chunguang and Jiang Junzhiwei for their companionship in Canberra. Ban Xiaojie offered invaluable guidance in navigating archives related to Kuomintang international propaganda. I would also like to thank Peng Dinan, Shen Yusu, Hong Lingyan, Liu Yuxuan, Liang Xiaodong and Chen Shuxian for their kindness and hospitality. Liu Heng and Gong Dasong gave thoughtful advice regarding academic careers in China. In Auckland, I received unshakable endorsement from Xu Miao. I am also grateful for the friendship of Liu Bolun and Cao Zhenpeng, whose company made the long journey of doctoral study more bearable. Mark Roman and Ian Watt offered both encouragement and friendship over many shared meals and conversations. Tim Atkin and Jesser Susi have been enduring companions, and I thank Amy Huang, Andy Ren, and their dog Boysen for their kindness and support during a critical time.

I am profoundly grateful to my family. My grandfather and uncle first sparked my interest in history, transforming what might have seemed distant or dry into something deeply engaging and alive. Their knowledge and encouragement laid the foundation for my scholarly path. My parents have been unwavering in their support, never doubting my commitment to history even when the road ahead was unclear. Their belief in me has been the source of my strength. And finally, to my partner, Zhao Yuanhui – thank you for your patience, care, and quiet strength, which have sustained me throughout this journey and beyond.

Above all, the original thesis was written under the shadow of the COVID-19 pandemic, which first emerged in my hometown of Wuhan. The memory of the uncertainty, fear, and sorrow of that time deeply affected me and still is raw. I wish to express my deepest appreciation to those who stood by Wuhan, and I honour the memory of those we lost.

# List of figures

# Introduction

At the close of World War II in 1945, the Australian headquarters of the Kuomintang (國民黨, Chinese Nationalist Party) in Sydney published a remarkable book, a mosaic of contributions from elated Chinese and Australians, spanning a diverse array of political ideologies and social backgrounds. *A Book to Commemorate a Common Victory* hailed China's wartime contributions, lauded the bright future of Sino-Australian relations, and celebrated the joint victories in China's War of Resistance (1931–45) and the Pacific War (1941–45).[1] This collective commemoration, an anomaly in the fraught history of relations between China and Australia, marked an unprecedented moment of harmonious solidarity – one that transcended political rifts, racial divisions, and class distinctions. It was, without a doubt, the rarest of breakthroughs in the history of the Sino-Australian relationship since the colonial and imperial eras. Yet, for all the jubilation, China during World War II is often framed as a "forgotten ally". History remembers China and Australia as distant allies in the struggle against Japan, who interacted through third parties and never truly grasped each other's strategic value nor expected each other's help.[2] But this book tells a different story – one that rewrites this

---

1    Yuan 1945.

1

narrative of distant allies by placing a spotlight on the role of Chinese propaganda, or *xuanchuan* (宣傳), in Australia.

This book explores the complex dynamics between China, Australia, and the Chinese diaspora in the 1930s and 1940s, focusing on Chinese propaganda in Australia, which was significantly shaped by Chinese Australians and their diasporic experiences and identities. It is a study of Chinese efforts to make their voices heard in Australia during China's War of Resistance and to forge a close China–Australia relationship, effectively challenging the conventional view of China and Australia as allies in name only. It argues that the relationship was not just shaped by war exigency and racial solidarity against a common enemy – Japan – but by the nuanced and evolving landscape of Chinese propaganda efforts in Australia. These endeavours were deeply intertwined with the Chinese Australian diaspora, drawing on their complex experiences and identities. The resulting tripartite relationship between China, Australia and diasporic Chinese was far more intricate than the simplistic solidarity portrayed in the 1945 publication. It was one of contested narratives, competing agendas and constant collaboration. *Patriots and Propaganda* thus expands the long-term focus on the great powers and their connections with less prominent nations and delves into the often-overlooked dimension of how these two geographically distant, relatively weak nations forged a much closer but also nuanced and tangled bond than is typically acknowledged.[3]

## The Chinese diaspora in Australia

The history of Chinese Australians has long been written predominantly as a narrative of race relations, framed against the

---

2   For China as a forgotten ally, see Mitter 2013. For the narratives of distant allies, see Albinski 1965; Andrews 1985; Stevens 2005. For similar descriptions applied to the wartime Canada–Australia relationship, see Hilliker 1984.

3   For research on wartime major powers and their relationship with the less prominent, see Beaumont 1996; Catherwood 2003; Day 1992; Saunders 1997; Stoler 2000; Todman 2020; Vehviläinen 2002.

backdrop of the racialised immigration regime commonly known as the White Australia policy. Early and some continuing scholarship has tended to dichotomise the experience of ethnic Chinese and white Australians, focusing heavily on immigration controls and the policing of racial boundaries.[4] The story of Chinese Australians, in this framing, has often been filtered through the lens of White Australia, with racial relations as its dominant motif.[5]

However, following Jennifer Cushman's call to situate Chinese Australians on their own terms within the Australian context,[6] a new wave of research has broadened and deepened the field. Recent studies have moved beyond the simplistic binary of oppressor and oppressed, introducing transnational perspectives that foreground the agency and complexity of diasporic Chinese experiences. Historians such as John Fitzgerald and Mei-fen Kuo have argued that Chinese Australians actively negotiated racial boundaries, deploying their own cultural resources and diasporic identities – patriotic devotion that was no less sincere than that professed by their white Australian counterparts.[7] This has been strengthened by a gendered dimension, deftly excavated by scholars such as Kate Bagnall, Julia Martínez and Alanna Kamp, who illuminate how diasporic Chinese women navigated the porous borders of inclusion and exclusion by White Australia. Through voluntary associations, sociability, and the fabric of family life, these women asserted agency in spaces less visible.[8] Meanwhile, Chinese Australians across a variety of professions – market gardeners, shopkeepers, cabinet-makers – as revealed by researchers, including Sophie Loy-Wilson and Peter Gibson, played an active role in reshaping the socio-economic landscape of White Australia.[9]

Collectively, these studies dismantle the enduring caricature of Chinese Australians as passive subjects and expand the oversimplified interpretations of the White Australia policy. They reveal a landscape

---

4     Markus 1994; Price 1968; Williams 2021; Yarwood 2008.
5     Cronin 1982; Giese 1999; Huck 1968; Loh 1989; Yong 1977.
6     Cushman 1984, 101.
7     Couchman and Bagnall 2015; J. Fitzgerald 2007; Kuo 2013.
8     Bagnall 2011; Bagnall and Martínez 2021; Gassin 2021; Kamp 2022; Kuo 2018; 2024.
9     Boileau 2017; Gibson 2020; Gibson 2022; Loy-Wilson 2014.

of fluid, hybrid, and often blurred racial boundaries between ethnic Chinese and white Australians. Furthermore, they challenge the entrenched orthodoxy that the formation and consolidation of the nation-state served as the primary architect of human identity, solidarity, and loyalty in Australia.[10]

Parallel to the rethinking of Chinese Australian history has been a critical re-examination of the relationships between diasporic Chinese communities and their homeland. Traditional assumptions have often adopted a China-centred approach. Much of this scholarship focused either on the active participation of overseas Chinese in significant political events in China or on the sojourner narratives emerging from 19th-century settler colonies, often framed within contexts of racial confrontation.[11] Although earlier studies acknowledged a degree of ethnic heterogeneity in diasporic Chinese communities, they tended to imply a political and cultural homogeneity among the Chinese diasporas.

The emergence of transnational perspectives and methodologies attentive to diasporic agency on their own terms has significantly expanded existing understandings. By challenging a rigid nation-state framework, recent scholarship has revealed the fluidity and hybridity of diasporic Chinese identities and loyalties that were often independent from, and at times in tension with, those of the homeland.[12] While historians have increasingly rejected the simplified "impact–response" model to characterise the China–diasporic Chinese relationship, other studies continue to emphasise the coexistence of multiple overlapping layers of connection.[13] Together, these insights foreground the complexity and dynamism underpinning the interplay between China and Chinese overseas.

Researchers working from an Australian perspective have similarly broadened their analytical lens, moving beyond a narrow focus on racial confrontation to position White Australia within wider social

---

10  Gabaccia and Hoerder 2011, 8.
11  Godley 1981; Wang 1991; Yen 1976.
12  S. Fitzgerald 1996; Gao 2017; Jones 2005.
13  Austin 2020; Byrne, Ang and Mar 2023; Cheng 2022; Fitzgerald and Kuo 2017; Kuhn 2008; Lydon 1999; Williams 2018.

and political frameworks. Traditional approaches to Australia's engagement with China and Asia, which were heavily filtered through a Eurocentric perspective of cultural superiority, have been critically reassessed. Under a transnational Asia-Pacific framework, new scholarship has explored the mutual and evolving interactions between Australia and its Asian neighbours. Historians such as Lachlan Strahan and David Walker have highlighted the profound ways in which Australia's encounters with China and broader Asia shaped Australian cultural and national identity, revealing deep and longstanding connections across the region.[14] Meanwhile, scholars including Gregor Benton and Drew Cottle have exposed the multiple layers of collaboration between Chinese migrants and Australian leftist movements, particularly in the realm of cross-cultural labour activism.[15] In addition, displaced experiences of white Australians in Asia – including travellers, internees and expatriates – have been studied by researchers such as Joan Beaumont, Agnieszka Sobocinska, and Christina Twomey. Their work has further enriched the historiography of the relationship by offering new insights into how Australians understood and negotiated their interactions with Asia during periods of upheaval and transformation.[16]

*Patriots and Propaganda* continues these evolving discussions by adopting a broader analytical perspective that considers the complex interplay between China, Australia and the Chinese diaspora. This book demonstrates that the Chinese diaspora, though deeply engaged in both Chinese and Australian affairs, did not uniformly align with the national agendas of either state. At the same time, the actions of both Kuomintang China and White Australia reveal a complexity that destabilises the prevailing narratives that Australia was indifferent towards Chinese affairs, that China merely exploited overseas Chinese for political ends, and that China and Australia were distant allies. By foregrounding these dynamics, this work contributes a transnational Chinese perspective to the existing scholarship on wartime experiences

14    Strahan 1996; Walker 2012.
15    Benton 2007; Cottle 2003; Loy-Wilson 2011.
16    Bagnall 2015b; Beaumont 1988; Loy-Wilson 2017; Sobocinska 2014; Twomey 2007.

of countries like Australia, challenging nation-centric historiographies and revealing a more intricate web of interactions across national and diasporic spaces.

## Chinese propaganda in Australia

The strategic significance of propaganda in shaping both domestic and international affairs is well established. Contemporaries such as E.H. Carr understood its power as a "modern instrument of power over opinion".[17] Frederic Eggleston, Australia's first minister to China, echoed this sentiment, emphasising that propaganda, when used wisely, could be a highly effective tool.[18] Historians have extensively examined the role of propaganda in wartime, focusing largely on the major powers.[19] However, the use of propaganda was not the sole domain of great powers; less powerful nations like China also recognised its importance. In the Chinese context, propaganda was not seen negatively, as it often was (and still is) in the West, but rather as a tool for public education and the pursuit of national independence.[20]

Recent scholarship has challenged the perception that Chinese wartime propaganda was neither proactive nor effective, instead highlighting how China used it to mobilise domestic and international support to restore its sovereignty in the absence of military and economic might.[21] Indeed, China faced a formidable adversary when, in September 1931, the Japanese military detonated a section of the southern Manchurian railway at Mukden (奉天, now 沈陽) and blamed China for the incident. The incident marked the beginning of Japan's swift occupation of North-East China. Faced with overwhelming odds, the Chinese government in Nanking (南京), led by Chiang Kai-shek (蔣介

---

17  Carr 1939, 3–5.
18  Eggleston to Minister of External Affairs, 1944, A989, 1944/554/7/1, 184465, National Archives of Australia (NAA), Canberra.
19  Berkhoff 2012; Brooks 2007; Cole 1990; Cull 1995; Hench 2010; Jowett and O'Donnell 2015; Kushner 2006; Wilcox 2005.
20  Liu 2020, 129, 164, 167.
21  Baumler 2020; Shu 2015; Wei 2017; 陳建新 2006.

石 ), adopted a policy of "internal pacification before external resistance".[22] This approach, deeply contested within the Kuomintang and the country, aimed to avoid a direct confrontation with Japan while seeking assistance from stronger powers.[23] However, the global responses to China's plight were marked by apathy, as the major powers and those less prominent, like Australia, hoped to resolve the crisis without alienating Japan.[24] In this context, propaganda became indispensable to breaking through indifference in the West and procuring sympathy to stop Japan's invasion.

While scholarly attention has largely focused on Chinese propaganda directed towards major powers, the efforts undertaken in regions like Australia have been notably underexplored. Although Australia lacked the global influence of Britain or America, it occupied a unique position within China's strategic framework. As a key member of the British Empire, a "white cousin" to America, and a close commercial partner with Japan, Australia occupied a space neither central nor peripheral to China's interests. Securing Australian sympathy, therefore, could exert pressure on both Britain and the United States, while simultaneously undermining Japan's economic influence.

The Chinese propaganda experience in Australia, however, was distinct. In major powers, such as the United States, the Chinese government played a central role in propaganda campaigns.[25] In diasporic Chinese areas, like South-East Asia, local Kuomintang networks were crucial to the effort.[26] In Chinese treaty ports, non-state actors and their transnational media networks were vital.[27] But in Australia, Kuomintang China's presence was relatively weak. Moreover, the lack of intensive interracial collaboration between Chinese and non-Chinese communities meant that Chinese propaganda in Australia was largely driven by Chinese Australians themselves and drawn from their complex diasporic experiences and identities.

---

22    Boyle 1972, 27–32; So 2002, 213.
23    Taylor 2009, 97–137.
24    Andrews 1981, 307; Beaumont 1996, 26–53; Fairbank and Twitchett 2002, 502.
25    Daniels 1988, 197.
26    Wang 1991; Yen 2008; Yong and McKenna 1990.
27    Wei 2017, 6.

Chinese propaganda in Australia unfolded along two interconnected veins: the divided mobilisation of Chinese Australians between Kuomintang-centred patriotism and broader homeland-oriented patriotism, and their shared efforts in anti-Japanese propaganda aimed at garnering sympathy from white Australians. Given the limited influence of Kuomintang China in Australia and the diversity of diasporic identities among Chinese Australians, both the Nanking government and pro-Nanking Chinese residents made it a priority to secure loyalty from the diaspora in support of China's war effort and advanced official propaganda campaigns directed towards the white Australian public.

Chapter 1 explains how Kuomintang China sought to initiate patriotic mobilisation among Chinese Australians primarily through Chinese-language newspapers and schools. However, this mobilisation was neither homogeneous nor entirely subordinated to China's national agenda; rather, it intersected with the agency of Chinese Australians, who pursued priorities at times independent from Nanking's directives.

Nanking's efforts to cultivate loyalty and exert leadership over Chinese Australians also encountered fierce resistance, transforming official endeavours to unify the Chinese diaspora into open rupture and turmoil within the community. Much of the opposition to Nanking's initiatives stemmed from a rejection of Chinese patriotism under the party-state ideology of Kuomintang China. Despite Nanking's attempts to suppress these dissidents, most efforts proved ineffective, largely due to the reluctance of Australian authorities to intervene – especially when anti-Nanking Chinese framed their resistance through appeals to Australian democratic values.

Chapters 2 through 4 examine these bitter clashes between Nanking and its critics, revealing a contested vision of Chinese patriotism expressed through fierce journalistic battles, competing memorial services, and struggling fundraising activities. Temporary unity was achieved only after the outbreak of the full-scale war between Japan and China in 1937, yet even then, deep divisions persisted.

The intensification of the wars in China, Europe, and the Pacific led to the emergence of new Chinese Australian community leadership composed of individuals from diverse social, gendered, and political backgrounds. They reshaped the social and political landscapes within the community and, under the mounting exigencies of war, further fragmented the diaspora whose internal divisions, long smouldering beneath the surface, ultimately disrupted their fragile solidarity. Despite persistent tensions, collaboration in support of China's, and later Australia's, war efforts continued. Although Kuomintang China made renewed efforts to unify Chinese Australian communities and suppress internal dissent through the 1940s, these attempts were largely unsuccessful.

Chapter 5 presents case studies illustrating the rise of new community leadership, comprising Chinese women, leftists, and Australian-born Chinese. Their practices of Chinese patriotism and community leadership were profoundly shaped by their diasporic experiences and hybrid identities. Even as political disagreement hampered their efforts, this newly established community leadership forged an efficient fundraising web for China and Australia.

Simultaneously, Chinese Australians and Kuomintang China found themselves engaged in uneasy collaboration, working together on propaganda campaigns to procure Australian public sympathy and counter Japanese propaganda, which sought to justify Japan's aggression and foster goodwill with Australia. Both Chinese and Japanese propaganda machines operated at full throttle in an extremely competitive contest across Australian soil. Complicating the clash was the active participation of white Australians, whose motivations varied widely.

Chapter 6 examines the Chinese–Japanese propaganda contest within Australia, highlighting how each side mobilised its diasporic webs and transnational networks to maximise their reach. White Australians not only shaped but were also shaped by this propaganda contest through their proactive involvement, leading some to reconsider Australia's changing interests and position within the international order. In this context, White Australia became entangled in the politics of North-East Asia well before the outbreak of the Pacific War, largely through the shifting dynamics of its Asian communities.

Although Chinese propaganda relied heavily on deep cooperation between local Chinese authorities and the Chinese diaspora, central government-directed efforts were by no means absent. The escalation of China's War of Resistance saw the centralisation of China's international propaganda apparatus, while the Pacific War saw the rapid expansion of these official endeavours into Australia. Transnational channels formed by Chinese and non-Chinese Australians became critical conduits for propaganda materials entering Australia from China. Strategic efforts to shape the perceptions of Australian visitors to China were deployed to align them with China's political agenda.

Within Australia, propaganda networks were increasingly institutionalised and professionalised, marked by the establishment of a Chinese publicity office and the proliferation of pro-China lobbying organisations. Yet, despite the rising strength of official propaganda operations, much of this activity remained deeply embedded within diasporic Chinese networks that continued to bridge China and white Australian society. Chapter 7 will examine the emergence of official Chinese propaganda in Australia, tracing the shift in publicity narratives from exposing Japanese atrocities to promoting ideals of racial and national equality between China and Australia.

# 1
# Loyalty to Kuomintang China

Fully aware of the international indifference and the frustrating disparity of strength between China and Japan, Nanking attempted to solicit maximum support from Chinese people overseas, including those in Australia, for its war effort. But by the 1930s the Chinese Australian population's demography and political and cultural identification with China had undergone significant changes. The Chinese Australian population had plummeted dramatically from 38,258 in 1861 to 10,846 by 1933. It further reduced to 9,144 in 1947, about 41 per cent of whom were Australian-born, not counting those considered part or half-Chinese.[1] Their identities were more mixed than those of their predecessors: many pledged their exclusive loyalty and affiliation to Australia, not China; others continued to prioritise their homeland; and then there were those whose identity was more fluid and hybrid, between or beyond being Chinese and Australian.[2] The increasingly diverse affiliations and loyalties among Chinese Australians thus posed a challenge to the Kuomintang government in Nanking, which had to solicit support from the diaspora by asserting leadership over them and mobilising their loyalty.

---

1   Choi 1975, 22, 42, 47; Williams 2021a, 196.
2   S. Fitzgerald 1996, 171, 175; Giese 1997, 86, 150, 180–2, 192; Kennedy 2015;
    Ling 2001, 49; Loh 1989, 13–14, 26, 51, 68, 131; Shen 2001, 1–64.

This chapter delves into the endeavours undertaken by the local Chinese authorities and their advocates in Australia to mobilise the loyalties of local Chinese in order to secure their support for the Kuomintang government's pursuit of national salvation. Local Chinese-language newspapers sympathetic to Nanking from 1931 to 1937, the *Chinese Times* (民報) and the *Chinese Republic News* (民國報), attempted to galvanise Chinese Australian communities through their transnational networks. A resurgence in Chinese-language schools across Australia also saw attempts to elicit support through transnational educational programs.

## Chinese Times

Founded in Melbourne in 1902 and relocated to Sydney in 1922, the *Chinese Times* had been the Kuomintang's official Australian organ since 1919. Circulated within the South Pacific and to China,[3] the newspaper was sold at a cost-effective price for those readers earning a basic weekly wage of £2 2 shillings in 1907, with each copy at 5 pence, a half-year subscription at 11 shillings and 3 pence, and an annual subscription at £1 10 shillings.[4] The paper was the only one of its own kind in Australia to endure until 1950, after the Kuomintang lost the Chinese Civil War and withdrew to Taiwan.[5] It was also the only paper that included an English supplement page,[6] thanks to collaboration between local Chinese and white Australians, and the management of P.J. Leader, an Australian journalist.[7]

Being Kuomintang China's official mouthpiece, the *Chinese Times* foregrounded the party's authority. Not only was the newspaper's Chinese title inscribed in calligraphy by Sun Yat-sen (孫中山, the Father of Republican China), but Sun Yat-sen's Will (總理遺囑) was

---

3    陳志明 1935, 142.
4    *Chinese Times* 22 April 1933, 1, SP320/4, TA50/3673, 7846106, NAA; for the basic weekly wage, see https://tinyurl.com/mh6th6nm.
5    *Chinese Times* 1950, SP320/4, TA50/3673, 7846106, NAA.
6    Lowenthal 1937, 2.
7    Kuo and Brett 2013, 78.

also featured on the front page to establish a unique and prestigious position within Chinese Australian communities. This endorsement was reinforced by the paper's claimed aim to foster "the spirit of Nationalism among Chinese overseas".[8] As such, the *Chinese Times* was devoted to delivering political information, party ideology and news concerning China. The paper's editorials, usually less than 2,000 words, often dealt with Sun Yat-sen's "Three Principles of the People" (三民主義, Sanmin Zhuyi) and news primarily centred on China's resistance to Japan's aggression.

Trans-Pacific networks connected the paper to the broader world and collected news from China and abroad. Reports were harvested from news agencies, including the International News Agency, Overseas News Service, Kiu Fung News Agency and China News Agency, from papers like the *Ta Kung Pao* (大公報) and the *Kuo Min Yat Po* (國民日報) in Hong Kong, the *Sydney Morning Herald* and the *Daily Telegraph* in Australia, and from Mandarin broadcasts in Chungking (重慶), Kueiyang (貴陽), Shanghai (上海), Nanking and the United States.[9] The arrangement aimed to provide readers with a wide range of news coverage that offered more diverse perspectives than those typically found in white Australian newspapers.[10]

The Australian Kuomintang headquarters elected a board of five to seven members each year to manage the *Chinese Times*' operation.[11] The paper's editors were generally selected and appointed by Nanking and operated under the supervision of the Overseas Department (海外部) of the Kuomintang Central Executive Committee (國民黨中央執行委員會) to ensure the *Chinese Times* continually followed and efficiently communicated the Kuomintang's line, in contrast to the rest of the newspapers which made their own appointments. Five of the known eight editors in the 1930s were appointed, with the others sometimes positioned as caretakers until a new editor was chosen: Lau Tze Him (劉子謙, 1929–32), Chen

---

8    *Chinese Times* 22 April 1933, 1, SP320/4, TA50/3673, 7846106, NAA.
9    *Chinese Times* 1941, C320, C8, 1495438, NAA.
10   陳志明 1935, 140.
11   陳志明 1935, 139.

Chih-ming (陳志明, 1933–34), Mar Leong Wah (馬亮華) and Peter Lee Chut (李少勤) (both as caretakers, 1934–35), Wong Chih-hwa (王持華, 1935–37), Loh Kai-tze (駱介子, 1937–38), Lew Jang Lean (1938, caretaker), Loh Kai-tze (1938–41) and Yuan Chung-ming (袁中明, 1941–45). Yuan likely received assistance from three other editors during the early 1940s: Jong Ngock Bew (張嶽彪), See Ping and Lew Jang Lean (who also doubled as the secretary and the manager of the *Chinese Times*).[12] The last editor – Henry Ming Lai (余國樂) – ended his term in 1949.[13]

According to the *Tung Wah Times* (東華報), this policy of having editors appointed from China seemed practical in that the newspaper largely echoed Nanking's changing policy on Japan. Lau's strong anti-Japanese position shifted to the contrary and parroted Nanking's internal pacification before external resistance policy. Until Wong assumed the role, the paper's posture became more ambiguous, following Nanking's emphasis on "preparation before resistance".[14] Nevertheless, what the *Tung Wah Times* noted seemed problematic, probably because its fierce opposition to the *Chinese Times* twisted the latter's views (see Chapter 2). Written documents from Australian authorities indicate a different picture: namely, that the *Chinese Times* appeared to be consistently anti-Japanese. When China's War of Resistance against Japan (also known as the "Second Sino-Japanese War") escalated in 1935, the paper's opposition to Japan was so evident that it disturbed the Lyons government, threatening the revocation of permission for publication.[15]

---

12   Reports of F.J. Quinlan and Thos. V. Maher, 1932–1933, A1, 1933/307, 1123059; Reports of Chen Wei-ping, H.B. Cody, and Pao Chun-jien, 1936–1938, A433, 1950/2/6890, 3103597; Report of Yuan Chung-ming, 24 November 1941, C320, C8, 1495438; L.T. Gamble to the Boarding Inspector, 8 January 1941, A433, 1950/2/6890, 3103597, NAA; Summary of Share Capital and Shares, 18 January 1942, Chinese Times Ltd, 1922–1949, 12951, 7978, NSWSAR.

13   Publication of Newspapers in Foreign Languages, 1949, A445, 232/4/18, 1963798; Memorandum, 22 April 1940, A2998, 1951/4501, 3106028, NAA.

14   *Tung Wah Times*, "誣人造謠無理取鬧," 11 January 1936, 8.

15   G.F. Pearce to the *Chinese Times*, 24 March 1936, A367, C1822, 428437, NAA.

It was not the first time the *Chinese Times* had attracted the attention of Australian authorities. In the 1920s, it had already been considered a propaganda conduit for the Kuomintang in alliance with Soviet Russia to unite China. Canberra believed the paper was anti-British and embraced communism and befriended the Australian Communist Party, labelling it as "troublesome", "harmful" and "most dangerous". Other Chinese-language newspapers conveyed political views identified as "harmless".[16] Such contrast underscores Canberra's profound concerns, not only about the dissemination of communist and anti-British sentiments, but also the potential for a newspaper with an official foreign background and support to spread propaganda.

The warning in 1935 was by no means the last time the *Chinese Times* unsettled the Australian government. In 1941, for example, the paper condemned the United States and the United Kingdom for their appeasement of Japan, encouraged community solidarity of Chinese Australians and promoted Chinese racial equality by urging Canberra to abolish the notorious immigration restrictions.[17] These challenges reveal the proactive agency of the diaspora press and the Kuomintang government in their pursuit of protection and racial equality for Chinese Australians, highlighting an interplay of agendas more complex than a traditionally known one-sided integration into the white host society, crystallising Australia as the suppressor and diaspora Chinese as the suppressed.

As it was the official mouthpiece of the Kuomintang, it is unsurprising to see the *Chinese Times* entrusted with a nationalist mission to bolster Nanking's authority and leadership over Chinese Australian communities. It was vital to ensure the Kuomintang regime, which attempted to extract patriotic support from Chinese Australians, enjoyed prestige among them. The paper was thus dedicated to: the promotion of news favouring Chiang Kai-shek, the national solidarity to be reached between various Chinese Australian parties under the Kuomintang's guidance, and the "Three Principles of the People" as indispensable in China's nation-building and in justifying Nanking's dictatorship.[18] In 1933, Chen Chih-ming even sought to augment

16  Reports of Investigation Branch, 1923–1927, A367, C1822, 428437, NAA.
17  *Chinese Times*, 1941, C320, C8, 1495438, NAA.

propaganda efforts by increasing the publication frequency and reformulated the newspaper from a weekly journal, published on Saturdays, to a biweekly one, appearing on Wednesdays as well.[19] Believing that recurrent promotion of the "Three Principles of the People" was vital to serving "national salvation", Chen intended for his intensifying efforts to drum "Chinese patriotism" into local Chinese to rejuvenate "our glory national spirit" and restore China's sovereignty, lost during the Japanese invasion. Along these lines, Chen stressed the importance of solidarity among the Chinese diaspora and requested that Nanking lobby for better treatment of Chinese migrants in Australia.[20]

Robust promotion aside, efforts to elevate China's prestige encompassed endeavours to suppress contested viewpoints from Nanking's political rivals. Wong Chih-hwa of the *Chinese Times*, for instance, launched a vigorous attack on the *Tung Wah Times* and the *Chinese World's News* (公報), accusing them of fabricating news regarding the unsuccessful assassination of Wang Ching-wei (汪精衛, the Prime Minister of China) in November 1935. Wong perceived the assassination attempt as a threat to the Kuomintang's authority and an indication of political instability in China, the reporting of which by political detractors would exacerbate the perceived threat. His criticism soon escalated into a full-blown dispute between these three papers over Nanking's role in China's War of Resistance, with each side exchanging verbal sparring.[21]

But, with Nanking's dictatorship and controversial policy of appeasing Japan's aggression, both promotion and suppression were unsuccessful. Chen's so called "new epoch" reform proved short-lived,

18  *Tung Wah Times*, "斥反對歡迎蔡將軍失敗之老羞成怒者," 16 March 1935, 2; "斥反對歡迎蔡將軍失敗之老羞成怒者 (續)," 23 March 1935, 2; Reports of the *Chinese Times* and Yuan Chung-ming, 1941, C320, C8, 1495438, NAA.
19  G.M. Kio to Postmaster General, 24 July 1934, SP320/4, TA50/3673, 7846106, NAA.
20  *Chinese Times*, "本報增刊改版宣言," 22 April 1933, 2, SP320/4, TA50/3673, 7846106, NAA; 陳志明 1935, 140.
21  *Tung Wah Times*, "誣人造謠無理取鬧," 11 January 1936, 8; "斥民報記者之謬妄," 18 January 1936, 8; "再斥民報記者之謬妄," 25 January 1936, 8.

and the paper reverted to its previous publication schedule within a year, despite appreciation from the Australian headquarters of Kuomintang and the Chinese consul general in Sydney.[22] The antagonism caused by Wong's attacks caused the Kuomintang's opponents to contemplate legal action against the *Chinese Times*, compelling the leaders of Chinese Australian communities to mediate to avert court hearings that could exacerbate their internal disputes.[23] The *Chinese Times* reportedly received more catcall than applause from Chinese Australians.[24]

Wong's and Chen's backfired strategies resulted in a continual loss of readership and consequent financial difficulties. Sales promotion strategies were deployed – for example, an advertisement offered customers who bought the *Chinese Times* a discounted price for a fabulously decorated box of washing compound called "SSS"[25] – but the paper's circulation saw a decline from 2,000 copies per week in 1934 to about 1,000 copies in 1940, which generated £5,015 in turnover but a debt of £400 to the Australian headquarters of Kuomintang.[26] Sales further decreased to less than a thousand copies in the following year, with the Australian Kuomintang also grappling with financial predicaments that made it hard to continue the sponsorship. A not unproblematic calculation based on incomes from yearly subscription and sales from May 1942 to the same month 1943 of the *Chinese Times* suggests that there were 251 annual subscribers and 115 half-year subscribers, in addition to up to 6,113 copies sold. Most of those subscribers were Kuomintang members.[27] The endeavours failed to realise their aims and paradoxically upgraded the popularity of the anti-Kuomintang papers and strengthened their voices, as discussed in Chapter 2.

---

22  Chen Wei-ping to the Secretary of the Department of the Interior, 5 March 1934, A1, 1933/307, 1123059, NAA.

23  Report of D.R.B. Mitchell, 20 December 1935, A367, C1822, 428437, NAA.

24  *Tung Wah Times*, "斥民報記者之謬妄," 18 January 1936, 8.

25  *Chinese Times*, 12 April 1933, 1, SP320/4, TA50/3673, 7846106, NAA.

26  Report of Investigating Officer, 8 March 1934, A1, 1933/307, 1123059; Report of L.T. Gamble, 4 April 1940, A433, 1950/2/6890, 3103597, NAA.

27  *Chinese Times*, 1941, C320, C8, 1495438, NAA. Balance Sheet, 1942–1943, Chinese Times Ltd, 1922–1949, 12951, 7978, NSWSAR.

Even with these challenges, the *Chinese Times* survived until August 1950. It benefited from the downfall of competitors overwhelmed by insurmountable pressures, including a scarcity of essential materials for printing and financial ruin caused by the escalating war in China and the Pacific. Their readership generally transitioned to the *Chinese Times*, and an estimated one-third of the Chinese residents in Australia purchased it during the Pacific War.[28] Support from the Chinese authorities in Australia and at home was likewise instrumental. In 1932, Nanking allocated 300 yuan to the *Chinese Times* to relieve the latter's financial dilemma.[29] In the late 1930s, the then Consul General Pao Chun-jien (保君健) secured permissions from Canberra to transfer two highly competent individuals, Lin Hao Kang, a well-educated and astute editor, and Dong Fong, a skilled compositor, from the *Chinese Republic News* to the paper. Lin Hao Kang received £2 5 shillings per week with lodging, and Dong Fong received lodging and £3 per week as assistant secretary for four to five hours' work and no salary as a part-time compositor for 2 hours a week. Such a move was twofold in purpose: to employ the individuals when their previous employers faced liquidation and to succour the *Chinese Times* to better serve an expanding readership and Nanking's propaganda campaigns.[30]

The *Chinese Times* also profited from sponsorship by the Australian headquarters of the Kuomintang, which issued debentures to collect funds. Except for a rent waiver for using the Kuomintang building as the paper's premises, about £100 was allocated in 1939 to facilitate the newspaper's operations; by 1942, headquarters had already extended loans totalling approximately £1,791 to sustain its activities.[31] This advantage was cemented by extensive financial resources based on the networks that the Kuomintang had established in the South Pacific. While longstanding political fragmentations between these

---

28  S. Fitzgerald 1996, 118.
29  陳志明 1935, 138.
30  Lin Hao Kang and Dong Fong, 27 November 1940; Pao Chun-jien to the Department of Interior, 2 February 1940, A433, 1950/2/6890, 3103597, NAA.
31  Balance Sheet, 20 November 1939, 30 June 1942, Chinese Times Ltd, 1922–1949, 12951, 7978, NSWSAR.

Kuomintang branches exacerbated the Australian headquarters' financial difficulties,[32] these branches supported the newspaper financially. Each Kuomintang member in Australia and New Zealand (except those in need) was obliged to purchase at least two shares in the paper (each valued £1) and those in Pacific islands at least one share.[33] In 1942, a nominal capital of £5,000, divided into 5,000 shares valued at £1 each, was raised for the *Chinese Times,* and the Kuomintang branches and individual buyers purchased about 3,511 shares. Many of these investors, from merchants to hawkers and tailors, held Kuomintang memberships, including D.Y. Narme (歐陽南), the manager of On Yik Lee (安益利公司) and Mar Leong Wah, the manager of Wing Sang (永興公司). It was not the first time the *Chinese Times* procured support from the Kuomintang's overseas offices. In 1929, each branch was secured to subscribe to a designated number of copies to increase the newspaper's circulation substantially.[34] When financial difficulty arose in subsequent years, party members and branches were encouraged to promote the paper's sale through purchases and publicity.[35] In 1933, the Fifth Convention of the Australasian Kuomintang decided that each branch should support the *Chinese Times* with at least one penny.[36]

The Australian Kuomintang additionally implemented an internal restructuring of the paper to deal with the imminent risk of bankruptcy and make the *Chinese Times* "more powerful".[37] The paper's ownership was moved in 1943 to three prominent members of the Kuomintang (Mar Leong Wah, D.Y. Narme and Jang Wai Shui), who secured a £135 loan from headquarters, reformulating the paper into an independent media company known as Chinese Press Pty Ltd. The company raised £500 in capital from its shareholders and increased the newspaper's price to 7 pence to ensure its financial sustainability. The executive committee of the Australian Kuomintang oversaw the company's board of directors

---

32    Kuo and Brett 2013, 79, 107.
33    陳志明 1935, 138–39.
34    Memorandum, 26 March 1929, A1, 1933/307, 1123059, NAA.
35    澳洲總支部執行委員會秘書處 1931, 183, 187.
36    陳志明 1935, 55.
37    Vanguard of the Overseas, 1943, A989, 1944/554/7/1, 184465, NAA.

to maintain control of their operations. Jang Wai Shui was installed as the general manager, Lin Hao Kang as the vice-manager and Tan Chut (譚楫) as the assistant manager. Except for the general manager, all received regular salaries. The weekly pay for the chief editor was £7 10 shillings, £6 for Lin and £2 10 shillings for Tan.[38]

Although the financial capacity seemed reduced compared to the 1942 funding initiative, separating itself from sponsorship by the Kuomintang headquarters relieved the Australian Kuomintang's financial dilemma and offered itself greater flexibility in dealing with future challenges. The paper was thus better placed to fulfil the Kuomintang's ambition for it to be the single legitimate mouthpiece for Chinese Australian communities. The *Chinese Times* reported achieving a circulation of "950 copies per day" (it is more likely the circulation was calculated "per week", given it was a weekly publication).[39]

## Chinese Republic News

First established in 1914 and published weekly on Saturdays at the more affordable price of 3 pence compared with its counterparts, the *Chinese Republic News* was said to boast a wide readership in various locations, including the South Pacific, the Strait Settlements and China, including Hong Kong and Canton (廣州). The paper and another three Chinese Australian press publications comprised eight pages at a size of "92×61 centimetres", and the text was printed with "type no. 4". News was harvested from sources in both Chinese and English and remained focused on China and home villages around Canton. Although the coverage of local news was minimal, the newspapers published large portions of commercial advertisements for Chinese and non-Chinese Australian commodities, information on shipping timetables for passengers travelling between China and Australia, details about books

---

38  Chinese Migration and Overseas Chinese, 1943–1944, A989, 1944/554/7/1, 184465, NAA; Chinese Press Pty Ltd, 1943, 12951, 21745, NSWSAR.
39  Chinese Migration and Overseas Chinese, 1943–1944, A989, 1944/554/7/1, 184465, NAA.

available for sale at stores and through the newspapers themselves, and the prices of food items at local Chinese grocery stores – information that readers wanted.[40]

Such common characteristics between Chinese Australian newspapers suggest a standardisation of themes, news and information, and the widespread acceptance of modern printing culture among Chinese Australian intellectuals and proprietors. But the degree to which these newspapers emphasised the link between diasporic Chinese, Australia and China varied. The *Chinese Times* portrayed a more intimate tie between China and Chinese overseas and named the column on news about China *"Zuguo Yaowen"* (祖國要聞, Key News in the Homeland). It referred to the column reporting local news as *"Aozhou Xinwen"* (澳洲新聞, News in Australia), clearly demarcating the distinction. In comparison, the *Tung Wah Times* used *"Zhongguo Xinwen"* (中國新聞, China News) and *"Benzhou Xinwen"* (本洲新聞, Local News), indicating a relatively neutral relationship with China and relative closeness with Australia. The *Chinese Republic News* struck a balance between its two counterparts, using *"Guoshi Jiyao"* (國事紀要, Key Summary of National Affairs) to indicate a close bond with China and *"Benzhou Xinwen"* suggesting a close link with Australia as well.[41]

While predominantly homeland-oriented, these Chinese-language newspapers did not ignore their connection to Australia. For example, they often used both traditional Chinese and Western concepts of time in parallel. In the *Chinese Republic News*, Chinese lunar and Western Gregorian calendars were presented alongside a Republican China chronology, the display of which was also observed in a special Chinese New Year issue that listed both Chinese and Australian festivals. This implied a diasporic lifestyle for Chinese Australians more than a temporary sojourn or complete assimilation. This practice also symbolised the desire of local Chinese intellectuals for harmonious ethnic relations between resident Chinese and white Australians, aiming to foster a "more sympathetic understanding between the Chinese race and the Australian people".[42]

---

40  Lowenthal 1937, 1–2.
41  *Chinese Times*, 22 April 1933, 2–3, SP320/4, TA50/3673, 7846106, NAA.

While allegedly representing no political party and only Chinese republicans in Australia and New Zealand, it is not uncommon to see the *Chinese Republic News* aligned with the *Chinese Times*: it frequently reprinted news dispatches and official notices from the *Chinese Times* and Kuomintang headquarters.[43] In fact, the Australian Kuomintang was attempting to bring the paper under its influence. Part of this was realised through a significant share purchase by Wong Coy (黃永輝) and D.Y. Narme, who became the managers of the paper for the purpose of strengthening the Kuomintang's voice.[44] P.J. Leader, one of the directors of the *Chinese Times,* was given the same position at the *Chinese Republic News* along with P.J. McGaulley, who became the manager and secretary.[45] This meant that the newspaper was primarily run by shareholders and directors in support of the Nanking government.[46]

But it would be an oversimplification to assume the *Chinese Republic News* was a mere puppet of the Australian Kuomintang and the *Chinese Times.* In the early 1930s, under the editorship of Young Suey Chong (楊瑞祥, an experienced Chinese journalist who came to Australia to join his brother, Yung Hook, and assumed the editorship in 1920), the paper was indeed in chorus with the *Chinese Times* (under Lau Tze Him) in displaying a strong anti-Japanese position,[47] while criticising Nanking's inefficiency in anti-Japanese campaigns. In subsequent years, while the *Chinese Times* acted as a cheerleader for Nanking's controversial Japan policy and its promotion of one-party

---

42 Letter to the Secretary of Department of Home Affairs, 22 August 1930, A433, 1947/2/6297 Part 2, 4037888, NAA.
43 *Chinese Republic News,* "特電," 27 February 1932, 8.
44 陳志明 1935, 144.
45 D.Y. Narme to G.F.A. Mitchell, 27 October 1936, A2998, 1951/4501, 3106028, NAA.
46 Chinese Republic Newspaper & Trading Co. Ltd., 1938, 12951, 9834, NSWSAR.
47 Memorandum of Department of Home Affairs, 9 October 1930, A433, 1947/2/6297 Part 2, 4037888; Quei Tze-King (魏子京) to the Secretary of Home and Territories Department, 30 January 1923, the Secretary of Home and Territories Department to the Collector of Customs, 15 January 1923, A433, 1937/2/6297 Part 1, 3095444, NAA.

rule, the *Chinese Republic News* took the opposite stance, advocating for political inclusiveness and democracy-building,[48] as well as criticising factional conflicts within the Kuomintang and calling for party unity and solidarity between Chinese authorities and people.[49] In essence, what the *Chinese Republic News* argued echoed the concerns of anti-Nanking camps, as discussed in Chapter 2.

Regarding Japan's invasion, the paper's position, which aligned with the Nanking government, proved short-lived. Unlike the *Chinese Times* becoming milder in 1932, the *Chinese Republic News* continued to display anger over China's ineffective response to the Japanese invasion after Young left his offices.[50] Such criticism reached its zenith when China's failure to defend Shanghai against Japan's attacks was confirmed in a subsequent truce in May. Both the *Chinese Republic News* and the *Tung Wah Times* were profoundly disappointed and vehemently criticised the Chinese government, pressuring for political reform.[51] Both shared similar admiration for patriotic Chinese figures and reservations about the effectiveness of the League of Nations in restraining Japan's aggression.[52] Their fervent protests disturbed the Chinese leadership, and Prime Minister Wang Ching-wei swiftly cabled the Chinese consulate general to clarify that "no political agreement was reached" and that the government had "consistently adopted a policy of both negotiation and resistance".[53] It was not only a display

---

48  *Chinese Republic News,* "抗日救國運動中官吏之責任," 7 November 1931, 5; "義勇軍抗暴之重大意義," 20 February 1932, 2; "由訓政達到真憲政之質疑," 2 July 1932, 2.

49  *Chinese Republic News,* "痛心的話," 31 October 1931, 5; "痛心的話," 21 November 1931, 5; "所謂新的外交方案," 5 March 1932, 2.

50  Young Suey Chong to the Collector of Customs, 12 February 1932, SP42/1, C1932/2295 [Part 1 of 3], 9631581, NAA.

51  *Chinese Republic News,* "政府果和乎," 7 May 1932, 2; "救亡與訓練青年," 14 May 1932, 2; "前途黯淡之停戰撤兵會議," 21 May 1932, 2; "一致共赴國難," 28 May 1932, 2; "追悼滬戰殉國將士," 9 July 1932, 2; *Tung Wah Times,* "中國軍人之奇恥," 16 July 1932, 2.

52  *Chinese Republic News,* "吾人對於國聯最後之認識," 30 January 1932, 2; "馬占山無恙耶," 26 March 1932, 2; "冀北匪氣之嚴重性," 30 September 1933, 2; *Tung Wah Times,* "國人只有自救壹途," 31 October 1931, 2; "國難中之剿共," 9 April 1932, 2; "勗東北義勇軍," 10 December 1932, 2.

of the vague loyalty of the *Chinese Republic News* towards the Nanking government but also a demonstration of Chinese Australians' proactive agency and aversion to being a passive and marginalised recipient of instructions from their homeland government.

This is not to say the *Chinese Republic News* had become a staunch rival of the Australian Kuomintang and toed the line with anti-Nanking camps, as seen with the Chinese Chamber of Commerce (中華總商會) and the Chinese Masonic Society (致公堂) in Sydney (explored in Chapter 2). The newspaper's various views differed significantly from these groups. For example, while it expressed anti-Communist stances,[54] the *Chinese Republic News* expressed sympathy and appreciation for Chiang Kai-shek's efforts to restore relations and seek an alliance with the Soviet Union to counter Japanese aggression in 1932 when major Western powers placated Japan's invasion.[55] The paper based its scepticism on China's historical experiences of the West and its roles in the ongoing war. The Nine Power Treaty, signed by all participants at the Washington Naval Conference in 1922 and meant to safeguard China's sovereignty, was portrayed as a manoeuvre of significant powers to compete for colonisation in China.[56] The disarmament negotiations discussed in Geneva from 1932 to 1934 were likewise viewed as "hypocritical", because the prominent states had little genuine desire to implement them.[57]

These complex views indicated that the *Chinese Republic News* had a strongly independent agenda that neither fully allied with the Australian Kuomintang nor its opponents, making the *Chinese Republic News* stand out among the Chinese-language newspapers published in Australia. The change of the paper's editorship largely accounted for

---

53  *Chinese Republic News*, "駐澳總領事館緊要通告," 21 May 1932, 8; *Tung Wah Times*, "駐澳總領事館緊要通告," 21 May 1932, 8.

54  *Chinese Republic News*, "冀北匪氣之嚴重性," 30 September 1933, 2; *Tung Wah Times*, "國難中之剿共," 9 April 1932, 2.

55  *Chinese Republic News*, "中俄復交問題," 12 March 1932, 2; "論對蘇復交與防遏共產," 25 June 1932, 2; "從國際情勢談到中蘇復交," 16 July 1932, 2; "中蘇復交與國際現勢," 21 January 1933, 2.

56  *Chinese Republic News*, "外交危言," 13 February 1932, 2.

57  *Chinese Republic News*, "炮擊山海關與新軍縮案," 14 January 1933, 2; "紙上制裁," 1 July 1933, 2; "文明的矛盾," 2 March 1935, 7.

such independence. The successor to Young Suey Chong in 1932 was Quan Mane (關明), a reliable partner and a close friend of Young at the *Chinese Republic News*. Both were shareholders of the paper's owner – the Chinese Republic News and Trading Company – and Quan was also named as one of the executors of Young's will when he passed away in August 1932.[58] Despite Quan's extensive experience, suggesting steadfast support of Chinese republicanism, he did not hold the Kuomintang's leadership in high regard, and his views were at odds with Nanking, which probably caused leading pro-Nanking members of the company to engineer his departure from the editorship. Lin Hao Kang was appointed as his replacement in 1933.[59]

The new appointment brought only a subtle shift rather than an outright reversal in the newspaper's coverage of China's affairs. Lin Hao Kang appeared to balance demonstrating loyalty to Nanking and preserving the *Chinese Republic News*' independence. The publication attempted to mitigate potential criticisms of Nanking's "non-resistance policy" by refraining from offering commentary on it and focusing more on international news, while occasional disapprovals were allowed.[60] Meanwhile, the paper aligned closely with Nanking on Chinese domestic affairs. When Feng Yu-hsiang (馮玉祥), who had been a prominent warlord and Chiang's rival, was pressured to disband his troops after Feng successfully defended Chahar (察哈爾), strong criticisms were outpoured by anti-Nanking camps that accused Chiang of obstructing resistance against Japanese forces there.[61] In comparison, the *Chinese Republic News* was satisfied with Nanking's endeavours to

58 R.G. Dun & Co. 1925, 25; New South Wales State 1933, 1226.
59 Memorandums of the NSW Collector of Customs and the Department of the Interior, 1932–1938, SP42/1, C1932/2295, 9631581, NAA. For the dismissal of Quan Mane, see *Chinese Republic News* to Chen Wei-ping, 15 February 1935, A433, 1947/2/6297 Part 2, 4037888, NAA.
60 *Chinese Republic News*, "日蘇軍事對立," 18 March 1933, 2; "德國政變所給與東方問題之影響," 1 April 1933, 2; "日本對華外交之新陣勢," 15 July 1933, 2; "日本外交之新轉向," 19 August 1933, 2; "中東路蘇偽談判與遠東和平," 2 September 1933, 2; "九一八二週年回顧," 16 September 1933, 2; "願明年今日有以告慰孫先生," 6 January 1934, 2.
61 *Tung Wah Times*, "察省存亡之關系," 19 August 1933, 2.

suppress warlords and consolidate its authority, contending that Feng had been unwilling to engage in anti-Japanese battles and holding him responsible for exacerbating intra-party conflicts. Similar support was given to Nanking for taking tight control of Sinkiang (新疆).[62]

The adjustment in views seemed unsatisfactory to the Australian Kuomintang, who decided to extend complete control over the paper and transformed it into a mouthpiece for Nanking. In 1934, after serving as the editor of the *Chinese Times*, Chen Chih-ming was appointed the editor of the *Chinese Republic News*.[63] He efficiently reformulated it into a tirelessly enthusiastic cheerleader for the Chinese government's policies and ideologies. A dedicated column called "*Qingbai*" (青白, Blue and White, referencing the Kuomintang's emblem and authority) was created for this purpose.[64] As Chen claimed, the newspaper would "take the 'Three Principles of the People' as the supreme tenet to guide the Chinese in Australia in assisting the Chinese government in reviving the Chinese nation."[65]

It was no surprise to see that the *Chinese Republic News* generally omitted things that did not follow the Kuomintang's interests. China's setbacks in the resistance against Japan's aggression were downplayed, with Nanking's authority shielded. In 1933, the signed Tangku Truce (塘沽協定) effectively facilitated Japanese expansion into North China and tacitly recognised Manchukuo (Japan's puppet regime in North-East China), which was portrayed by the paper as an unfortunate but unavoidable compromise.[66] Rather than holding Chiang and Wang accountable, like anti-Nanking newspapers, the supportive *Chinese Republic News* blamed the Chinese people: their

62  *Chinese Republic News*, "華北兩問題," 12 August 1933, 2; "願明年今日有以告慰孫先生," 6 January 1934, 2; "新疆事變感言," 26 August 1933, 2.
63  *Chinese Republic News*, "本報緊要啟事," 27 January 1934, 7.
64  *Chinese Republic News*, "全國公路建設," 17 March 1934, 7; "新生活運動的意義," 14 April 1934, 2, 4.
65  *Chinese Republic News*, "本報之使命," 27 January 1934, 7.
66  Dryburgh 2001, 43; Mitter 2013, 66; *Chinese Republic News*, "分裂乎? 團結乎?," 3 February 1934, 2; "傀儡稱帝之原因," 10 March 1934, 2; "怎樣紀念五九國恥," 12 May 1934, 2.

"degeneration" caused these frustrations, and the public ought to reflect on their duties and obligations.[67]

In addition, the *Chinese Republic News* confronted challenges to Nanking's authority that stemmed from Chiang's detractors. Widely applauded by Chinese Australian newspapers for his courageous defence of Shanghai in 1932, Tsai Ting-kai (蔡廷鍇), for example, defied the central government by establishing a breakaway regime in Fukien (福建) in late 1933 as a response to Chiang's attempts to disband his 19th Route Army (十九路軍). Along with the Australian Kuomintang's resentful condemnation of Tsai's rebellion jeopardising the Chinese nation before external threats,[68] the paper withdrew its admiration and denounced Tsai as a rebel, considering Nanking as the core of the nation, the leadership that the Chinese people should support. In contrast, the *Tung Wah Times* celebrated the new regime and cast Tsai's insurrection as revolutionary and Chiang's suppression as reactionary, attacking Nanking for being resolute in internal conflicts but cowardly towards external threats.[69] Coverage was the same when the central government clashed with the South-West Political Affairs Council (西南政務委員會), established by Chiang's opponents to advocate for Chiang's resignation and the overthrow of Nanking.[70]

But such staunch support did not endure more than a year. By 1935, the *Chinese Republic News*' disappointment with and disapproval of Nanking's performance were undisguised, as more concessions were being granted to Japan.[71] Placatory responses to fascist aggressions elsewhere in the world added to this dissatisfaction, including after

---

67    *Chinese Republic News*, "救國先從自己做起," 9 June 1934, 2; "救國先從自己做起," 16 June 1934, 2; "國民應有民族性的奮發," 30 June 1934, 2.

68    陳志明 1935, 59.

69    Hu 2024, 693–5.

70    *Tung Wah Times*, "貴州政變與西南政局," 7 January 1933, 2; "讀西南灰電後之感想," 23 September 1933, 2; "又多一張永不兌現支票," 4 August 1934, 2; "西南有電與言論自由," 10 November 1934, 2; "華北已矣華南如何," 20 July 1935, 5; "西南應貫徹其主張," 4 July 1936, 2.

71    *Chinese Republic News*, "從個讓字說起," 13 July 1935, 7; "睦鄰與善鄰," 21 September 1935, 7; "我為國脈懼," 26 October 1935, 7; "火花," 23 November 1935, 7.

the fall of Abyssinia (Ethiopia), whose dauntless resistance before formidable Italy in the same year formed a stark contrast to China's concessions to Japan. As the *Chinese Republic News* put it, Abyssinia's performance "shamed us Chinese" and placed China as the "most shameful country in the world".[72] The newspaper again aligned with anti-Nanking voices, such as the *Tung Wah Times*.[73]

One of the likely factors that incited this sudden reversal in attitude was Chen Chih-ming's departure from his editorship in 1935 to attend the Fifth National Congress of the Kuomintang in China as one of the delegates representing the Australian branch. His absence relaxed the Kuomintang-imposed ideological control over the paper, with the column *Qingbai* folding in September 1934. Concurrently, the newspaper limped through a financial crisis; there had been a constant decline in circulation from 5,000 copies per week in the 1920s to 1,200 by the 1930s.[74] It waned to 1,000 copies per week in 1936 and further plummeted to around just 875 over the subsequent two years.[75]

The funding shortage additionally precluded the *Chinese Republic News* from securing a qualified editor and probably manager after 1935, and D.Y. Narme – as the director of the Chinese Republic News and Trading Company – had to temporarily assume the role of honorary editor. Although Narme's expertise in editorship was unclear, it is likely that he was hindered by his juggling of other positions and responsibilities. During his tenure, the quality of the newspaper declined, and the publication of Australian news became irregular. In 1936, he chose to step down due to the pressures of "business and other interests". Lin Hao Kang again took on the editorship in November

---

72  *Chinese Republic News*, "我願做阿國人," 3 August 1935, 7; "赤腳軍," 14 September 1935, 7; "對阿國人表敬意," 2 November 1935, 7; "阿人的蠢," 16 November 1935, 7; "阿比西尼亞之民謠," 28 March, 1936, 7; "亡國的情緒," 4 July 1936, 7.

73  *Tung Wah Times*, "屈辱即可苟安乎," 13 July 1935, 5; "中國竟不如阿比西尼亞乎," 3 August 1935, 5; "黍離詞," 21 September 1935, 5.

74  Memorandums of Home and Territories Department, 1928–1930, A433, 1947/2/6297 Part 2, 4037888, NAA.

75  Memorandum of the Department of the Interior, 30 March 1938, A433, 1945/2/3557, 3093972; Memorandum, 3 July 1940, A2998, 1951/4501, 3106028, NAA.

of that year. His talent and education were expected to lift up the Chinese community.[76] Both the previous and current editors were wary of further alienating readers, fearing an exacerbation of the newspaper's financial instability. This concern was especially evident in Lin Hao Kang's decision to forgo editorials in 1937, except for the first issue, which emphasised the critical importance of national solidarity in the face of Japan's invasion.[77]

The newspaper proprietor actively sought assistance from financial institutions to cope with financial strains. In 1934, he obtained a mortgage of £250 from the English Scottish and Australian Bank to alleviate the overdraft account of the *Chinese Republic News*. Another mortgage of £425 was secured from the same bank the following year.[78] Despite these manoeuvres and the paper's revered editorial attitude, the financial dilemma continued with a grim excess of receipts over payments.[79] The proprietor's reported turnovers (£14,100 in 1936, £16,427 in 1937, and £1,616 in 1939) are not entirely reliable, because there is no corresponding information on overall profits or financial losses due to the unavailability of relevant archives.[80] But the company did decide to cease operations, winding up business in December 1938 and entering liquidation in 1939. In February of 1940, the newspaper ceased publication, and the company's name was officially removed from the register.[81]

---

76  D.Y. Narme to Boarding Officer, 27 October 1936, A2998, 1951/4501, 3106028, NAA.
77  *Chinese Republic News*, "感言," 2 January 1937, 2.
78  Debenture, 30 November 1934, 1 November 1935, Chinese Republic Newspaper & Trading Co. Ltd., 1938, 12951, 9834, NSWSAR.
79  Abstracts of receipts and payments, 1937–1938, 12951, 9834, NSWSAR.
80  Memorandum, 3 November 1936, 9 February 1938, A2998, 1951/4501, 3106028, NAA.
81  Office of the Registrar of Joint Stock Companies to the Register General, 6 June 1940, 12951, 9834, NSWSAR; Memorandum, 24 June 1940, A433, 1950/2/6890, 3103597, NAA.

## Chinese-language schools

By the 1930s, Australian-born Chinese presented to the Nanking government as a growing and significant strength. In ageing Chinese Australian communities, their share of over 40 per cent of the diaspora population indicated significant potential for China's expected long-lasting war effort. But the complex identities of these locally born individuals, evolved within White Australia, often bred a nebulous concept of "China" and a similarly nebulous emotional attachment that would certainly be at odds with such potential. Nanking was conscious of the urgency and challenges of reclaiming the Chinese heritage, fostering patriotism and securing the long-term allegiance of Australian-born Chinese. Local Chinese officials thus reiterated the necessity and exigency of preserving the Chinese heritage of residents and their Australian-born offspring, to safeguard them from assimilation into the host society or channelling their skills and successful careers to benefit the country of birth rather than their heritage homeland.[82]

One of the popular ways to realise this goal involved sending Australian-born Chinese children back to their ancestral villages in China to receive a traditional Chinese education. But this strategy faced substantial challenges. Australian immigration restrictions and customs service requirements aside,[83] education resources in China were mediocre and inaccessible to a broader population, as the government's unwavering commitment was continually undercut by its limited financial resources. For the few Chinese schools established in native-origin villages, frequently sponsored by wealthy Chinese

---

82  Correspondence from Chinese Consul General in Melbourne and Overseas Chinese Affairs Council in China, 1931, AU NBAC 111-9-4, Noel Butlin Archives Centre (NBAC), Australian National University, Canberra; *Chinese Republic News*, "華僑學校應用國語教授," 14 January 1933, 8; *Northern Territory Times*, "Banquet by Kuo Min Tang," 19 January 1932, 5; *Chinese Republic News*, "教育外交等部公布修正領事經理僑教規程," 9 June 1934, 7; *Tung Wah Times*, "僑務委員會附設僑生回國升學補習班入學簡章," 4 April 1936, 5.

83  Australian Born Chinese Limit Time for Education in China, 14 September 1932, A1, 1932/10538, 45450, NAA.

overseas, a unique education approach was applied to instil a sense of Chinese traditions and identity while embracing Western ideals and language skills.[84] Consequently, this approach served a crucial role in adapting Chinese emigrants to their adopted communities, which ran counter to Nanking's desire to nurture a distinct Chinese identity and unwavering loyalty to China.

Given these challenges, the Sinicisation and re-Sinicisation of local diaspora communities would instead be practically realised through Chinese education in Australia. It was not something that just sprang to mind for prominent Chinese Australian figures and Chinese authorities. There were Chinese-language schools in Sydney, Melbourne, Darwin and Perth already established through the years leading up to the 1930s. Local Chinese Australians volunteered to teach at the schools, and students were exempted from tuition fees. Nearly all of these were night schools, some of which operated libraries for students. These schools were tasked with the overarching goal of fortifying the local-born youths' Chinese heritage, enhancing community solidarity and empowering students to become formidable supporters of China.[85] But most of the schools were short-lived and the rest had continually low attendance.[86]

The Chinese were not the only ethnic group in Australia who sought to preserve the heritage of their younger generations. Notably, Japanese immigrants were more successful than the Chinese. Japanese-language teaching had already progressed as early as 1917 to the secondary education level in New South Wales, and it was introduced in 1919 at the University of Melbourne. During the interwar decades, the Japanese-language teaching sponsored by Tokyo expanded into the rest of Australia, where five sets of textbooks were donated to Perth Technical School in 1934. Japanese-language classes were introduced at the university and selected high schools in Queensland in 1937. Japanese history and language also became the subject of a popular program for the Australian Broadcasting Commission from

---

84    Benton and Liu 2018, 137; Cheng 2022, 69–70, 100, 105, 107–8, 112.
85    Kuo 2009, 232; Minute Book, May 1923, AU NBAC 111-1-1, NBAC; 陳志明 1935, 77, 124; 澳洲總支部執行委員會秘書處 1931, 17, 36, 171, 268.
86    Yong 1977, 215–16.

1935 until 1941.[87] The prominence of Japanese-language teaching, in contrast to its Chinese counterpart, was due more to Canberra's concerns about Japanese imperialism in the Pacific than genuine interest in interracial exchange.[88]

In the 1930s, the revival of Chinese-language schools in Australia was realised first in Sydney under the sponsorship of Chinese authorities and community leaders. One such institution was founded at the Australian Kuomintang headquarters in June 1931 – the Chinese Overseas Night School (華僑國文夜學). A board of 16 members was organised to govern it, and this number later increased to 46, comprising 22 standing and 24 honorary members. Community leaders (particularly those pro-Nanking) and Kuomintang officials were appointed to key roles, including D.Y. Narme as the chairman, Mar Leong Wah as the deputy chairman, and Li Mingyan (李明炎)[89] as the school's principal. The board held regular meetings at 7 p.m. on the first Saturday of each month. These arrangements indicated a growing interest and higher regard from the school's founders, as well as Nanking's determination to secure dominant control in the education program. About £480 was allocated by Nanking to sponsor the Australian Kuomintang's efforts in fields such as propaganda and education.[90]

Despite its official background, the school's establishment was not to challenge White Australia's educational system but to complement it. Classes were held from 7 to 9 p.m. every Monday, Tuesday and Friday, with two terms per year, typically starting in February and August. Using self-designed textbooks, the curriculum focused on oral and literary Chinese, history, geography, calligraphy and Kuomintang ideology. The lecturers were payment-free volunteers, often selected from prominent local figures, including Zheng Weiyao (鄭渭軺), Liu Boming (劉博明), Jang Wai Shui and Liang Lanxin (梁蘭新). These arrangements were identified as practical to implement, and a similar

---

87    Darian-Smith 2023, 186.
88    Baldwin 2019, 107.
89    Lau Tze Him, Loh Kai-tze and Mar Leong Wah would succeed these
       appointments.
90    澳洲總支部執行委員會秘書處 1931, 131.

Chinese-language school attached to local Kuomintang was established in Darwin the following year.[91]

The school encouraged local-born Chinese to enrol through financial manoeuvres. Tuition fees were waived for Chinese students, while a £2 fee was charged for white Australians. As this strategy would financially burden its sponsors, the school had to rely on support from Chinese Australian communities, such as regular donations. Students of Australian or mixed heritage also joined the institution. For example, a student whose name was written in Chinese as "密司笑容" (Miss Smile) was included in the roster. Given the rarity of such names among Chinese students, this individual was probably of Australian or mixed heritage.

Notwithstanding financial insufficiency, the Kuomintang-sponsored school made satisfactory progress. The number of enrolled students reached about 40 to 50; requiring five additional teachers to be housed at the headquarters' auditorium. Three of the seven well-educated staff had received tertiary education, which indicated the high expectations and value placed on the Chinese-language school by the Chinese authorities. The staff's skills strengthened commitment and led to a more diverse educational program, incorporating general knowledge, singing and elementary Chinese martial arts alongside the existing courses.[92]

Instructed by Nanking in 1930,[93] Chinese authorities made efforts in Melbourne. Proposed by Lee Hong (李鴻) from the local Chinese consulate and approved by the Chinese Ministry of Education, the Melbourne Chung Wah School (美利濱中華補習學校) was established at an Anglican church in August 1931. Although it operated under the leadership of the consulate, not the Kuomintang's Melbourne branch, the night school's subjects and aims were identical to those of

---

91  *Telegraph*, "Chinese Republic," 12 October 1932, 2.
92  *Chinese Republic News*, "澳洲雪梨華僑學校開學通告," 13 February 1932, 8; "華僑學校將開懇親會," 16 July 1932, 8; *Tung Wah Times*, "澳洲雪梨華僑學校開學通告," 13 February 1932, 5; "華僑學校通告," "僑校概況與發展前途," 30 July 1932, 5; "雪梨華僑學校通告," 11 February 1933, 5; "澳洲雪梨華僑學校募捐啟事," 8 July 1933, 8; "華僑學校消息," 27 January 1934, 5; 陳志明 1935, 45, 71.
93  陳志明 1935, 77.

the school in Sydney. The educational program was carefully tailored to the different needs of students of various age groups. Two sections were established: a regular course for students under 17 years of age, and a tutoring class for those over 17, each accommodating up to 40 students.[94] Slightly better at finding funding than its counterpart in Sydney, the school received 120 yuan in patronage from the Chinese government, alongside donations from resident Chinese, garnered by commissioners sent to seek potential donors door-to-door.[95] The staff of the Chinese consulate served as volunteer teachers.[96]

The closure of the Chinese consulate in Melbourne in 1933 changed the school's leadership. The Chinese Citizens Society (中華公會), the most renowned Chinese association in the city, took over the school's administration. The transition also resulted in a restructuring of the school's leadership, which now mirrored the Kuomintang-controlled school in Sydney. Chen Ruixi (陳瑞熙) was selected as the director of the education section, and P.W. Lew (劉譜雲) became the school's principal, replacing Tsiang Char Tung (蔣家棟) from the local Chinese consulate. While the educational program remained unchanged and continued to accept students of all age groups, improvements were introduced to better meet the needs of Australian-born Chinese children by establishing a special class for them.

The management of the new sponsor seemed well received, and the school soon gained popularity among local Chinese. It expanded, relocating to 121 Little Bourke Street, featuring larger classrooms and

---

94  Correspondence from Chinese Consul General in Melbourne and Overseas Chinese Affairs Council in China, 1931, AU NBAC 111-9-4, NBAC.

95  *Tung Wah Times*, "美利濱漢文學校招生," 30 January 1932, 5; "美利濱中華公會教育科董事會通告," 25 February 1933, 5; "美利濱漢文學校消息," 22 July 1933, 5; "教部已照準美利濱漢文學校備案," 29 July 1933, 5; "美利濱中華公會附設中華補習學校新校舍舉行開幕典禮誌盛," 3 March 1934, 5; "美利濱中華補習學校之近訊," 20 July 1935, 5; "敬謝惠捐美利濱中華補習學校經費宣言," 3 August 1935, 5; "敬謝惠捐美利濱中華補習學校經費宣言," 10 August 1935, 5.

96  W.P. Chen to H.C. Brown, 14 December 1934, A2998, 1951/2055, 1997161, NAA.

furnishings to accommodate the growing number of students. It was a three-storey building, with the first and third floor used for classrooms and the second as an auditorium, in the middle of which hung a Chinese national flag.[97] Courses including Cantonese, Chinese reading and writing, geography, history and music were conducted on Monday, Wednesday and Friday nights. China's traditional moral code and way of living were imparted alongside Sun Yat-sen's doctrines. This popularity was enduring, with the Chinese-language school introducing a new crash course in 1935 to meet the needs of children with limited study time.[98] By 1940, 46 young Chinese (about six of whom were girls), aged 13 years old on average, as well as three European children, attended. Each student was reportedly charged a fee of £2 per annum.

Furniture, such as desks and chairs, and gifts including annual prizes often in the forms of books or "oriental ornaments", were donated by various supporters, including white Australians, local Chinese, and Chinese societies such as the Kong Chew Society (岡州會館), Sze Yup Society (四邑會館), Melbourne Kuomintang and Masonic Society and the Chinese Herbalist Association (中醫公会).

The school's success caught the attention of both local Chinese and white Australians. Enthusiastic congratulations were received from Chen Chih-ming, and Australian newspapers including the *Sun News-Pictorial* paid close attention.[99] The school's success was also an encouragement for the diaspora community. A journalist for the *Chinese Republic News* enthusiastically called on his fellow countrymen from all over Australia to establish similar language schools to impart Chinese culture, thereby "preventing assimilation by other races and ethnicities".[100] The Chung Wah School survived until at least 1944, and

---

97  *Tung Wah Times*, "美利濱中華公會附設中華補習學校新校舍舉行開幕典禮誌盛," 3 March 1933, 5.

98  *Tung Wah Times*, "美利濱中華補習學校之近訊," 20 July 1935, 5; Memorandum, 30/9/1941, A2998, 1951/2055, 1997161, NAA.

99  陳志明 1935, 77; *Sun News-Pictorial*, "School for Chinese in Heart of Melbourne," 25 June 1934, 16.

100  *Chinese Republic News*, "美利濱中華公會附設中華補習學校新校舍舉行開幕典禮誌盛," 3 March 1934, 5.

providing remuneration for teachers who were not government officials was divided between Chinese authorities and diasporic community contributions.[101]

Despite their intentions to address the concern of Chinese Australian identity, the new schools differed from their predecessors. The 1930s schools aimed to inspire and mobilise exclusive Chinese nationalism to foster loyal affiliation to the Chinese government. Chinese Australians were constantly encouraged to attend these institutions to "carry forward the homeland's culture" to prevent potential alienation and cultural decline, thereby better serving their "motherland". A textbook titled *Guochou Qianshuo* (國仇淺說, *A Short Introduction to the National Feud*) was developed by the Society of Chinese Residents in Australia (對日救國後援會) with nationalist tones to "awaken children and strengthen their patriotism".[102] Alongside the inoculation of nationalism rooted in anti-Japanese discourse, the Australian Kuomintang made Chinese education more accessible to local Chinese by replacing the textbooks written in classical style with those in the vernacular.[103] The music Chinese students learned was mostly war songs, including China's national anthem today, *March of the Volunteers*.[104]

Endeavours to mobilise homeland-oriented patriotism were not homogenous but followed a diversity of approaches. Because of the Kuomintang's sponsorship, the Chinese-language school in Sydney overtly focused on promoting party-state rule, affirming the Kuomintang's indisputable prestige and authority. All schools affiliated with the Australian Kuomintang prioritised party doctrines.[105] Rituals such as singing the party song became a regular part of the school's

---

101  Miss Tso Yung Chen, 2 November 1944, BP242/1, Q30575, 466983, NAA.

102  *Chinese Republic News*, "華校茶會紀盛," 26 December 1931, 6; "僑校懇親會誌盛," 23 July 1932, 6; *Tung Wah Times*, "救國會第十五次常會紀," 30 January 1932, 8; "救國會第二十一次常會," 12 March 1932, 8; "美利濱中華公會教育科董事會通告," 25 February 1933, 5; "澳洲雪梨華僑學校募捐啟事," 8 July 1933, 8; "教部已照準美利濱漢文學校備案," 29 July 1933, 5.

103  澳洲總支部執行委員會秘書處 1931, 153–54.

104  *Herald*, "They learn to answer father back," 27 April 1940, 16.

105  澳洲總支部執行委員會秘書處 1931, 139, 268.

tea parties and parent–teacher meetings. Academic excellence awards included texts like *Sun Yat-sen's Doctrine* (總理遺教), further enshrining the party's authority.[106] In comparison, the school operated by the Chinese Citizens Society in Melbourne placed less emphasis on party-state ideology and more on a broader notion of "Republican China". It included practices such as bowing formally to the national flag and singing patriotic songs at the beginning and end of gatherings.[107]

Apart from preserving heritage and fostering loyalty, the Chinese-language schools were commissioned to expand the Nanking government's authority by promoting Mandarin as the primary Chinese language to replace Cantonese dialects for communication within Chinese Australian communities. Social networks of diaspora Chinese were frequently based on family and clan affiliations, rather than a broader national identity,[108] of which Cantonese dialects were indispensable to serve as a marker of heritage, loyalty and identity. While instrumental in interweaving the community for solidarity, these dialects posed a challenge to the emerging Chinese national identity. They worked against acceptance of the authority of the Kuomintang regime by demarcating the boundary between Cantonese-speaking immigrants and Mandarin speakers (most of whom were Chinese officials), precluding Chinese Australians from being integrated into China's official narrative and the discourse of a united Chinese nation guided by the Kuomintang's doctrines and ideology (discussed in subsequent chapters).

Therefore, Nanking reiterated in the early 1930s the use of Mandarin for all courses in overseas Chinese-language schools, in place of Cantonese, to unify diaspora communities and reinforce their connection with and commitment to China.[109] The new policy seemed

---

106 *Chinese Republic News*, "華校茶會紀盛," 26 December 1931, 6; "僑校懇親會誌盛," 23 July 1932, 6.
107 *Tung Wah Times*, "美利濱中華公會附設中華補習學校新校舍舉行開幕典禮誌盛," 3 March 1934, 5.
108 Lydon 1999, 67.
109 Correspondence from Chinese Consul General in Melbourne and Overseas Chinese Affairs Council in China, 1931, AU NBAC 111-9-4, NBAC; *Chinese*

practical and also well received by students in Australia, due not only to the popularity of Chinese phonetic notation in the 1930s (helping learners to understand Chinese characters), but also to the valuable rewards – including cameras and gilded picture frames – for those who excelled academically.[110]

Many students at the Kuomintang-sponsored school in Sydney could also accurately pronounce and speak Mandarin, and their public speeches at a parent–teacher association meeting in 1932 impressed the audience. Chen Wei-ping (陳維屏), the Chinese consul general, proudly claimed that the improvement in and popularity of Mandarin was both a personal success for the students and a sign of the increased status of Chinese culture in Western society.[111] This perspective was echoed by Loh Kai-tze and local community leaders, who argued that education improved social status and was indispensable for their national salvation and ethnic equality.[112] In essence, Chinese education was politicised to realise Nanking's agenda to exert leadership over and exact support from the Chinese Australian community. It simultaneously symbolised Chinese modernisation to counter the White Australia policy. This idea was continually prioritised and emphasised in subsequent Kuomintang moves to integrate the Chinese diaspora into China's political agenda throughout its War of Resistance.[113]

## Conclusion

Historians have correctly argued about the heterogeneity of "Chinese identity" and that Chinese-ness varied according to socio-economic

*Republic News*, "華僑學校應用國語教授," 14 January 1933, 8; *Tung Wah Times*, "華僑學校應用國語教授," 7 January 1933, 5.

110  *Chinese Republic News*, "華校茶會紀盛," 26 December 1931, 6; "僑校懇親會誌盛," 23 July 1932, 6.

111  *Chinese Republic News*, "僑校懇親會誌盛," 23 July 1932, 6.

112  *Tung Wah Times*, "僑校概況與發展前途," 30 July 1932, 5; "美利濱中華補習學校歡送會誌盛," 18 August 1934, 5.

113  *Chinese Republic News*, "新運視察員駱介子," 16 January 1937, 4.

Figure 1.1 Chen Wei-ping (*Methodist*, "With Dr. Chen at Canberra and Queanbeyan," 9 May 1936, 12).

position, legal status and political affiliations.[114] The underscored diversity highlights heterogenous loyalties within Chinese Australian communities that challenged Kuomintang China's traditional claim of leadership over them and efforts to garner their support to counter Japanese aggression. Both Chinese-language newspapers and schools were thus utilised as conduits for propaganda to encounter this challenge, to reclaim and educate diaspora Chinese about their heritage and mobilise homeland-oriented patriotism. Despite progress, it was not very easy, and even backfired with the changing political landscapes among China, the Sino-Japanese relationship and Chinese Australian communities.

---

114 Kamp 2022, 125; Williams 2018, 160–2.

# 2
# Nanking's voices contested

The efforts of Chinese authorities and their supporters in Australia to encourage homeland-oriented patriotism had unintended consequences. Their engagement backfired – intensely – by triggering political ruptures rather than fostering solidarity within Chinese Australian communities. It thereby jeopardised the relationship between the diaspora and the regime governing their homeland. Chiang Kai-shek's controversial policy of "non-resistance" was held accountable for much of this paradoxical outcome. The Chinese Chamber of Commerce and Chinese Masonic Society in Sydney – two of the three most prominent Chinese diaspora associations – spearheaded campaigns challenging Nanking's claim to leadership over Chinese Australians. The Chinese Chamber of Commerce was established by Chinese merchants in 1913 and had once been hostile to republicanism, while the Chinese Masonic Society was once allied with the Kuomintang during the republican revolution but broke ties in the 1920s.[1] The 1930s also saw anti-Japanese campaigning by Chinese Australian newspapers simultaneously advocating for different political agendas.

This chapter will explore the intricate dynamics within Chinese Australian communities and their relationship with China, exemplified

---

1   Yong 1977, 90, 113–68.

by the co-existence of their bitterness towards the Nanking government and its policy of placating Japanese aggression. It examines the evolving anti-Nanking narratives of the *Tung Wah Times*, followed by a discussion of the fierce clash between the anti-Nanking *Chinese World's News* and the Chinese government's attempt to suppress these dissenting voices. The chapter examines the anti-Japanese campaigns endorsed by these newspapers and the active engagement of their readers in these campaigns. It sheds light on the Chinese Australian experience during a period of political turmoil, not uncommon throughout Chinese diasporas in the 1930s.[2] This chapter thus contributes to scholarship refuting the simplified narrative of assumed diaspora loyalty to China.[3]

## Tung Wah Times

Established in 1898 and later serving as the official organ of the Chinese Chamber of Commerce in Sydney, the *Tung Wah Times* ardently championed the progressive elements of Confucianism and propagated anti-Kuomintang sentiments. Available at the same price as the *Chinese Times*, the paper boldly claimed to have "agencies in all principal towns" across Australia, New Zealand, China, Hong Kong and the United States. It also boldly claimed to have the largest circulation in Australia, New Zealand and the Pacific Islands.[4] The *Tung Wah Times* notably employed a distinctive dating method that combined the birth anniversary of Confucius and the Republic of China, incorporating solar and lunar calendars. While information about the paper's personnel through the 1930s is scarce, records indicate that in 1938 at least four individuals were employed: Stanley South (translator and editor); Pang Fong (manager); Violet Young (secretary) and Jong Foo

---

2   Chinese Americans had similar experiences, see 麥禮謙 1992, 187, 207, 223.
3   For scholarship that challenges the essentialised view of China–diaspora relations as a simple dominant–dominated binary, see Chan 2015; 2018.
4   Letter to the Home and Territories Department, 2 March 1931, A433, 1945/2/3557, 3093972, NAA.

Figure 2.1 Compositors at the *Tung Wah Times* (*ABC Weekly* (1942) 4(9): 6. National Library of Australia).

Chong (compositor and assistant editor, who also played an important role in the control of the newspaper).[5]

The *Tung Wah Times* was often perceived as a representative of conservatism, primarily due to its veneration of Confucianism, which was seen as an obstacle to Chinese modernisation in the 1920s.[6] This paper and the *Chinese Republic News* had previously been in opposition, especially concerning whether Chinese monarchy or

---

5    J. Fitzgerald 2007, 102; Kuo 2013, 128; Memorandum of Home and Territories Department, 24 January 1928; Memorandum, 28 June 1938, A433, 1945/2/3557, 3093972, NAA; *Tung Wah Times*, "總商會祝孔祝節紀盛," 12 October 1935, 8.
6    For how Confucianism was perceived during 1920s Chinese modernisation, see 劉建軍 2012, 112–13.

republicanism should shape the future of their homeland in the early 20th century.[7] Under the prestigious chamber's sponsorship, the paper wielded significant influence in the 1930s and became a formidable rival to Nanking's advocates in Australia. Due to this sponsorship, Canberra labelled it as being controlled by an external source, like the *Chinese Times*, while the *Chinese World's News* of the Chinese Masonic Society was seen differently.[8]

One of the newspaper's consistent positions was pressing the Chinese government to replace the "non-resistance" policy and declare war on Japan. As major imperialist powers that owned significant interests in China would be jeopardised by a Sino-Japanese war, a declaration of war was deemed necessary to compel Japan to halt its aggression. In contrast, the newspapers doubted the ability of the League of Nations to stop Japan's invasion.[9] The newspaper also suggested that Nanking should simultaneously convene a Pacific conference to involve interested countries in confronting Japanese aggression, particularly encouraging the United States and possibly the Soviet Union to join.[10]

Despite the *Tung Wah Times* echoing the *Chinese Republic News* in advocating international intervention against Japanese aggression, the two papers diverged greatly on which prominent power(s) China should procure support from. Compared to the favouring of the Soviet Union and the distrust of the West of the *Chinese Republic News*, the attitude of the *Tung Wah Times* was generally the opposite. It preferred to use Western powers for China's benefit and was reluctant to recommend seeking the Soviet Union's help. It bitterly opposed communism and Chiang's attempts to restore the Sino-Soviet relationship.[11] The *Tung Wah Times* viewed the Soviet Union as no better than Japan, arguing that a Sino-Soviet alliance would encourage the expansion of the Chinese Communist Party. Introducing the Soviet

7    Yong 1977, 93.
8    Memorandum, 7 December 1939, A2998, 1952/253, 3107692, NAA.
9    *Tung Wah Times*, "中日關係與世界和平," 25 November 1933, 2; "造成國際嚴重局面," 26 May 1934, 2.
10   *Tung Wah Times* "東北問題如何解決," 6 August 1932, 2.
11   So 2002, 215.

Union to counter Japan was akin to "rejecting a tiger while welcoming a wolf".[12] Nevertheless, the paper did not entirely trust the West, believing that its potential interference would further its existing privileges and encroachment on Chinese sovereignty obtained in China's century of humiliation: great powers were predisposed to "bully the weak".[13]

Such ambivalence about the strategy of playing off one or more significant powers against the others indicated a helpless dilemma for Chinese Australian intellectuals whose desires to have China emerge from the national calamity had to rely upon countries that were still committed to infringing Chinese sovereignty. Establishing a potent China was a possible and realistic way to address this predicament. It is therefore not difficult to find that the *Tung Wah Times* placed greater emphasis on the importance of successful Chinese nation-building and cultivation of an independent national spirit, staunchly insisting that "God helps those who help themselves".[14] Many news pieces and editorials dealt with managing social, economic and military development while pursuing political and national unity to succeed in China's War of Resistance. Most instigated a clamour for a comprehensive "reform" and "revolution" to fortify China's position against Japanese aggression, seeing those catastrophic concessions due to the Kuomintang's inefficacious bureaucratic system.[15]

Reform or revolution meant a complete reformulation of the Kuomintang principal doctrine in a one-party-rule dictatorship in the political organisation of China. Indeed, the *Tung Wah Times* diligently advanced democratisation in building a Chinese nation-state that significantly emphasised the negotiation between various political parties, state apparatus and civil society. For example, Chiang's line of "internal pacification" was reinterpreted as unity between parties

---

12  *Tung Wah Times*, "中俄復交問題," 25 June 1932, 2; "中俄復交問題," 2 July 1932, 2.

13  *Tung Wah Times*, "東北四省之前途," 15 July 1933, 2.

14  *Tung Wah Times*, "國人只有自救壹途," 31 October 1931, 2; "今後之遠東問題," 28 May 1932, 2; "天助自助之," 21 January 1933, 2.

15  *Tung Wah Times*, "偏安與興革," 12 August 1933, 2; "如何能根本肅清共禍," 1 December 1934, 2.

through a coalition government to dismiss the Kuomintang's dictatorship and to resist Japan's aggression instead of an eradication of political rivals as promoted.[16] It rejected Nanking's perspective to see all rivals as fundamentally menacing and argued for an evaluation of the performance of these parties before deciding whether they were hindrances to a unified anti-Japanese effort.[17]

Meanwhile, the paper assiduously promoted a cordial and collaborative relationship between the Chinese government and the public. The nation, rather than the state, was considered the backbone of the war. Public opinion and strength were believed to deserve particular attention through establishing a government "by the people" and "for the people", to institutionalise the state-nation relationship and ensure the authorities were well informed about public interests in order to prioritise them.[18] Accordingly, mobilising public participation to the fullest extent in China's war effort was called for. Not only could this be realised through social organisations, such as volunteer militias and self-support civilian societies,[19] but declaring war on Japan would rejuvenate the "low ebb of Chinese national spirit and the fading will of the people", as struggle was the "supreme philosophy of peace".[20] As such, China could realise "true solidarity" and stop Japan's invasion.[21]

These demands additionally reflected conspicuous and persistent critiques of the Kuomintang regime in a plethora of editorials, news articles and literary compositions that focused on Nanking's

16  *Tung Wah Times*, "由對日交涉之所感," 26 September 1931, 2; "對日兵強占滿洲之觀感," 3 October 1931, 2; "廢止內戰與外交," 1 October 1932, 2.
17  *Tung Wah Times*, "安內之限度問題," 16 February 1935, 2.
18  *Tung Wah Times*, "對日兵強占滿洲之觀感," 3 October 1931, 2; "沉悶局面如何打破," 30 April 1932, 2; "中國人之奇恥," 16 July 1932, 2; "請行政院通電書後," 23 July 1932, 2.
19  *Tung Wah Times*, "對日兵強占滿洲之觀感," 3 October 1931, 2; "國人只有自救壹途," 31 October 1931, 2; "國人應註意日方之夾攻形勢," 1 October 1932, 2; "新政府成立感言," 25 February 1936, 2.
20  *Tung Wah Times*, "不抵抗與自殺," 28 November 1931, 2; "拯救和平," 12 December 1936, 2.
21  *Tung Wah Times*, "中華民族能保生存乎," 1 August 1936, 2; "其盡豆焦釜亦破裂," 5 September 1936, 2.

unsuccessful state-building and resistance. Even Chiang Kai-shek's efforts to modernise China were perceived as methods to actualise and consolidate the Kuomintang dictatorship.[22] His policy of "non-resistance" was certainly bitterly denounced and taken to challenge the regime's professed role as the "custodian" of the Chinese populace.[23] The *Tung Wah Times* embarked on a deconstruction of the Nanking government's legitimacy. It switched the narrative of the Kuomintang's abortive resistance from what was initially characterised as *"wuguo"* (誤國, misleading the nation) and *"guochi"* (國恥, national humiliation) to a graver connotation as *"maiguo"* (賣國, betraying the nation) and *"guonan"* (國難, national calamity).[24] These altered terms underscored the profound deterioration of Chinese sovereignty under Nanking's leadership and, more importantly, a shift in the perception of the regime from a leadership with errors to one deemed national traitors. The changing terms indicated diminishing prospects and capabilities for the Chinese government to rectify itself, suggesting that the leadership of the Kuomintang posed a grave threat to the Chinese nation's survival and that overthrowing the Nanking regime was the sole viable solution.

In response to persistent and hardening opposition, Nanking repeatedly sought to reassure dissidents of Chiang Kai-shek's determination to resist Japanese aggression, hoping to gain their endorsement and build solidarity between China and its diaspora.[25] But tensions between Nanking's followers and their rivals in Australia

---

22  *Tung Wah Times*, "蔣介石口中之禮義廉恥," 31 March 1934, 2; "憲法與憲政 (上)," 12 May 1934, 2; "憲法與憲政 (下)," 19 May 1934, 2; "五四紀念," 9 June 1934, 2; "西南之謎," 16 June 1934, 2; "國事感懷,"18 August 1934, 5; "蔣中正所謂禮義廉恥之新註腳," 15 September 1934, 5; "復興民族當註重一誠字," 13 April 1935, 2.

23  *Tung Wah Times*, "蔣日妥協之五條件(上)," 17 June 1933, 2; "蔣日妥協之五條件(下)," 24 June 1933, 2; "停戰協定簽字後," 8 July 1933, 2; "傀儡溥儀果不成為討伐對象乎," 21 April 1934, 2; "國家危亡之癥結在於官," 18 August 1934, 2.

24  *Tung Wah Times*, "當局何以對國民," 23 June 1934, 2; "國恥與國難," 13 June 1936, 2.

25  *Chinese Republic News*, "公電," 18 March 1933, 8.

escalated into devastating ruptures during the visits of Tsai Ting-kai in 1935. Tsai Ting-kai – celebrated for defending Shanghai in 1932 but later involved in the 1933 anti-Chiang Kai-shek mutiny in Fukien – became a contested figure in Australia. Chiang's critics viewed Tsai as a patriot; his supporters, a traitor. When Tsai applied to enter Australia in 1935, tensions between opposing factions within Chinese Australian communities resurfaced. Canberra navigated these dynamics carefully – granting him entry while restricting any political activity that might undermine Nanking's authority.[26] As the subsequent section shows, Canberra continued to play a delicate role in navigating complex political dynamics within Chinese Australian communities.

The dispute over Tsai's visit quickly devolved into a bitter and vitriolic journalistic war between the *Tung Wah Times* and the *Chinese Times*. Even after Tsai's return to China, the fallout lingered: friendships were fractured, trust eroded and bitterness became pervasive. Patriotic agendas based on divergent concepts of "China" paradoxically spoiled each other's pursuit of solidarity for China's war.[27] The *Tung Wah Times* continued to stress the duty of overseas Chinese to hold Nanking accountable and criticised the *Chinese Times* for toeing the Kuomintang's official line, questioning its legitimacy as a qualified newspaper expected to be independent from government interference.[28]

Written documents suggest the *Tung Wah Times* continued to publish until April 1942, when the decision to wind up the business was made.[29] The precise reasons for its discontinuation are unknown, due to a dearth of records available for review. A confluence of factors

---

26   Longfield Lloyd to H.E. Jones, 25 February 1935, 173584, NAA.
27   Hu 2024, 668–704.
28   *Tung Wah Times*, "誣人造謠無理取鬧," 11 January 1936, 8; "爲奉派來澳視察新運告僑胞同志書," 19 December 1936, 2.
29   For documents that confirmed the paper's closure, see *Dun's Gazette for New South Wales* 67, no. 21 (1942): 239; "The Tung Wah Times Newspaper Co. Ltd.," *Government Gazette of the State of New South Wales*, no. 59 (1943): 1371. For the traditional view, see Bagnall, 2015b; Gilson 1962, 1; Huang and Ommundsen 2015, 9; Jones 2005, 65; Kuo 2013, 6. For the document from Australian censors, see Address to Censorship Office, 29 July 1941, C320, C8, 1495438, NAA.

could partly account for this conclusion. One could have been the insufficient supply of news information essential for publication. By 1941, Japan had successively taken Kwangtung (廣東) and Hong Kong, pivotal transportation hubs for Chinese emigrants and their material exchanges, and this may have severely disrupted the circulation of news to Australia. It is likely that this exacerbated the paper's pre-existing financial dilemma, as the war constrained the chamber's activities.[30] By the end of June 1937, the newspaper had incurred a net loss of £144, with a small circulation of approximately 500 copies per week and income of about £1,211. In comparison, it had reported a net profit of around £332 in 1927 and a weekly circulation of about 2,000 copies in 1928.[31]

Moreover, as subsequent chapters show, the diaspora community leadership was in the process of transition during the 1940s. The Chinese Chamber of Commerce and the Masons were experiencing an ebb, as many new organisations sponsored by Chinese authorities, local Chinese Australian elites and leftist immigrants were established for patriotic purposes, becoming new intermediaries between China, Australia and Chinese Australian communities.

## Chinese World's News

The antipathy of the *Tung Wah Times* was joined by another prestigious Chinese-language newspaper – the *Chinese World's News* – that rallied resistance against the Kuomintang and its claim of leadership over Chinese Australians. Sold at a rate of 5 pence per issue, with an annual subscription cost of £1 for readers in Australia (with an additional 2 shillings for postal service within the South Pacific and a 4 shilling postage fee for the rest of the world),[32] the paper claimed to have a global circulation within Chinese communities and to be distributed

---

30  Chinese Societies in New South Wales, November 1941, 3051769, NAA.
31  Balance Sheet, 30 June 1927; Memorandum from H.B. Cody to the Director of NSW Customs, 24 February 1938; Jong Foo Chong, 11 March 1938, A433, 1945/2/3557, 3093972, NAA.
32  *Chinese World's News*, 22 August 1936, SP42/1, C1936/5686, 31112332, NAA.

directly to Chinese storekeepers and merchants in Australia and the Pacific Islands.[33]

The *Chinese World's News* was the official organ of the Chinese Masonic Society – "definitely anti-Nanking government"[34] – which joined the Chinese Chamber of Commerce and the Kuomintang as the most prestigious three organisations within the diaspora community in Australia, likely owing to its extensive membership that constituted a substantial portion of local Chinese. In New South Wales, for instance, the Masons boasted approximately 1,000 members, predominantly concentrated in Sydney, where the Chinese population was estimated to be between 1,000 and 2,000. In stark contrast, the Kuomintang had only reported about 70 financial members in the region, most of whom were from the "market-dealer class" and financially constrained.[35]

The potent membership numbers laid a robust foundation for the Masons' financial capacity and for mobilisation capabilities committed to anti-Kuomintang campaigns. Although few files on their financial operation in the 1930s have survived, a glimpse of those in the 1940s demonstrates their financial competence. A special appeal by the Masons to their branches in Melbourne and Ballarat yielded a collective sum of £2,228 from their membership in 1943 so as to offset a financial loss of around £12 incurred in 1942.[36] But the primary financial source for the Masons consistently came from membership donations.[37]

The operational structure of the *Chinese World's News* in the 1930s was notably distinct from the four Chinese-language newspapers. The other three papers enjoyed the patronage of their respective sponsors, but the relationship between the *Chinese World's News* and the Masons was more of a leasehold nature than financial sponsorship. The actual owner of the paper was a press company called Chinese News Ltd,

---

33　Quan Mane to Joseph Lyons, 17 September 1935, A445, 232/4/18, 1963788, NAA.
34　D.R.B. Mitchell to the Secretary of the Department of External Affairs, 20 December 1935, A367, C1822, 428437, NAA.
35　D.R.B. Mitchell to the Secretary of the Department of External Affairs, 20 December 1935, A367, C1822, 428437, NAA.
36　*Chinese World's News*, 22 August 1936, SP42/1, C1936/5686, 31112332, NAA.
37　Revenue Account, 31 December 1943; Book of Account, 31 December 1944, Chinese World's News Ltd, 1922–1938, NSWSAR.

the proprietor of which was the then-editor, Quan Mane. Although his company entered liquidation in 1930 and was still in liquidation by 1935, Quan and the Masons had an arrangement wherein he leased the printing equipment and premises owned by the Masons annually on behalf of the *Chinese World's News*.[38]

Prioritising the authority of the organisations it represented as the *Chinese Times* did, the *Chinese World's News* featured the calligraphic inscription of Tsai Ting-kai who was also a distinguished member of the Masons in China.[39] Tsai's complex dual roles, as both a patriotic symbol of resistance against Tokyo and a prominent figure advocating the overthrow of Nanking, were strategically leveraged through his inscription in the newspaper, thus positioning the *Chinese World's News* as the embodiment of Chinese patriotism opposed to both Japanese aggression and Nanking's rule.

A notable personnel overlap underscored a close alliance between the *Chinese World's News* and the *Tung Wah Times*, much like the relationship between the *Chinese Times* and the *Chinese Republic News*. Editor Quan Mane had previously served in the same position at the *Tung Wah Times*, and the roles of translator and assistant editor (or possibly editor – the precise title is not clear) at *Chinese World's News* were held by Stanley South, a Chinese immigrant who had resided in Australia before Federation and had led the editorship of the *Tung Wah Times*. Stanley South died in June 1939 and his position at the *Chinese World's News* was taken by Jung Chick Yee.[40] This arrangement ensured a collaborative effort in disseminating propaganda opposing Nanking and promoting patriotism.

While few copies of the *Chinese World's News* from the 1930s have endured, a surviving issue published on 22 August 1936 provides a window into the newspaper's political narrative that unequivocally demonstrated anti-Kuomintang voices. By favouring Chang Tai-yen

---

38   Yu Kwan, 5 April 1935, A433, 1947/2/6297 Part 2, 4037888, NAA.
39   Fees for Certificate, 26 August 1936, SP42/1, C1936/5686, 31112332, NAA.
40   Memorandum, 27 July 1933, A2998, 1952/253, 3107692; Chen Wei-ping to the Secretary of the Department of External Affairs, 9 August 1935, A445, 232/4/18, 1963788; Memorandum from H.B. Cody to the Director of NSW Customs, 24 February 1938, A433, 1945/2/3357, 3093972; C.F. Marks to the Boarding Inspector, 5 July 1939, A2998, 1952/253, 3107692, NAA.

(章太炎) – a prominent revolutionary philosopher and a staunch opponent of Sun Yat-sen – in an editorial, the *Chinese World's News* bluntly and fiercely criticised Chiang Kai-shek's dictatorship and Sun Yat-sen's doctrine. Sun's "Three Principles of the People" were derided as "nonsense"; alliance with Soviet Russia and Chinese communists in the 1920s was characterised as *"huoguo"* (禍國, detrimental to the nation); and education policy was portrayed as destructive. These bitter condemnations clearly showed the radical rejection by the newspaper and the Masons of the Kuomintang's claimed legitimacy in ruling the Chinese nation.[41] Such views went even further than the *Tung Wah Times*, whose disapproval centred on rejecting Nanking's authority rather than denying the whole Kuomintang.

The *Chinese World's News* threatened the Chinese government more significantly than the *Tung Wah Times*. Unlike the declining circulation that many of its counterparts in the United States and Australia experienced,[42] the cooperative rather than affiliate relation between *Chinese World's News* and the Masons proved effective in countering financial challenges by allowing Quan Mane to enjoy better flexibility and exert more agency in boosting the press. This approach saw growth in sales in the 1930s.[43] A statement provided by the company in 1935 indicated that the newspaper maintained a monthly circulation of approximately 6,000 copies, generating a turnover of £2,741. But a financial deficit of £49 was recorded after accounting for deductions, including an amount of £300 allocated to Quan and his five children.[44]

The contradiction indicates an exaggeration in the company's stated copies in circulation, but the claimed growth of circulation and profits appeared to be factual. Inspection officials observed that the paper's weekly circulation was around 1,250 copies in 1933, increasing to about 1,750 copies by 1939. The upward trend continued in subsequent years, with another increase of 500 copies in circulation, particularly after the *Chinese Republic News* ceased functioning in

---

41  Fees for Certificate, 26 August 1936, SP42/1, C1936/5686, 31112332, NAA.
42  For Chinese American newspapers, see 麥禮謙 1992, 225.
43  Notice, 28 January 1930, Chinese World's News Ltd, 1922–1938, NSWSAR.
44  Yu Kwan, 5 April 1935, A433, 1947/2/6297 Part 2, 4037888, NAA.

February 1940. By 1941, the circulation had expanded to approximately 2,500 copies per week. The circulation growth was accompanied by a spike in turnover, rising from £1,700 to £2,741 between 1932 and 1934. When the circulation culminated in 1941, it became capable of supporting eight staff members.[45] In comparison, the *Chinese Times*, having a weekly circulation of only 1,000 copies, employed only four staff members, a number that Australian authorities considered "rather large". The employment of additional staff by the *Chinese Times* was only possible because the paper was the Kuomintang's official voice.[46]

It is essential to acknowledge the challenges in accurately determining the total circulation of these Chinese newspapers, as surviving documents are not always reliable. Not only was exaggeration typical in the statements from these papers, but it was also insufficient for Australian authorities to authenticate their circulation, which was usually based on those overstatements (the manager of the *Chinese Republic News* in the 1920s told the Australian government that it had 20,000 copies circulated per week, while Australian customs reported about 5,000 copies).[47] Nevertheless, these figures align reasonably with what contemporaries in the 1930s generally speculated. When the publishers informed Rudolf Lowenthal that their total circulation per issue was 12,000, he expressed "without doubt" that this number was "greatly exaggerated". If the Chinese population, many of whom were illiterate, numbered "below 16,000" in Australia and New Zealand, the total circulation would scarcely exceed 3,000 to 4,000 for the entire region.[48]

The evident popularity and financial advantage of the *Chinese World's News* enabled it to initiate capable and sustainable anti-Kuomintang propaganda whose influential sway perturbed the Chinese government. The Chinese consul general, Chen Wei-ping, was instructed to take action to close down the respective anti-Nanking

---

45  Lowenthal 1937, 2. H.B. Cody and Thos. V. Maher to the Boarding Inspector, 1933–1935, A433, 1947/2/6297 Part 2, 4037888; Paul Wong, 9 May 1941; H.B. Cody and L.T. Gamble to the Boarding Inspector, 1933–1941, A2998, 1952/253, 3107692, NAA.
46  Memorandum, 22 April 1940, A2998, 1951/4501, 3106028, NAA.
47  Yu Kwan, 24 November 1934, 1947/2/6297 Part 2, 4037888, NAA.
48  Lowenthal 1937, 2.

voices of the Masonic Society and the Chamber of Commerce.[49] While historians have argued that the warming Sino-Australian relationship in the 1930s elevated the consul general's authority and leadership role,[50] the evidence from the dispute between the *Chinese World's News* and the consul general illustrates a different scenario: the strengthening diplomatic ties did not necessarily translate to a better position for local Chinese authorities within Chinese Australian communities.

In order to attract attention from Canberra and wind up those anti-Nanking newspapers, Chinese authorities in Australia emphasised the severity of their damage to the Chinese government's prestige. In 1935, Chen Wei-ping and his associate Wang Kung-fang (王恭芳) brought to the attention of Prime Minister Joseph Lyons a series of criticisms published by the *Chinese World's News* in July and December. These articles referred to Chiang Kai-shek and Wang Ching-wei as national "quislings" and "betrayers" who were "selling" China to Japan, calling for united actions to "down Chiang". These attacks were so offensive that they antagonised the Australian headquarters of the Kuomintang, whose members were claimed to be prominent leaders of the Chinese community.[51] Wang Kung-fang also accused the staff at the *Chinese World's News* of attempts to undertake anti-Kuomintang propaganda.[52] This was partly proved when some Chinese approached G.A. Monticone – the chief government interpreter – to seek translation of the article into English for a wider readership. Monticone declined, citing his unwillingness to get involved in disputes within the Chinese diaspora community.[53]

49   Chen Wei-ping to A.R. Peters, 19 February 1935, A433, 1947/2/6297 Part 2, 4037888, NAA.
50   Kuo and Brett 2013, 98.
51   Chen Wei-ping to George Pearce, 22 July 1935, A367, C1822, 428437; K.F. Wang to the Secretary of the Prime Minister's Department, 6 December 1935, A455, 232/4/18, 3093972; K.F. Wang to the Secretary of the Prime Minister's Department, 13 December 1935, A445, 232/4/18, 1963788, NAA.
52   K.F. Wang to the Secretary of the Prime Minister's Department, 13 December 1935, A445, 232/4/18, 1963788, NAA.
53   D.R.B. Mitchell to the Secretary of the Department of External Affairs, 20 December 1935, A367, C1822, 428437, NAA.

The consul general also highlighted one of Canberra's concerns (although without concrete evidence) that both the *Chinese World's News* and the *Tung Wah Times* incited discord within the diaspora community in Australia through their shared anti-Nanking propaganda. Chen sought clauses to fortify his argument that this propaganda violated the rules stipulated in the Commonwealth Publication of Newspapers in Foreign Languages Regulations, urging Australian authorities to consider shutting down the operations of both newspapers. To further these points, he claimed that the Chinese readership would be satisfied with the *Chinese Republic News* and the *Chinese Times*, which provided sufficient information about China and their native-origin villages, considering the defined literacy rate of Chinese Australians.[54]

Alongside efforts to convince Australian leadership, there was an endeavour to limit the growth of the *Chinese World's News* by preventing it from hiring additional employees, particularly compositors. In the early 1930s, Quan Mane, the paper's editor, and Charles Ng Kin (伍根), the grand master of the Masons in Sydney, hired Yu Kwan (also known as Yick Kwan or Wong Yak Kwan, recently dismissed after a legal dispute with the *Chinese Republic News*) as compositor and paid the fee to obtain exemption from the immigration laws designed to maintain the White Australia policy. The *Chinese Republic News* vehemently protested Yu Kwan's new employment under the sponsorship of the *Chinese World's News*, seeing this collaboration as "the most unscrupulous method to injure their company".

An additional staff member would cement the already substantial propaganda capacity of the Masons and the *Chinese World's News*. When Canberra sought the informal opinion of Chen Wei-ping regarding the legitimacy of the accusations, the consul general decided to politicise the controversy by indicating his disapproval of the *Chinese World's News'* employment of a new compositor, primarily based on the paper's strong opposition to Nanking and the political unrest it had stirred within the Chinese diaspora community. But such efforts

---

54 Chen Wei-ping to George Pearce, 22 July 1935; Chen Wei-ping to the Secretary of the Department of External Affairs, 9 August 1935, A455, 232/4/18, 3093972, NAA.

proved to be in vain, as Australia dismissed both the claims made by the *Chinese Republic News* and Chen Wei-ping's recommendations, and approved Yu Kwan to work for a new employer. The decision was based more on financial than political concerns about the *Chinese World's News* because the Department of the Interior was "not concerned with the dissensions existing amongst these Chinese".[55] Hiring Yu Kwan in 1935 improved the newspaper's circulation by another 1,000 copies per month, as Chen had feared.[56]

China's efforts to silence anti-Nanking voices also failed due to active resistance from the *Chinese World's News*. A firm belief in modern democracy had been ingrained in the Chinese diasporic experience in Australia from the early 20th century.[57] Reflecting this sensibility, Quan Mane launched passionate protests against Canberra's attempt to shut down the newspaper at China's request. Quan argued that the political dissent expressed in the newspaper was no different from the disagreements between white Australian newspapers that had sparked controversies in the past and present. Meanwhile, the published news was taken verbatim from Chinese newspapers in Hong Kong and approved by local authorities,[58] indicating that Britain had no objection to the authenticity of the news. Quan Mane warned Canberra not to intervene too much in diaspora community affairs, as shutting the *Chinese World's News* down would signify Australia taking a side in the "domestic affairs of a foreign country", while siding with the Kuomintang would imply Canberra was at odds with seven major local Chinese societies.[59] Despite offending Australian authorities, Quan

---

55  Chen Wei-ping to A.R. Peters, 9 November 1934; Chen Wei-ping to A.R. Peters, 19 February 1935; Yu Kwan, 5 April 1935, A433, 1947/2/6297 Part 2, 4037888, NAA.

56  C.F. Marks to the Boarding Inspector, 5 July 1939, A2998, 1952/253, 3107692, NAA.

57  Kuo 2013.

58  The *Chinese World's News* did not have cable service as the *Chinese Times* did, so it translated news from papers received from Hong Kong and Shanghai and republished them, see Memorandum, 7 December 1939, A2998, 1952/253, 3107692, NAA.

59  Quan Mane to the Secretary and Prime Minister, 1935–1936, A455, 232/4/18, 3093972, NAA; *Tung Wah Times*, "中華總商會茶會紀盛," 15 October 1932, 5.

Mane insisted on expressing his nation-first patriotism, arguing that Chinese Australians were greatly concerned about their beloved China's future in the context of the Kuomintang's successive concessions to Japan's invasion.

Quan Mane's representation proved more than convincing to Canberra, who ruled out Chen Wei-ping's demands despite the latter's persistence and pressures. The situation put Chinese authorities at a disadvantage. Not only did the China-hoped-for prohibition of newspaper publication not eventuate (and was replaced by suggestions to seek legal action), but Australian authorities also began to doubt the consul general's motivation in seeking to shut the newspaper down, believing he had "certainly" used his position to further the disputes between Chinese-language newspapers. On the one hand, little evidence other than the dissenting news was offered to justify Chen Wei-ping's accusations. On the other, Canberra was informed by "leading Chinese" that the consul general did not represent Chinese Australians effectively. The Australian Kuomintang's authority within the diaspora community was likewise called into question. Australian officials were conscious of Nanking's unpopularity and the Masons' popularity among resident Chinese, as well as internal divisions within those groups (including the Kuomintang headquarters) favouring the Chinese government.[60]

The Australian government was also in a predicament. Nanking might interpret the rejection of Chen Wei-ping's request as an unfriendly gesture, while an acceptance on ill-founded grounds would certainly antagonise a majority of Chinese Australians. Canberra needed to somehow balance the decision, making it less offensive to Chinese authorities, and thus issued official warnings to both dissident newspapers, threatening to revoke their publication permissions in Australia if future coverage of China was controversial. The papers were

---

60   From W.R. Hodgson to H.E. Jones, 12 December 1935; J.H. Starling to the Chinese Consul General, 4 July 1935; D.R.B. Mitchell to the Secretary of the Department of External Affairs, 20 December 1935, A367, C1822, 428437; *Chinese World's News*, 20 December 1935, A445, 232/4/18, 1963798; Memorandum from H.B. Cody to the Director of NSW Customs, 24 February 1938, A433, 1945/2/3557, 3093972, NAA.

also forbidden from conducting propaganda that could harm Nanking's authority and foment disaffection in Australia. To ensure their compliance, both were required to submit a copy of each future issue to official inspectors.[61] The strategy of rejecting China's demand but restraining Nanking's rivals revealed Canberra's tactful approach to managing the transnational politics within local Chinese communities by maintaining equilibrium between political groups in conflict, to ensure Australia's harmonious links with Chinese Australians and the Chinese government. The complexity of the clash between Nanking and the *Chinese World's News* that implicated multiple players contradicts what researchers have overly simplified as a manifestation of Australian democratic inclusiveness.[62]

The *Chinese World's News* likely understood the delicacy while it continued to oppose the Nanking government. Objectionable content was cloaked in "correct and decorous" language. Equally interesting was that Canberra did not follow through on what it had ruled. Half a year later, in March 1936, Chen Wei-ping again protested to the Australian Department of External Affairs against the *Chinese World's News* for the latter's anti-Nanking reports. The evidenced article reiterated the paper's long-term rebuke of Chiang Kai-shek's policy of "non-resistance" by comparing the Chiangs to a historical but notorious arch-traitor figure – Wu San-kwei (吳三桂) and his disreputable concubine during Imperial Qing. Despite Australian authorities identifying this article as one that "exceeded the limits of reasonable political comment", they only issued another stern warning rather than withdrawing the newspaper's publication permission as promised. The highly questionable effectiveness of such warnings somehow indicated Canberra's unwillingness to reformulate the equilibrium strategy. It was no wonder that Chen Wei-ping expressed his "misgivings" about the ambivalence of Australian authorities and noted his additional but futile efforts to pressure Canberra to take more drastic action.[63]

---

61    Secretary to Chen Wei-ping and Publication of Newspapers in Foreign
        Languages Regulations, 19 August, 13 September 1935, A455, 232/4/18,
        3093972, NAA.
62    Coatney 2021, 97, 99.

The equilibrium strategy indicated Canberra's intention to maintain distance from conflicts between Chinese Australian communities and the Kuomintang government. This strategy encouraged community democracy but also emboldened anti-Nanking camps to challenge Nanking further, intensifying the political divisions within Chinese Australian communities. Indeed, many anti-Nanking advocates began to manoeuvre to procure support from white Australians for their agenda.

One such manoeuvre was illustrated in the case of Vivian Chow's tension with Chinese authorities. Born in Australia in 1906, Chow travelled to Canton in 1925 and later moved to Shanghai, where he worked as a journalist. A staunch critic of the Nanking government, Chow was keenly aware of, and took pride in, the protections conferred by his Australian birthright. These protections shielded Chow from Chen Wei-ping's petition in 1932 to have him arrested upon his return to Australia.[64]

Chow further leveraged the advantages of his transnational identity in 1935, when he intensified his anti-Nanking campaign by revealing to the Australian *Sun* the Kuomintang's suppression of Chinese journalists, thereby ensuring international attention to their plight.[65] This tactic worked well, leading to protests from Australian readers, including the League of Australian Writers, against the Chinese government. Wang Kung-fang, by now the acting Chinese consul general, brought this matter to the attention of Joseph Lyons in order to silence Vivian Chow and advance China's complaint about Chow taking shelter in Australia. Wang's efforts met the same fate as Chen's: he received only a vague reply, advising him to obtain legal counsel.[66]

The struggles between the Kuomintang regime and the *Chinese World's News* ultimately ended in 1942 when the newspaper suspended publication due to wartime disruptions of newsletter transmission and

---

63  Chen Wei-ping to the Secretary of the Department of the External Affairs, 9 April 1936, A445, 232/4/18, 1963798, NAA.
64  J. Fitzgerald 2007, 114.
65  *Sun*, "To face death on Xmas Day," 22 December 1935, 9.
66  J. Fitzgerald 2007, 115; K.F. Wang to J.A. Lyons, 23 December 1935, A981, CON314, 174499, NAA.

printing supplies.[67] Although the paper briefly revived from 1949 to 1951 under the sponsorship of Yee Ben (余炳), the grand master of the Masons and former director of the Chinese Chamber of Commerce, it eventually moved into liquidation in May 1955 because of financial difficulties and was later withdrawn from publication permission.[68]

Financial dilemmas likewise overtook the Chinese Masonic Society for most of the 1930s and 1940s. Financial losses of £41 occurred in 1938 and in 1939. Despite a significant spike in profits from membership donations and special appeals in 1943 across Australia, as mentioned earlier, overall profits declined in the following years. Profits in 1944 shrank to just £478, resulting in a loss of £88 in 1945. There was a slight recovery in 1946 and 1947, with profits of £48 and £224, respectively. Yet an excess over income was again incurred in 1948, amounting to about £149. The fluctuations in fiscal conditions were partly because of a continual loss of membership and limited special appeals, as many left for China after the Pacific War. Renovation and repair of the Masons building at 18 Mary Street, Sydney, also accounted for significant costs, while extra expenditure on a charitable trust fund and Charles Ng Kin's travel to the Melbourne branch may also have harmed their financial condition.[69]

---

67   M.L. Tuan to the Secretary of the Department of the Interior, 21 August 1942, A2998, 1952/253, 3107692, NAA. For the financial condition of the *Chinese World's News*, see Chinese World's News Ltd, 1922–1938, 12951, 8021, NSWSAR.

68   T.H. Heyes to Yee Ben, May 1955, A445, 232/4/18, 1963798, NAA; Report of Annual Return of a Company not having a Share Capital, 31 December 1944, Chinese World's News Ltd, 1922–1938, NSWSAR.

69   Balance Sheet, 31 December 1939; Book of Account, 31 December 1944; Book of Account, 31 December 1945; Yee Ben to Registrar General, 31 December 1946; Directors' Report, 31 December 1947; Revenue Account, 31 December 1948; President Report, 25 July 1949, Chinese World's News Ltd, 1922–1938, NSWSAR. For the financial condition of the Chinese Masonic Society, see Chinese Masonic Society, 1922–1949, 12951, 8177, NSWSAR.

## Anti-Japanese solidarity

The political dynamics within Chinese Australian communities not only featured fragmentation over Chinese affairs but also solidarity against external threats. These diasporic newspapers accommodated their feuds, like their counterparts in America,[70] in the midst of propaganda campaigns against Japanese aggression in China. Through news updates on the war, editorials elaborating Japan's ambition, and literary supplements delivering patriotic narratives, these Chinese-language newspapers created an imagined transnational community that gave Chinese Australians, whose heritages and dialects varied, a sense of unity, linked them to their imagined homeland, and contested white Australian newspapers, which were subjected to Japanese influence publishing incorrect information and failing to grasp the Japanese invasion's gravity.[71]

The most compelling anti-Japanese narratives emerged from the literary writings featured in newspaper supplements. These works portrayed the courage and resilience of Chinese defenders in arresting detail, often intertwining accounts of military valour with Confucian values to construct heroic images that resonated with the Chinese Australian public. The glorious history of resisting Japanese pirates from the 13th to 16th centuries, along with the brave Chinese opposition to Japanese incursions in the late 19th century, was repeatedly invoked. Complementing these uplifting narratives were those steeped in scornful language, condemning the brutality and savagery of the Japanese and vilifying Chinese collaborators who submitted to Japanese authority.[72] The sanctification of Chinese resistance was thus constructed in tandem with the demonisation of the enemy. Didacticism, patriotism, and anti-Japanese sentiment converged in these literary pieces. While some contemporaries criticised them for overshadowing lesser-known figures in favour of

---

70  Zhao 2002, 106–7.
71  For Australian newspapers subjected to Japanese influence, see Macmahon Ball 1938, 10–13; Murray 2004, 16; Putnis 2012, 426–7. For the concept of "imagined community", see Anderson 2006.
72  Hu 2021, 105–9.

martyrs and heroes,[73] this body of Chinese-language literature ultimately served to connect Chinese Australians more closely to their homeland than to their adopted society – unlike much of the Chinese American literature of the time.[74] It inspired morale, strengthened confidence in China's eventual victory over Japan, and deepened patriotic attachment to China while intensifying hostility towards Japan.

The production of patriotic literature was not solely the work of editors, but a collaborative endeavour involving Chinese Australian readers. Much of this literary output was characterised by sentimental, nostalgic and nationalist undertones. Its forms varied considerably, including folk songs written in Cantonese vernacular, such as *Yueou* (粵謳) and *Bailange* (白欖歌), many of which were likely authored by Pang Zijun (龐子峻) in Sydney.[75] These accessible and melodious ballads, imbued with patriotic spirit, were easily sung and transmitted among the community. The popularity of Cantonese vernacular literature centred on Chinese affairs underscores the intersection of local and national dimensions within diasporic Chinese identities. This use of vernacular literature as a vehicle for political expression was not unprecedented; similar strategies had been employed during the anti-Qing revolutionary movement in Kwangtung in the early 20th century.[76]

Chinese poetry and couplets constituted another well-received form of patriotic expression. There were a few particularly active contributors in these genres, including Guo Jiegong (郭潔公) from Sydney, Zhu Longqiu (朱隆裘) from Geraldton, and Zhu Linchang (朱林昌) from Melbourne.[77] Much like their counterparts in the United States,[78] poetic works by Chinese Australians were often composed in

73   黃紹竑 1990, 294.
74   For Chinese American literature, see Yin 2000, 158.
75   *Chinese Republic News,* "持不抵抗," 30 July 1932, 5; *Tung Wah Times,* "哀國恥," 19 December 1931, 5; "黨人怨," 23 March 1935, 5.
76   程美寶 2006, 160.
77   *Chinese Republic News,* "感事七絕十二首," 26 December 1931, 5; *Tung Wah Times,* "中外近事詩," 21 December 1935, 5.

a freer rhythm and a more colloquial tone, distinguishing them from the tightly structured and elevated style of the classical *wenyan* (文言) tradition.

Additionally, opinions on Chinese politics and international affairs were sent to the newspapers and published in line with careful editorial selection based on political alignment and quality of expression. The *Tung Wah Times* frequently featured letters from dissidents critical of the Nanking government to bolster its own legitimacy in opposing Chiang Kai-shek and asserting the need for regime change.[79] The *Chinese Republic News*, in comparison, covered wider motifs in similar tactics. Alongside discussions about Nanking's concessions, the newspaper published letters addressing racial exclusion, diasporic solidarity, and national salvation – each reinforcing its editorial agenda.[80] These literary and commentary writings gave exclusive moral authority to patriotic rhetoric, which didn't just heighten arguments between competing factions but also fostered a self-consciousness among readers, prompting them to scrutinise both their own conduct and that of others through the lens of patriotic responsibility.[81]

These literary creations also facilitated cultural exchange among Chinese communities across Australia and beyond. In 1933, a little-known patriotic organisation in Western Australia – the Society for the Eradication of Japanese (鋤倭社) – organised a patriotic couplets competition that drew 51 entries from 43 participants (including three women) of Cantonese and Shantung (山東) heritage residing in Australia and New Zealand. The renowned Singaporean Chinese intellectual Khoo Seok Wan (丘菽園) acted as chief commentator and judge, awarding Zhu Longqiu the top prize.[82] The

---

78  Yao 2010, 80.
79  *Tung Wah Times*, "對日妥協," 24 June 1933, 5; "蔣華啟事," 31 March 1934, 5; "唔好犯眾怒," 30 March, 1935, 5.
80  *Chinese Republic News*, "日人之恫嚇手段," 29 April 1933, 2; "海外僑胞提防將來的排華," 30 September 1933, 8; "國民應有民族性的奮發," 30 June 1934, 2.
81  For the exclusiveness of morality, see 趙靜蓉 2015, 136.
82  *Chinese Republic News*, "徵聯揭曉," 9 December 1933, 5; "徵聯揭曉," 16 December 1933, 5.

competition's popularity and reach challenged conventional assumptions about the marginal role of Western Australia within the broader Chinese Australian community. Moreover, it highlights transnational literary and cultural networks linking the Chinese in Australasia with those in South-East Asia. Importantly, the participation of women also offers a rare window into the cultural lives of Chinese Australian women beyond their more frequently studied roles in domestic, political, and commercial spheres.[83]

As Japan's invasion of China intensified, the urgency to instil nationalism and foster patriotism among younger generations of Chinese in Australia grew, leading to the expansion of Chinese educational initiatives in the early 1930s. Unlike earlier efforts led by Kuomintang China, these renewed undertakings stemmed primarily from local Chinese elites motivated by anxiety over national identity and the homeland's crisis. In April 1937, the first Chinese-language school in North Queensland, the Overseas Chinese Voluntary School (華僑義學), was established in Townsville, generously funded by local Chinese merchants. It was led by Miss Jang Chen-so (鄭省德), a former teacher at the Central Government School in Hong Kong with 12 years of experience. Approximately 30 pupils attended classes free of charge after regular hours at state schools.[84] The school remained active at least until 1941, when a teacher from China joined the educational initiative, which was by then associated with On Sing Loong, a business owned by Wong Poo Sang in Cloncurry, Queensland.[85] Although the Kuomintang also called on its Australian branches to advance Chinese education,[86] there is little evidence of substantive follow-through.

Following the official outbreak of China's War of Resistance in 1937, efforts at (re-)Sinicisation – spearheaded by prominent figures within Chinese Australian communities – expanded steadily across

---

83   For studies on the abovementioned roles of Chinese Australian women, see Bagnall and Martínez 2021; Kamp 2022.
84   *Telegraph*, "Chinese school opens at Townsville," 19 April 1937, 17; *Morning Bulletin*, "Chinese school at Townsville," 22 April 1937, 8; *Chinese Republic News*, "湯士威爐埠華僑義學開幕," 1 May 1937, 2.
85   Memorandum, 27 November 1941, A433, 1950/2/6890, 3103597, NAA.
86   陳志明 1935, 54.

both urban and rural regions. In 1939, Albert Hing (朱松慶) as the president of the Chinese Chamber of Commerce founded the Sydney Chinese School and recruited Wing Ling Lee, who had previously studied at a Japanese university before the war, to instruct approximately 30 students four evenings per week at the Chinese Chamber of Commerce. Many of these young students possessed only limited knowledge of Chinese and struggled with their studies.[87] In 1940, Miss Chan from the Chinese Catholic Action Group joined the teaching team.[88] That same year, Thomas Chensee, a former president of the Chinese Catholic Action Group, established a Chinese Sunday School in Sydney aimed at teaching both the Chinese language and the Catholic faith. Teachers were drawn from among respected community members, including Wong Siang Wong – a Melbourne vegetable vendor and one of 42 overseas Chinese delegates who attended the Chinese National Assembly in Chungking. In 1942, the school aspired to establish a day school for Chinese children, primarily those of Catholic faith, and sought to recruit a bilingual teacher proficient in both English and Chinese.[89] The ongoing growth of Chinese-language education prompted Yuan Chung-ming of the *Chinese Times* to further encourage the local community to elevate educational standards in Chinese.[90]

Chinese-language schools in Australia experienced renewed vitality during the Pacific War, bolstered by an influx of literate Chinese refugees and the strengthening of the Sino-Australian alliance. In 1941, Lo Shui Kwong arrived in Darwin from Hong Kong and established a Chinese-language school there. After being evacuated from the city, he relocated first to Townsville, where he reopened the school, and later to Sydney, where he and his wife continued teaching Chinese at home.[91] That same year, plans were set in motion to establish Chinese-language

---

87    *Daily Telegraph*, "Chinese taught own language," 26 November 1939, 7.
88    *Catholic Freeman's Journal*, "Chinese nun professed in Sydney," 1 August 1940, 13.
89    *Daily Telegraph*, "'Fight on,' say Chinese here," 31 July 1940, 1; *Catholic Freeman's Journal*, "Chinese catholic action group," 8 January 1942; *Catholic Weekly*, "Catholic action among Sydney Chinese," 20 May 1943, 6.
90    *Chinese Times*, 4 October 1941, C320, C8, 1495438, NAA.
91    *Daily Mercury*, "Chinese clergyman," 16 March 1943, 5.

MR ALBERT HING, President of the New South Wales Chinese Chamber of Commerce, who is conducting a patriotic and goodwill mission on behalf of the Chinese Government.

Figure 2.2 Albert Hing (*Morning Bulletin*, "Chinese patriotic and good will," 22 July 1938, 6. State Library of Queensland).

schools in both Sydney and Melbourne following the visit of Yu Chuen-Hsien (余俊賢) – a member of the Kuomintang Executive Committee and the director of Overseas Chinese Education attached to the Overseas Chinese Affairs Commission (侨务委员会). His tour aimed to promote schools that complied with local educational requirements while offering courses in Chinese culture, history and traditional customs.[92] In Brisbane, Chinese university graduates were reported to have conducted evening classes at elementary and intermediate levels in 1944, organised by the Chinese Youth League (侨青社, discussed in Chapter 5).[93]

92 大公報(香港), "余俊賢飛澳," 13 August 1941, 4; *Age*, "School for young Chinese," 30 August 1941, 8.
93 *Courier-Mail*, "Advertising," 21 April 1944, 6.

The sustained commitment of influential community leaders to instil and preserve Chinese patriotism among younger generations of Chinese Australians remained evident throughout the period. However, most of these initiatives, including those of the 1930s, lacked unified coordination. This suggests that Chinese-language education in wartime Australia was largely shaped by historical contingency caused by war exigency, and therefore that collaboration between Chinese authorities and local communities was coincidental as each side advanced its own agenda of cultural preservation and national identity.

Measuring the efficacy of Chinese-language schools in cultivating patriotism is difficult; however, written records suggest that patriotic sentiment among Australian-born Chinese youth should not be underestimated. For example, Zhu Huimin (朱惠民), the son of Albert Hing, demonstrated notable nationalist zeal at just ten years old. He frequently urged his younger siblings not to "forget national humiliation" or buy Japanese goods, expressed deep concern for China's War of Resistance, donated £1 from his pocket money to Chinese fundraising campaigns, publicly condemned Japanese aggression and questioned the League of Nations' failure to restrain it.[94] In 1937, Arthur Leedow, a student at a Chinese-language school in Sydney, donated £10 at a Chinese Australian ball.[95] In Brisbane in 1938, 16-year-old Master H. Sue, actively involved in relief efforts for China, enthusiastically expressed his aspiration to "speak for the youth of China." Such expressions of patriotism likely reflect the influence of Chinese-language institutions, which claimed to have successfully nurtured patriotic sentiment among their students.

Despite their impressive progress, Chinese-language schools in wartime Australia faced numerous obstacles that hindered their effectiveness. Limited financial resources, inconvenient locations and exclusion from the Australian education system all curtailed their potential impact.[96] At the same time, the act of teaching Chinese can be

---

94  *Tung Wah Times,* "小學生熱心可嘉," 5 March 1932, 5; "小學生朱惠民之演 說詞," 18 April 1936, 5; "小學生朱惠民之演說詞," 25 April 1936, 5.

95  *Chinese Republic News,* "青年華僑跳舞籌款," 25 September 1937, 2.

96  The exclusionary nature of the white Australian education system did not result in the complete eradication of Chinese cultural presence in schools. In

interpreted as a subtle form of resistance against cultural assimilation.[97] Yet many Chinese Australians were wary that speaking their native language might lead to further social exclusion in White Australia.[98] The lower-than-expected student enrolment suggests that some families were either ambivalent about or resistant to the nationalist ideology promoted in these schools. Even among those who did enrol, motivations were often driven more by practical concerns than by anxiety over assimilation. As observed in the Chinese American context, many families hoped that their children's bilingual education might improve future employment prospects in China, especially as domestic opportunities often failed to match their qualifications.[99]

Wartime exigencies further exacerbated existing difficulties. After Australia entered the Second World War, fluctuating currency exchange rates and the challenge of obtaining locally printed materials compelled the Chung Wah School in Melbourne to request books and maps, rather than financial aid, from the Chinese government.[100] The curriculum at both the Chung Wah School and the subsequently established National Alliance School – located on the top floor of 14 Heffernan Lane, Melbourne – was later deemed inadequate by some members of the local Chinese community.[101]

China's prolonged War of Resistance hindered the fulfilment of educational aspirations. Cantonese remained one of the languages used in instruction, and attending Chinese-language schools was sometimes motivated more by religious needs than patriotic sentiment. Several schools failed to survive the Pacific War. By 1944, it was reported

---

some regions, such as Queensland, local schools admitted Chinese pupils and permitted them to speak Chinese in the playground and wear traditional clothing. The staff at these schools were often culturally diverse, including individuals of Anglophone, Chinese, and Indian heritage, which may have contributed to a more tolerant and multicultural school environment than is commonly assumed. See *Evening News*, "Queensland principal," 4 March 1935, 9.

97　Kamp 2022, 123.
98　Giese 1997, 149.
99　Yin 2000, 129.
100　*Herald*, "They learn to answer father back," 27 April 1940, 16.
101　Miss Tso Yung Chen, 2/11/1944, BP242/1, Q30575, 466983, NAA.

that the only remaining Chinese-language class in New South Wales was organised by the Australian Chinese Association of NSW (中澳協會, explored in Chapter 5). Miss Irene Young conducted weekly Thursday night classes, offering instruction in both spoken and written Cantonese to Australians and Chinese alike. The most advanced pupil would be awarded with prizes valued at "one guinea."[102] The school appeared to be well received, as Pearl and Minna Chung joined the teaching staff the following year.[103] The school later received efforts from pro-China Australian lobbies in 1945 for two Chinese-language classes under the tutorship of Jame Y. Chaung to be established by the Australia–China Association (澳華協會, explored in Chapter 7), costing students £1 for a term. The association was starting another two classes for the advanced and beginners to be taught by David Ting from the Chinese consulate general and another young Chinese teacher.[104]

The proactive Chinese educational enterprise was at odds with the host society's prevailing conception of "Australianness", deeply rooted in notions of a shared Anglo-Saxon heritage. The political and public discourse in white Australia demanded that immigrants forsake their native languages in favour of English.[105] The Chinese-language schools were then perceived as making Chinese Australians "un-Australian", reinforcing suspicions about the community's loyalty to Australia. Authorities often complained that Chinese communities "resent being brought under the compulsory education laws of modern states" and "want their schools organised and controlled by China" and Chinese students were "asked to resist assimilation and avoid naturalisation".[106] This persistent consciousness of China's ambitions, combined with widespread faith in assimilationist ideology, ultimately contributed to the decline of Chinese-language schools in Australia by the 1960s. Although sporadic language classes continued to be offered in churches

---

102 *Daily Mirror*, "Welfare worker's diary," 23 March 1944, 10; 4 April 1945, 16.
103 *Daily Mirror*, "Welfare worker's diary," 4 April 1945, 16.
104 Australia–China Association 1945a; 1945b.
105 Kamp 2022, 118.
106 Note on the racial equality issue, Chinese Migration and Overseas Chinese, 1944, A989, 1944/554/7/1, 184465, NAA.

and clubs, these initiatives served as a pale substitute for a comprehensive Chinese education.

This chapter does not suggest that patriotism among Chinese Australians was simply transplanted from the homeland. For instance, in China, patriotism was often a central feature of commercial marketing, with advertisers promoting their products by appealing to their contribution to the nation.[107] However, such institutional advertising – framing consumer choices as acts of national virtue – was rarely found in Chinese Australian newspapers. Although strategies to promote patriotism among Chinese Australians bore a resemblance to those identified by historians working within a nation-state framework,[108] the diasporic context presented here complicates and enriches conventional understandings. It highlights the distinctive dynamics of Chinese Australian agency, shaped by intersecting and often conflicting loyalties. The diasporic experience in Australia was not merely a backdrop but a constitutive element of how patriotism was expressed and practiced.


## Conclusion

This chapter demonstrates proactive agency by anti-Nanking voices within Chinese Australian communities. The dynamic formulation presents a different landscape compared to the accepted wisdom that the Chinese diaspora had a passive affiliation with the Chinese government. Leveraging social transnational networks, the Chinese Australian press effectively resisted the expansion of the Kuomintang's leadership over the community and articulated their political agenda, revealing the inherent heterogeneity in China–diasporic Chinese relations. Political conflicts aside, the newspapers' unanimous opposition to Japanese aggression showcased the complexity of Chinese Australian political dynamics and social tenacity. This was constantly complicated, with the participation of Chinese Australian readers. The

---

107  Tsai 2010, 103–26.
108  Alford, 1995, 21; Cohen 1987, 89; Forchtner 2016, 31; Kallis 2005, 4; Lee and Yang 2007, 9; Mittler 2004, 413.

changing political landscape and vibrant social vigour within the Chinese Australian community challenges the traditional narrative of a "dying" and "marginalised" local Chinese society during the 1930s and 40s.[109]

---

109  Andrews 1985, 85; S. Fitzgerald 1997, 11; Markus 1994, 141; Tavan 2005, 26.

# 3
# War commemorations in Chinese Australian communities

The inaugural Chinese National Humiliation Day commemoration was held on 18 September 1932 in Sydney to mark the first anniversary of the Mukden Incident. At a gathering at the Australian headquarters of the Kuomintang in Sydney, Chen Wei-ping delivered what the *Labor Daily* described as "one of the most emotionally disturbing speeches" on behalf of Chinese residents in Australia who were loyal to the Nanking government; his speech mobilised patriotic support in response to China's War of Resistance.[1] Through quasi-official commemorations that politicised diasporic memory, the Kuomintang sought to mobilise support for the homeland among overseas Chinese in the early 1930s. This was particularly essential for the Kuomintang, being an unpopular party within Chinese Australian communities that faced increasing frictions with their rivals in Australia. In Darwin, for instance, the Wah On Society (華安會館), the most influential society in the region, was at odds with local Kuomintang, culminating in a significant physical altercation involving members from both parties.[2]

Significantly inspired by research on memorial services,[3] festive cultures,[4] and war memory in Australia and China,[5] this chapter investigates three key commemorative events organised by Chinese

---

1   *Labor Daily*, "China's National Day of Humiliation," 19 September 1932, 4.
2   *Tung Wah Times*, "互相控告之華人團體鬥毆案," 16 April 1932, 8.

authorities and local elites in Australia, revealing the fragmented political loyalties within the Chinese Australian community in response to the Kuomintang's efforts to consolidate leadership abroad. Through a close examination of the memorial for the Manchurian dead held in Sydney in late 1931, alongside the observances of National Humiliation Day in Sydney compared to Melbourne in 1932 and 1933 respectively, this chapter traces how war memory was actively constructed and mobilised among Chinese Australians. These memorial practices served dual purposes: they were vehicles for galvanising support for China's war efforts and battlegrounds for political legitimacy. In both cities, the Kuomintang's attempts to assert hegemonic control over diasporic Chinese identity and loyalty met resistance, as rival groups contested the meaning and ownership of Chinese wartime memory. In so doing, this chapter expands current scholarship on Chinese Australian festivities.[6]

## Commemoration of the Fallen Manchuria

Ending the unfavourable friction between different groups and establishing exclusive leadership over Chinese Australians became crucial in Nanking's desperate need to mobilise the patriotism and loyalty of the resident Chinese towards their homeland. Alongside China's efforts through the press and language schools was the commemoration in Australia of the compatriots of the Chinese who had fallen in the course of the Japanese occupation of Manchuria. On the afternoon of 15 November 1931, members of the Sydney Chinese community held a three-hour commemoration at the Opera House,

---

3   Anderson, 2006; Ashplant, Dawson and Roper 2000; Bell 2009; Connerton 1989; Edkins 2003; Hobsbawm 2013; 2006; Mayo 1988, 64; McDonald 2010; Winter 1995; Winter and Sivan 1999.
4   Brettell and Reed-Danahay 2014; Gutiérrez and Fabre 1995; Hazareesingh 2004; Jacobson 1995; Ozouf 1991; Reis 2003; Sinn and Wong 2005; Turner 1982.
5   Govor 2005; Kildea 2007; Light 2018; Seraphim 2006; Wellington 2017; Yoshida 2006; 郭辉 2019.
6   For studies on Chinese Australian festivities, see G. Edwards 2013; Rasmussen 2004; Roper 1985; Tsai 2016; 郭美芬 2019.

supported by the Society of Chinese Residents in Australia, a patriotic Chinese organisation sponsored by the Australian headquarters of the Kuomintang.

The commemoration strategically served as a propaganda vehicle, partly encouraged by the Chinese Ministry of Information,[7] to garner sympathy from Chinese and white Australians through publicity of the Mukden Incident. More than a thousand people gathered – mainly Chinese, but many white Australians also attended. The Opera House was already full an hour before the event began. The memorial service was well received by both Chinese and white Australians. It also caught the attention of many mainstream and regional Australian newspapers, although most printed incorrect facts about it and failed to understand the significance of the Mukden Incident.[8]

The service was a demonstration of the solidarity of the Chinese Australian community and a sign of the end to residents' decades-long political differences. Prominent community members from nearly all major Chinese groups in Sydney attended, including Chen Wei-ping, the Chinese consul general; Albert Hing, the president of the Chinese Chamber of Commerce; James Chuey (黃柱), the grand master of the Masons; and D.Y. Narme, a key member of the Australian Kuomintang. These prominent figures in the Chinese Australian community were unlikely to risk adverse publicity that could jeopardise the semblance of unity and stability that "warranted their acceptance" in Australia.[9]

The commemoration aimed to achieve multiple goals. On the one hand, it connected the living to the dead through a "liturgical community" and created an outlet for the audience's emotions.[10] In this public way, "collective remembrance" would be realised. Large numbers of condolence cables, couplets and letters were sent to the memorial meeting, where long vertical white linen banners (representing condolence and respect for the dead) floated above the dais, with

---

7   *Chinese Republic News*, "要電," 26 September 1931, 8.
8   Andrews 1981, 307; *Barrier Miner*, "Reference at meeting of Chinese in Sydney", 16 November 1931, 1; *Daily Telegraph*, "China and her woes", 16 November 1931, 8; *Inverell Times*, "Chinese ceremony", 16 November 1931, 1; *Sydney Morning Herald*, "Manchurian dispute", 16 November 1931, 10.
9   Jones 2001, 64.
10  Connerton 1989, 58–9.

Chinese eulogies tied to them. Chinese Australians mourned China's loss of Manchuria and their deceased Chinese compatriots with deep grief and profound respect.

At the same time, the memorial service was intended to strengthen the identification of Chinese Australians with their heritage and homeland, thus mobilising their loyalty and patriotism for China's war effort. As one article published in the *Tung Wah Times* argued, the commemoration was initiated not only to "console the spirit of the deceased" and "convey the brotherhood of compatriots" but also to rally Chinese residents to "put up a desperate fight" against the Japanese.[11]

Moreover, the ceremony promoted the indisputable leadership of the Nanking government and the Chinese Kuomintang. The Kuomintang party flag was positioned in the centre above the dais and under a huge banner emblazoned with "Chinese Memorial Service in Commemoration of the Fallen Compatriots in Manchuria" in Chinese and English. Chinese elegiac couplets were placed on either side of it, and a big wreath of lilies tied with crepe was propped against it. The commemoration conflated the ideals of Chinese nationalism, patriotism and the Kuomintang's dominance, establishing an elevated sense of reverence and awe. As Anthony R. Pratkanis and Elliot Aronson suggested, the way an object is portrayed is a propaganda-defined label that pre-persuades recipients even before the propaganda starts.[12]

The conflation of these ideals went beyond special symbolism. The memorial ceremony ritualised and transformed the symbolic elements into an official memorial narrative of the Mukden Incident. The ceremony had five parts: a bell rang at 2 p.m. and the ceremony began with a dirge; attendants rose as a mark of respect and bowed to the Chinese national flag; a wreath was unveiled, the Chinese national anthem played, and three minutes' silence was observed for the dead; memorial orations from Chinese groups were read and patriotic speeches were delivered in English, Mandarin and Cantonese; a group photo was taken and the dirge was repeated before the close.[13] Through

---

11    *Tung Wah Times,* "為追悼東北殉難同胞泣告僑胞書," "追悼會各體團祭文," 28 November 1931, 7.

12    Pratkanis and Aronson 2001, 72.

the ceremonial enactments, the ritual performers and the audience's participation, the "liturgical community" was constructed from ritualising symbols. As a result, ritual-invented sacredness and grandeur were articulated in the physical manifestation of dramatic symbols and integrated thought and action, thus defining the memorial as having moral value. It thereby conveyed a remembrance of the past, the deceased, the centrality of Chinese identity and the Kuomintang's authority. Integrating history and values, the commemoration intended to constitute a China-centred social order emphasising the leadership of the Kuomintang among ethnic Chinese living outside China.

Patriotic orations by honoured speakers were a core feature of the commemoration. Standing in the centre of the dais before the party flag and the elegiac words and couplets, speakers (including prominent Chinese figures and white Australians) assumed authority in interpreting the past and shaping the audience's memory of war.[14] Assiduously peddling the idea of the "Chinese nation first", the prominent figures of the Chinese diaspora appealed to resident Chinese to unite in solidarity and support China's struggle with the enemy to remove "national humiliation" from the Chinese mentality.[15] Nanking's failure to thwart Japanese aggression was emphasised in an emotional appeal to national and individual sentiment, in an attempt to impose on the Chinese audience the dominance of their Chinese heritage over their Australian aspect. It is highly possible that the speaking prowess of the Chinese leaders who gave speeches was strong, as many had once joined a Chinese debating society founded in the 1920s to train their oratory skills.[16]

---

13   *Chinese Republic News*, "澳洲雪梨華僑追悼東北殉難同胞大會攝影," 5 December 1931, 5; *Daily Telegraph*, "China and her woes," 16 November 1931, 8; *Tung Wah Times*, "澳洲雪梨華僑追悼東北殉難同胞大會詳情," 21 November 1931, 5; "澳洲雪梨華僑追悼東北殉難同胞大會攝影," 5 December 1931, 7.

14   *Sydney Morning Herald*, "Manchurian dispute," 16 November 1931, 10.

15   *Chinese Republic News*, "澳洲雪梨華僑追悼東北殉難同胞大會詳情 (續)," "追悼東北殉難同胞急應註意的三個要點," 28 November 1931, 5, 7.

16   Minutes of the Chinese Debating Society, 1921–1922, AU NBAC 111-5A, NBAC.

Figure 3.1 *Tung Wah Times*, "澳洲雪梨華僑追悼東北殉難同胞大會攝影,"
5 December 1931, 7. State Library of New South Wales.

News coverage from the Chinese-language newspapers at that time informed their audiences of China's concession of Manchuria to Japan, as discussed in Chapter 2, among which anti-Nanking voices criticised China's non-resistance. Letters from readers provide evidence of the Chinese in Australia showing their anger and disappointment. The Kuomintang-held commemoration tried to avoid mentioning Nanking's incapability – that is, mention was avoided of China's withdrawal of military force from Manchuria without initiating any resistance. The commemoration attempted to distract the audience from Nanking's military performance, focusing instead on their shared sorrow for the deceased, common outrage at the aggressor, and the broader significance of the Japanese invasion in Manchuria to the stability of East Asia and international security. First-person collective pronouns, like "we" and "us", were frequently used by the speakers to establish an apparent unity between Nanking and the resident Chinese in Australia. Furthermore, the global importance of imperial Japan's military thrust in China could also target the white Australian audience members in attendance, seeking their sympathy and alerting them to concerns over potential threats from Japan. The Kuomintang's mistakes in conducting the war were strategically not brought up.[17] In other words, remembrance of the past through the memorial service was also a means of forgetting.

Much like their Italian counterparts in Australia, whose support and responses to Mussolini's regime during the 1920s and 1930s were deeply divided,[18] the Chinese community was markedly fragmented, as dissenters resisted the authority Nanking attempted to impose. Not all Chinese Australians were in line with Nanking at the ceremony, and the Australian Kuomintang was embarrassed by challenges to its authority. These political rivals of Nanking, mainly identified with numerous members of the Chinese Chamber of Commerce and Chinese Masonic Society in Sydney, differentiated themselves from the official narrative promoted by pro-Nanking supporters.[19] The condolence couplets and

---

17 *Chinese Republic News*, "澳洲雪梨華僑追悼東北殉難同胞大會詳情 (續)," "追悼東北殉難同胞急應註意的三個要點," 28 November 1931, 5, 7; *Tung Wah Times*, "為追悼東北殉難同胞泣告僑胞書," 28 November 1931, 7.
18 Cresciani 1980, 23–67; Gerado 2020.

articles they wrote and sent to the memorial service were read out at the event and published in the Chinese-language newspapers, complaining of China's incompetence and internal disorder that had offered Japan the opportunity to invade.[20] Despite their disagreement with the Kuomintang's narrative at the memorial service, they restrained their dissent in order to preserve the public solidarity of the Chinese Australian community. Meanwhile, the Chamber of Commerce and the Masons attacked the Nanking government and the Kuomintang bitterly through their official organs, the *Tung Wah Times* and the *Chinese World's News*, as discussed in Chapter 2.

The portrayal of an object is carefully designed to influence the thinking of those it is intended for. The pro-Nanking exponents in Australia and their opponents articulated their different political sentiments through their interpretations of "China". Advocates of the Kuomintang toed the official line of the *dangguo* (黨國, the party-state) that centralised the Kuomintang in Nanking as equivalent to "China". Pleading for the solidarity of Chinese Australians and their retaliation against Japan, they emphasised that the purpose of these appeals was to console the *dangguo*, clearly prioritising the Kuomintang above all else. In comparison, the Kuomintang's opponents saw "China" as *Minguo* (民國, Republican China) without explicitly referring to the Kuomintang.[21] Emphasising democratic principles and Chinese national interests rather than the party-ruled dictatorship and the Kuomintang's interest, the opponents of the Kuomintang effectively denied Nanking's authority. As Mei-fen Kuo observed, drawing on their diasporic experience in Australia, Chinese residents in the early 20th century already recognised the values of the rule of law and democracy.[22] Notably, such political disagreement was not new to overseas Chinese but rather an inheritance of the debates about China's political future envisaged by Chinese intellectuals in the late imperial era.[23]

---

19  Memorandum of the Department of the Interior, 30 March 1938, A433, 1945/2/3557, 3093972, NAA.

20  *Tung Wah Times*, "追悼會各體團祭文," 28 November 1931, 7.

21  *Tung Wah Times*, "追悼會各體團祭文," 28 November 1931, 7.

22  郭美芬 2011, 194.

## National Humiliation Day in Sydney

Memorial services became contests between different groups to give public articulation to and gain recognition for competing narratives and the memories they structured. With the situation in China worsening in 1932 and 1933, the previously less visible competition of war memory between pro-Nanking supporters in Australia and their rivals became explicit in the commemorations of National Humiliation Day. The concept can be traced back to the Memorial Day of National Humiliation established in 1915 by Yuan Shih-kai (袁世凱, who was the then president of Republican China), as a non-governmental commemoration of the humiliation of the Twenty-One Demands imposed by Japan in the same year. Yuan aimed to demarcate Chinese self-consciousness by manipulating the collective memory of the public by politicising rituals and recollection. This event was often not held at the official level until the Kuomintang came into power in 1927, when the Nanking government designated 21 national memorial days, six of which were related to national humiliation. It would be difficult not to notice that the Chinese government categorised these commemorations of national humiliation as events of national significance and great value.

Established on 25 August 1932 to commemorate national trauma and consequent undermining of the pride and esteem of the Chinese people, the anniversary of the Mukden Incident was of great significance to Nanking as a means to further mobilise patriotism for China's war effort.[24] Not only was this anniversary observed in China, where people were required to stop recreational activities and stand in silent mourning for five minutes at 11 a.m., but Nanking also instructed the Australian Kuomintang to observe it (at 11 a.m. on the same day).[25] These war commemorations also intended to garner the sympathy of white Australians for China's hardship.[26] Likewise, Australian

---

23   For their imagination of "Chinese nation" and debates that followed in the late Qing era, see 王建朗與黃克武 2016, 974–1002.
24   郭輝 2019, 142.
25   *Chinese Republic News*, "九月四號上午十時半接南京電," 10 September 1932, 8.

newspapers paid extensive attention to this China-invented commemoration, reporting the ceremony with either a neutral or sympathetic tone. The *Labor Daily* commented that there is "no Australian Labourite who does not wish China well".[27]

In 1932 and 1933, about two hundred people attended the commemorations at the Australian headquarters of the Kuomintang in Sydney. While the venue was less grand than the Opera House, it was easier to ensure an audience of the Kuomintang's loyalists, emphasising the centrality of the party and creating an impression of groundswell support. Special symbols were pivotal in expressing and motivating traumatic and patriotic emotions. With the elevation of "party-rule" to the core of the Australian Kuomintang's engagement with local Chinese communities, subsequent events were more overtly Kuomintang-dominated than the Fallen Manchurian commemoration in 1931, foregrounding the Kuomintang's core leadership over China and Chinese overseas. The building's flags were flown at half-mast to mourn the national loss, and the headquarters' hall was hung with paper streamers with prominent Chinese characters expressing grief and patriotic fervour. A portrait of Sun Yat-sen was prominently placed in the foreground and draped with national party flags to stress the authority and legitimacy of the Kuomintang regime in Nanking. This was the setting in which the Chinese attendees assembled.[28]

The solemnity and stateliness apparent at the commemorations were crystallised in the ceremonial rituals established at the events. The rituals of the 1932 and 1933 commemorations were similar, except for a slight difference in their sequence:

- As a mark of respect, attendees stood in silence for five minutes to mourn the national calamity, while a Chinese mourning march played.

---

26  *Sydney Morning Herald*, "Humiliation Day," 19 September 1933, 10.

27  *Chinese Republic News*, "雪梨華僑舉行九一八國難紀念會," 23 September 1933, 6; *Labor Daily*, "China's National Day of Humiliation," 19 September 1932, 4.

28  *Daily Telegraph*, "Sydney Chinese mourned with China on Day of Humiliation and tears," 19 September 1933, 9; *Sydney Morning Herald*, "Sydney Chinese," 19 September 1932, 9.

- The audience stood and bowed three times to the national flag and the portrait of Sun Yat-sen, while a Chinese mourning march played.
- Proclamation of Sun Yat-sen's Will (Sun's writing in his will became an enshrined fundamental document for the Kuomintang and his legacy was crucial in the construction of the orthodoxy of the party).
- Speeches were delivered by renowned figures, including Chen Wei-ping, and pro-China Australians such as John Sleeman (editor first at the *Kalgoorlie Sun* and *Brisbane Sun* then later *Labor Daily* and then *Beckett's Budget*) and C.H. Currey (president of the New South Wales Public School Teachers' Federation and lecturer at the University of Sydney).
- The Chinese national anthem was played and sung.
- A group photo was taken before attendees were dismissed.[29]

These rituals essentially formalised commemorations, implying continuity with the past. The commemorations linked the memory of the Sino-Japanese War to the shared social values and principles of the present, reaffirming the Kuomintang's centrality and legitimate leadership. Chinese submission to and respect for the Nanking government were re-declared, moulding the bygone ordeal of the Japanese invasion of China into the loyalty and patriotism to the homeland by Chinese Australians.

The commemorations provided platforms for local Chinese leaders to reinforce Nanking's official narrative of the war. In order to deal with Nanking's embarrassing concessions to Japan, the commemorative texts and speeches either avoided blaming the central government or attributed the submission to Japanese brutalities. The Society of Chinese Residents in Australia, for example, claimed that a "civilised nation" could not resist a rapacious and ruthless "brigade".[30] Meanwhile, the commemorations aimed to shore up the audience's

---

29  *Chinese Republic News*, "雪梨華僑舉行九一八國難紀念會," 23 September 1933, 6; *Tung Wah Times*, "澳洲雪梨各界僑胞舉行九一八國難周年紀念熱烈情形," 24 September 1932, 5. For Sun Yat-sen, see Du 2019.

30  *Chinese Republic News*, "澳洲雪梨華僑抗日救國會為九壹八國難二週年紀念宣言," 23 September 1933, 8; *Tung Wah Times*, "澳洲雪梨各界僑胞舉行九壹八國難周年紀念熱烈情形," 24 September 1932, 5.

spirit in case the gloomy news from China made them lose heart. Chen Wei-ping's assurances to Chinese Australians of China's counterattack against Japan successfully "roused the audience to enthusiasm".[31] The broader significance behind Japan's invasion of China was again exploited. William Liu (劉光福) said Australia should be alert to the approaching incursion and not become "a second Manchuria".[32] The commemorations of the Kuomintang were encoded with special symbols, ritualised actions and patriotic language intended to shape the audience's collective memory and reinforce their Chinese national identity. Thus, the effective expression of sacredness, solemnity and the appropriate discipline of emotion reflected the intimate bond between personhood and community.

While Nanking's supporters forged Kuomintang-centred memorial services, those in opposition constructed an alternative expression of memory and identity: their own commemorations of the anniversary of the Mukden Incident. This dissenting movement consisted primarily of six Chinese societies in Australia, including the Chamber of Commerce and the Masons. They established the Association of Anti-Japanese Warfare Provision (對日戰費籌備會) and carried out a separate program of commemorations in 1932 and 1933, claiming to awaken and unite Chinese Australians.[33]

The distinguishing feature of these separate commemorations was the removal of the party-ruled symbols and rituals. Instead, the ceremony was simple: mourning in silence, patriotic speeches, and calling out nationalist slogans.[34] The association not only decided to remove the reading of Sun Yat-sen's Will, it kept the ceremonial premise in simple decoration. Its reinterpretation of the war memory focused on Chinese national patriotism rather than submission to the Kuomintang's party rule. The commemoration also began at 11 a.m., a deliberate challenge to the authority of those organising Nanking's ceremony.[35] The reinvented "liturgical community" was used as

31  *Labor Daily*, "China's National Day of Humiliation," 19 September 1932, 4.
32  *Sydney Morning Herald*, "Humiliation Day," 19 September 1933, 10.
33  *Tung Wah Times*, "悲慘淒愴之國恥紀念會," 24 September 1932, 8.
34  *Tung Wah Times*, "悲慘淒愴之國恥紀念會," 24 September 1932, 8 ; "九一八國恥紀念," 23 September 1933, 8.

leverage to articulate independent Chinese diasporic interest and to indicate the resistance of Nanking's opponents in Australia to the authority and social order that Nanking tried to impose.

Although Nanking's party-ruled memorial program was rejected by its opponents, the Chinese officials in Australia did not stop trying to win the competition of war memory. They took the association's commemoration as a chance to defend Nanking's misconduct in the war with Japan and to maintain the Kuomintang's prestige among Chinese Australians. After his promotion to vice consul of the Chinese consulate general in Sydney, Lee Hong, formerly a popular Chinese consul in Melbourne,[36] seemed to be the ideal figure to take up this role.

Lee's speech at the commemoration in 1932 in defence of the Kuomintang's failure proceeded cautiously. It did not straightforwardly touch upon China's loss of Manchuria. He presented Japan's occupation of the land as an ambitious long-term plot facilitated by Chinese warlordism rather than by the Nanking government's weakness. Referring to the fact that China was unable to regain the lost territory, Lee encouraged his audience's Chinese patriotism by choosing specific words that evoked their "national spirit", such as "warcraft", describing their "heart" as a "warship", their "fortune" as "fortification" and their "flesh" as a "shell". He implicitly defended the weakness of the Kuomintang regime's resistance by contrasting China's and Japan's capacities and saying that China was bound by international law. He quoted the Kellogg–Briand Pact, signed in 1928, to justify China's non-resistance as respect for anti-war diplomacy; Nanking's preferred strategy was to encourage powers such as the United Kingdom to stop the Japanese invasion. Lee further argued that by not declaring war against Japan, China would protect its coastal provinces, anti-Japanese compatriots and the remittances of Chinese Australians.[37] In other words, the Kuomintang's passive defence against Japanese invasion was

---

35  Committee for the Collection of Donations to Help the Struggle Against Japanese Invasion Minute Book, 1932–1937, 8, AU NBAC 111-6-1, NBAC.

36  *Chinese Republic News*, "美利濱華僑歡送李領誌盛," 11 June 1932, 8.

37  *Tung Wah Times*, "悲慘淒愴之國恥紀念會," 24 September 1932, 8; "悲慘淒愴之國恥紀念會," 1 October 1932, 8.

the result of reasonable consideration, not a demonstration of incompetence.

Although it is hard to measure whether his defence might have been successful, Lee's effort was probably discounted by the cultural barrier between the Chinese officials and the Chinese who were long-term residents of Australia. The latter were bonded by a common Cantonese language, birthplace and diasporic experience in Australia, while the Chinese officials whose primary working language was Mandarin and who were appointed by an unpopular Chinese government, seemed to be outsiders. In a journalistic spat, the *Tung Wah Times* once mocked the editor of the *Chinese Times*, who was assigned to his position by the Nanking government, for his ignorance of Cantonese.[38] When Lee Hong, who came from Putsien (莆田) in Fukien, spoke in Mandarin,[39] he had to rely on local translators to reach the ears of speakers of Cantonese, continually othering himself (and indeed also his Mandarin-speaking colleagues) within the Cantonese-dominated diaspora community.

## Chinese National Humiliation Day in Melbourne

The Chinese community in Melbourne seemed less divided and antagonistic to the Kuomintang than its counterpart in Sydney. The Chinese Citizens Society represented the Melbourne Chinese community, supported by other Chinese groups. The Chinese Citizens Society was formed in Melbourne in 1904, with William Ah Ket (麦锡祥) as president and Mee How Ah Mouy as treasurer, to challenge the 1896 *Factories and Shops Act* in Victoria and promote social intercourse among members. It ceased to function in 1913, when both leaders departed for China, but reformed on 14 November 1931 in response to the Manchurian invasion, also known as the unofficial outbreak of China's War of Resistance.[40] The society admitted that Melbourne's

---

38  *Tung Wah Times*, "再斥民報記者之謬妄," 25 January 1936, 8.
39  For Lee's heritage, see 澳洲總支部執行委員會秘書處 1931, 5.
40  Yong 1977, 194.

Chinese lived harmoniously, yet no singular organisation could unite them.[41]

A couple of significant factors may account for the Melbourne Chinese community showing less division than their counterparts in Sydney. First, as Mei-fen Kuo has argued, community leadership in Sydney was based on prominent Chinese merchants and their commercial power, while leadership in Melbourne was founded on the Chinese working class.[42] As Melbourne's Chinese working class had no influential political representatives, the local Chinese were much less able to challenge the authority of the Nanking government than were their compatriots in Sydney.

Secondly, the Chinese authorities in Melbourne were much less influential over the Chinese Australian community than their superiors in Sydney. Sydney defeated the Melbourne branch of the Kuomintang in its bid for leadership within the Australian Kuomintang in the 1920s. Melbourne was reduced to a district office under the direction of the Sydney headquarters.[43] The relationship between the two branches was further strained over Chiang Kai-shek's Party Purification Movement in the 1920s, as the Melbourne branch staunchly opposed the Sydney headquarters' decision to endorse Chiang's reactionary campaign.[44]

In addition, the Chinese consulate in Melbourne experienced internal tensions. Pao Chun-how (保君曄), then vice consul general, had a dispute with his vice consul, Lee Hong, and the Sydney Kuomintang. Lee had to act cautiously to avoid offending his superior. In his notice in the newspaper, he requested that local Chinese address him as "Mr. Lee" rather than "Consul Lee," as the latter could be construed as an indication of his ambition to replace his superior.[45] Pao's relationship with the local Chinese in Melbourne also soured. The Chinese Citizens Society complained to Nanking that Pao's performance as the Chinese consul in Melbourne was "*wuguo yangmin*" (誤國殃民, endangered the nation and people). The

---

41  *Chinese Republic News*, "美利濱華僑歡送李領誌盛," 11 June 1932, 8.
42  Kuo 2011, 174.
43  陳誌明 1935, 20–4.
44  J. Fitzgerald 2006, 103–4.
45  *Chinese Republic News*, "李鴻啓事," 9 April 1932, 8.

Melbourne Chinese swore "not to admit his authority", and they pleaded for his removal from office.[46] In 1932, the Sydney Kuomintang engineered his dismissal from Melbourne.[47]

The relative lack of a precise political posture within the Chinese community in Melbourne contributed to the society's less conflicted program of commemorations for Chinese National Humiliation Day. The Melbourne gatherings did not present an overtly loyal or hostile position on the Nanking government. Nevertheless, the authority of Nanking appeared to fail to reach the community, whose memorial ceremonies highlighted the notion of the "Republic of China" in grand and solemn commemorations that deviated not only from the party-ruled line endorsed by the supporters of Kuomintang but also from the alternate versions adopted by the detractors of the Kuomintang. The Melbourne ceremonies in 1932 and 1933 were both attended by around 200 people. Flags of Chinese associations were lowered to half-mast, and the memorial rituals followed a similar format to those in Sydney but were slightly different in their sequence:

- The audience stood as a mark of respect.
- A mourning march was played, and the chairman of the commemoration announced the opening.
- The chairman announced the purpose of the meeting, and a patriotic song was sung.
- The Chinese national anthem was sung, and the audience stood in silence for three minutes to remember the dead.
- The memorial song of national humiliation was sung.
- Addresses.
- Slogan-shouting and patriotic singing.
- The event closed.[48]

---

46  Chinese Citizens Society, 美麗濱中華公會電國民政府為保領負國殃民僑等誓不承認今復誣陷李副領懇飭外交部依法查辦, 27 May 1932, 001-067101-00002-016, Academia Historica (AH), Taipei.
47  Kuo and Brett 2013, 72.
48  *Tung Wah Times*, "美利濱華僑舉行國恥紀念大會之盛況," 8 October 1932, 5; "美利濱中華公會開會紀念國恥," 30 September 1933, 5.

The commemorations created a sense of community centred on the idea of the Chinese nation. Sacred and unshakable national authority was expressed in ritual performances, engendering emotion through sounds, language and repetition. The mourning march and patriotic songs also prompted the audience's memory of the past and reaffirmed the social order that the ceremonies promoted. Chinese patriotism and nationalism in Melbourne, mobilised by the Chinese Citizens Society, mildly resisted Nanking's authority but avoided the political clashes that broke out in Sydney.

The society expressed Chinese Australians' dissatisfaction with Nanking less explicitly, trying to maintain the superficial solidarity among Melbourne Chinese. In addition to repudiating party-ruled rituals, the society's view of the Sino-Japanese clash did not align with that of the Chinese government. The society did not appeal to international justice from Western powers, as Nanking had attempted to do. Meanwhile, it prioritised Chinese national interest and solidarity over the Kuomintang's party rule, demanding that the Nanking government not concede to Japan.[49]

The Chinese Citizens Society's stance pushed the local Chinese officials tasked with promoting Nanking's prestige into an awkward position, as they had to rely on the society to proceed with their mission.[50] Wu Qinxun (吳勤訓), the successor of Pao Chun-how, was pressured by the society to conform to its aims and not disturb local Chinese unity. Therefore, Wu had to keep to the Chinese Citizens Society's stated themes in his address, stressing national solidarity and anti-Japanese efforts.[51] The moderate language that the society used in its discussion successfully reduced the visibility of those disagreements.[52]

---

49  *Tung Wah Times*, "美利濱華僑舉行國恥紀念大會之盛況," 8 October 1932, 5; "美利濱中華公會開會紀念國恥," 30 September 1933, 5; "九一八國恥告全體僑胞文," 22 October 1932, 8.

50  *Chinese Republic News*, "美利濱中華公會舉行國慶紀念," 22 October 1932, 8.

51  *Tung Wah Times*, "美利濱華僑舉行國恥紀念大會之盛況," 8 October 1932, 5.

52  *Chinese Republic News*, "美利濱中華公會廿一年周年國慶紀念宣言," 29 October 1932, 8; "美利濱中華公會廿一年周年國慶紀念宣言," 5 November 1932, 8.

It appeared that the Chinese government failed to monopolise the traumatic memory of the Chinese Australians and script it as a means of obtaining their loyalty and asserting Nanking's exclusive authority over them. War commemorations were not the only shapers of the collective memory of Chinese Australians; other social agencies, such as local Chinese-language newspapers, also participated in constructing and forming people's social consciousness. Unfavourable news and criticisms made by the Kuomintang's political rivals in Australia, as explored in Chapter 2, undermined the prestige of the Chinese Kuomintang and the Nanking government.

In addition to its disastrous management of domestic affairs in China, the Kuomintang regime also failed to protect the diasporic interests of Chinese Australians. Repeatedly urged to action by Chinese Australians, China put pressure on the Australian government throughout the 1930s to relax, if not remove, the White Australia policy and recognise the ethnic equality of the local Chinese. Such efforts proved fruitless.[53] The Chinese government also refused to reopen the Chinese consulate in Melbourne to attend to the interests of the local Chinese after the office closed in 1933.[54] These failures undoubtedly frustrated some Chinese Australians; the community in Australia was further divided politically before China's desperate confrontation of the full Japanese invasion in 1937. The Chinese Australian community was never united for the remainder of China's War of Resistance, even when Chiang Kai-shek's regime achieved enormous international prestige in the 1940s.[55] In other words, Nanking failed to unite the divided Chinese diasporic community; it in fact further intensified the division.

---

53  改善旅澳華僑待遇 (一), 1938, 020-011507-0002; 紐澳移民條例與華僑待遇, 1939, 020-070900-0035, AH.

54  中國國民黨五全大會設立駐外使館決議案, 25 December 1935, 001-061100-00001-018; 國民政府文官處函中國國民黨中央執行委員會秘書處為五全大會陳志明等提議於澳大利亞墨爾本設領事館一案據行政院呈復已交外交部酌辦函達查照轉陳, 1936, 001-061100-00001-022, AH. Based on the report of the Chinese legation in Australia that the jurisdiction of the Chinese consulate in Melbourne covered areas beyond Victoria, including Tasmania and South Australia, see Report, 24 June 1947, A1067, IC/15/11/5, 191828, NAA.

55  億中公司駐墨爾本經理趙約翰案, 1941–1943, 020-011507-0022, AH.

Furthermore, the memorial services were burdened by the need to adapt to the host society. Instructed by Nanking, for example, the initial starting time of 11 a.m. had to switch to 8 p.m. to ensure enough attendees and not disrupt the working day. Despite this, the Australian Kuomintang's war commemorations and the contests of war memory between these prominent Chinese organisations (along with the Chinese-language newspapers) were effective in the patriotic mobilisation of Chinese Australians towards their homeland. An enormous number of letters, essays and enquiries on China's war situation were sent from Chinese readers throughout Australia, overwhelming diasporic Chinese newspapers such as the *Tung Wah Times,* which had to apologise for its incapacity to publish all of them.[56] Publications extolling patriotic Chinese figures sold out quickly.[57] The *Mercury* newspaper observed that Chinese loyalty "seems to be for their Fatherland more than their fellow Chinese".[58] Due to financial hardship in the Australian headquarters of the Kuomintang,[59] the Chinese war commemorations in Australia were suspended in the mid-1930s (they would be revived in the 1980s by the Chinese Communist Party to remind its people at home and abroad "repeatedly of their history as a people"[60]).

Such commemorations were an integral part of everyday life for Chinese Australian communities. Beyond memorial services for the deceased, occasions like tea parties, farewell dinners, the anniversary of Confucius' birth and Chinese National Day were typically celebrated with festivities. Political struggles were also evident in the rituals associated with these events, as each party sought to shape Chinese Australian identities and loyalties for political ends. The Kuomintang, as ever, advanced its party-rule ideology and asserted its leadership, while its opponents championed the broader notion of "Republican

---

56  *Tung Wah Times,* "本報緊要啟事," 7 November 1931, 8; "誣人造謠無理取鬧," 11 January 1936, 8.
57  *Tung Wah Times,* "新到馬占山龍江血戰記," 30 July 1932, 8; "代郵," 13 August 1932, 5.
58  *Mercury,* "Chinese patriotism," 1 May 1933, 6.
59  Kuo and Brett 2013, 47, 66.
60  For the revival of war commemoration, see Denton 2007, 250, 269; Wang 2012, 6.

China"[61] However, the creation of such a liturgical community was not always effective in achieving its intended goals. Its success largely depended on the willingness of the targeted participants to engage. For example, the Australian Kuomintang's Newcastle branch expressed frustration that the majority of attendees at their commemorative events were white Australians, rather than local Chinese, who seemed primarily interested in the free tea and biscuits offered. This disillusionment was partly attributed to the anti-Kuomintang sentiment circulating among the resident Chinese community.[62]

These political rows in the Chinese diaspora were intense but no zero-sum game. Many Chinese embraced political flexibility and navigated between multiple loyalties. James Chuey of the Masons, for instance, was once involved in the Kuomintang-sponsored Society of Chinese Residents in Australia; notable merchants, such as Mar Leong Wah, William Liu and William Gock Young (郭劍英), engaged with both the Kuomintang and the Chamber of Commerce.[63] Leaders of the three prestigious Chinese Australian organisations also found themselves cooperating where they had shared interests. Supported by James Chuey, D.Y. Narme and Chen Wei-ping, Albert Hing visited Joseph Lyons to try to procure a lenient interpretation of the White Australia policy on the grounds of little public hostility towards resident Chinese.[64] In the 1940s, D.Y. Narme and Quan Mane, the old rivals in journalistic battles, cooperated to accommodate Chinese evacuees from Darwin in 1942 under the leadership of Chinese Consul General Tuan Mao-lan (段茂瀾).[65] These community leaders, too, attended each other's ceremonies to exhibit a sense of community

---

61　*Chinese Republic News*, "美利濱中華公會舉行國慶紀念," 22 October 1932, 8; *Northern Territory Times*, "Chinese Republic 1911–1931," 13 October 1931, 4; *Tung Wah Times*, "中華總商會茶會紀盛," 15 October 1932, 5.

62　澳洲總支部執行委員會秘書處 1931, 163.

63　*Chinese Republic News*, "澳洲雪梨華僑對日救國後援會通告," 7 November 1931, 8; Kuo and Brett 2013, 71.

64　*Tung Wah Times*, "中國人入澳洲條例," 22 September 1934, 5; Chen Wei-ping to J.A. Lyons, 29 January 1934; Immigration Act and Chinese Requests, 12 March 1934, 174497, NAA.

65　*Sun*, "House for Chinese evacuees," 19 February 1942, 8.

solidarity in front of the Australian public.[66] Chinese patriotism did not exclude loyalty to the British Empire and Australia. In welcome celebrations, congregations and Chinese weddings, tributes were paid to both "Republican China" and the "British Emperor".[67]

## Conclusion

This chapter provides case studies to suggest that Chinese Australians acted independently of the political agendas of their homeland,[68] partly contrary to historians' previous arguments. The Kuomintang-constructed commemorations of the Mukden Incident politicised the collective memory of Chinese Australians in order to diligently claim their loyalty and identification, generating a social order favouring Nanking. While effective, resistance from Nanking's rivals was evident, indicating the different concepts of "China" held by other Chinese Australians. This echoes John Bodnar's argument that diverse expressions, some more privileged than others, became possible during symbolic public expression of memory.[69] Nanking's efforts to unite Chinese Australian communities backfired and further partitioned them.

---

66 *Chinese Republic News*, "總商會舉行新委就職禮紀盛," 6 May 1933, 8; "駐雪梨總領事館慶祝雙十國慶紀念," 20 October 1934, 5.

67 *Chinese Republic News*, "雪梨僑胞歡迎蔡廷鍇將軍之熱烈," 2 March 1935, 8; "葉炳南翁女公子結婚之盛況," 2 May 1936, 8; *Tung Wah Times*, "總商會歡宴張尚仁," 23 May 1936, 8.

68 Jones 2005, 64–5.

69 Bodnar 1992, 245.

# 4
# Chinese fundraising campaigns

Chinese Australian patriotism materialised in the fundraising campaigns in support of China's war efforts against Japan. It was a reciprocal process in which Nanking sought to alleviate its financial hardships while diaspora Chinese practised their imagined patriotic duty. This manoeuvre was not unique to China. Irish immigrants to Australia, for example, also actively organised similar campaigns for comparable causes that proactively answered appeals from their homeland throughout the early 19th and early 20th centuries.[1]

Nevertheless, the challenges for Chinese Australians who were dedicated to fundraising for China were more significant than Australians of Anglo-Saxon heritage. In the context of White Australia, diaspora patriotism often made Chinese presence "un-Australian", justifying Australian racial exclusion.[2] This was added to by Canberra's policy of appeasing Japan's invasion, which restricted the Chinese diaspora from achieving more. Meanwhile, the collection of subscriptions constituted a dynamic arena in which diasporic Chinese actively asserted their own agendas, generating tensions akin to those observed in memorial rituals and journalistic conflicts. Unlike the relatively harmonious and nationally coordinated fundraising efforts

1    Campbell 2008.
2    Khoo and Noonan 2011, 110.

among Chinese Americans,[3] the Chinese Australian experience was markedly more politicised and contested.

This chapter investigates the political tensions embedded in Chinese Australian fundraising campaigns. It begins by examining the competitive dynamics between pro-Nanking organisations and their rivals. Both sides were persistent and unyielding in asserting their own agendas. The analysis then turns to the case of Melbourne, exploring how diasporic Chinese and their homeland was interwoven through patriotic discourse. Finally, the chapter considers how shifting developments on the war front prompted a momentary cohesion among disparate factions within the Chinese Australian community. In so doing, it adds a different dimension to the existing scholarship that has generally assumed that the war efforts of Chinese Australians were unified.[4]

## Fundraising in 1930s Sydney

Driven by China's War of Resistance in the early 1930s, several newly established associations aimed to sponsor China's war effort through fundraising. These included the Society of Chinese Residents in Australia and the Association of Anti-Japanese Warfare Provision in Sydney, as well as the reorganised Chinese Citizens Society in Melbourne. Their presence dramatically remade the Chinese Australian community's social networks and the political landscape previously dominated by native-origin (such as the Sze Yup Society) and social-economic-goals-oriented (like the Chinese Chamber of Commerce) organisations. Fundraising within the Chinese diaspora was further politicised and transformed as parties of divergent agendas contested for authority and community leadership. Financial relief and political enterprise were closely bonded to ensure individual donors contributed according to their political loyalty while lessening the

---

3   Chen 2006, 170; Ling 1998, 107.
4   Cottle 2003; S. Fitzgerald 1996; 2001; Giese 1999; Hall 1990; Khoo and Noonan 2011, 95; Loh 1989; Rankine 1995.

possibilities of inconsistent behaviours that damaged the interests of varied political camps.

Eleven days after the Mukden Incident, the Society of Chinese Residents in Australia (對日救國後援會) was founded at the Australian headquarters of the Kuomintang. It aimed to lead "all Chinese national salvation groups in Australia".[5] The society later removed the term "backup support" (後援) from its Chinese title to maintain consistency with its counterparts in China,[6] indicating a growing dedication to support China and confront Japan. Not only have historians suggested that the Chinese title indicated efforts to monopolise the role of legitimate spokesperson for the Chinese diaspora community,[7] but the difference between the Chinese and English titles also suggests endeavours to negotiate and balance their Chinese and Australian identities. In a similar instance, the Chinese name for the New South Wales Chinese Residents' Refugees' Relief Fund Committee (紐修威華僑救濟祖國難民委員會), established following the escalation of the Sino-Japanese conflict into full-scale war in 1937, likewise diverged from its English counterpart. The Chinese term for "homeland" (祖國) was intentionally omitted from the committee's name. The removal of nationalist Chinese terms by these societies suggested their English portrayals in a more Australian manner aimed to preclude suspicions about their allegiance to Australia. This inconsistency of language demonstrates Chinese Australian people's anxiety about their precarious position, navigating multiple identities and loyalties in White Australia.

The structure of the Society of Chinese Residents in Australia was designed in a spirit of democracy. Under the chairmanship of William Gock Young, the general manager of Wing On Company (永安公司), the society functioned through a 30-member committee consisting of 21 formal members and nine alternate members, with a small number of standing members selected from among them. To prevent abuse

---

5   陳志明 1935, 52.

6   *Tung Wah Times*, "澳洲雪梨華僑對日救國後援會緊要啟示," 23 January 1932, 8.

7   Kuo and Brett 2013, 73.

or fabrication of the society's decisions, official instructions and documents from the committee would only be considered valid with the signatures of more than two standing members. Regular meetings were conducted by William Gock Young, Mar Leong Wah and D.Y. Narme in rotation, typically held at 8 p.m. every Sunday. Several operational divisions were established to implement the committee's decisions, including a propaganda section and a finance office.[8] Much of the society's function relied on Chinese Australians' donations.[9]

One of the society's principal missions was to solicit financial support from Chinese Australians to succour China's fiscally grim situation and support the Chinese war refugees. Fundraising campaigns were initiated after the Shanghai Incident in 1932, when Japan's ambition to conquer China became pronounced. Subscription procedures were projected to secure donors to fulfil their pledged contributions. Each donor was provided with a register booklet to record his or her name and the specific amount of money pledged to subscribe before making subsequent payments. The names of these contributors would be published in local Chinese-language newspapers as a token of appreciation. Long-term subscriptions based on a fixed proportion of one's salary or business turnover were additionally promoted, highlighting the importance of a sustained financial flow to Nanking. The Chinese government was also asked to maintain a record of names of long-term subscribers whose donations were due at the end of each month. This list was used to issue certificates of appreciation and encourage more participation from previous contributors.[10] Donating to China was, therefore, a token of not just patriotism but

8   *Chinese Republic News*, "雪梨華僑對日救國後援會啟事," 10 October 1931, 8; "澳洲雪梨華僑對日救國後援會通告," 4 November 1931, 8; *Tung Wah Times*, "雪梨華僑成立對日救國後援會," 3 October 1931, 8; "雪梨華僑對日救國後援會啟事," 17 October 1931, 5; "救國會通告," 23 April 1932, 5; "雪梨抗日救國會第三十九次會議誌," 5 November 1932, 5; "救國會常會誌," 22 July 1933, 5; "救國會重要啟事," 30 June 1934, 5.

9   *Chinese Republic News*, "捐助澳洲雪梨華僑抗日救國會宣傳費續報," 9 April 1932, 8.

10  *Chinese Republic News*, "救國會第廿九次常會誌," 21 May 1932, 8; *Tung Wah Times*, "澳洲雪梨華僑抗日救國會籌募戰費簡章," 13 February 1932, 5; "為

respectability, in which official recognition of these contributions was also a means to promote Nanking's authority.

Propaganda efforts were integrated within the fundraising campaigns to galvanise cooperation in anti-Japanese actions among Chinese Australians and seek their unanimous support for China's fight. Fundraising balls and lion dances were organised as part of these initiatives to engage and captivate the audience, during which propaganda booklets were distributed. Echoing the calls of Chinese Australian newspapers,[11] repeated appeals were made to local Chinese to demonstrate solidarity and commitment by rejecting Japanese goods in Australia. These efforts appeared effective, as many Chinese grocers reportedly ceased procuring Japanese products, in a boycott that persisted throughout the 1930s.[12] However, despite these endeavours within Australia, the Sincere Company in Canton – owned by Chinese Australian merchants – was caught selling Japanese goods and penalised by the Kuomintang at provincial level.[13] This reinforced concerns voiced by Chinese Australian newspapers regarding the commitment of businesses to the boycott.[14]

Meanwhile, the propagandists intensified their ventures by composing and publishing a daily journal on Sino-Japanese relations. Priced at a sixpence and relying on translated wireless cables from Shanghai, it soon gained popularity among local Chinese. For example, a memorial volume produced by prominent community figures in 1932 to encourage donations had around 1,500 copies in circulation. The journal proved transient from 1931 to early February 1932, likely because it was less helpful when Chinese patriotism swept the community in subsequent years.[15]

催募捐款告各界僑胞書," 30 July 1932, 5; "澳洲雪梨華僑抗日救國會為提倡常年義捐宣言," 11 February 1933, 5; "救國會常會會議誌," 6 May 1933, 5.

11  *Chinese Republic News*, "要救國須靠自己力量," 14 November 1931, 5.

12  *Chinese Republic News*, "西澳普扶華僑抗日救國會籌款敬告僑胞書," 12 March 1932, 8; *Sydney Morning Herald*, "Chinese Chamber of Commerce appeal for action," 2 October 1937, 18; *Tung Wah Times*, "雪梨華僑成立對日救國後援會," 3 October 1931, 8; "快郵代電," 14 November 1931, 5.

13  *Chinese Republic News*, "先施公司仇貨案之省黨部批示," 27 May 1933, 7.

14  *Tung Wah Times*, "港商竟赴日巨頭會議耶," 15 June 1935, 2.

Despite the Kuomintang's sponsorship, the Society of Chinese Residents in Australia was by no means a cheerleader for the Nanking government. Many announcements diverged from the official line, blurring the connection with its sponsor and asserting its independence. Nanking was urged to declare war without making concessions to Japan, reclaim lost territories, and seek reconciliation with Kuomintang's opponents in a measured and diplomatic manner. The society sent a cable to the League of Nations in which it protested Russia's infringement on China's sovereignty; it also accused Japan of committing atrocities in China and requested stringent sanctions following an impartial investigation into Japan's aggression.[16] Some of these efforts met with positive responses, notably the recommendation submitted to Nanking advocating military mobilisation in Chinese schools, which was subsequently accepted.[17] By making its voice heard at local, national and transnational levels, the society intended to become the only legitimate and politically independent spokesgroup for Chinese Australians.

This ambition was not easily attained, and the society faced formidable challenges from those who disagreed with the Nanking government. One of the most proactive of these groups was the Association of Anti-Japanese Warfare Provision, which formed in Sydney on 12 December 1931, under the collective sponsorship of six local Chinese societies, including the Chamber of Commerce and the Masons. Compared with the Society of Chinese Residents, this organisation was concerned less with publicising itself to white

---

15 *Tung Wah Times*, "中日近日要訊出版廣告," 23 January 1932, 6; "本報緊要啟事," 13 February 1932, 5; "雪梨抗日華僑救國會籌賑上海戰區難民進支數列, 救國會三二次會議誌," 18 June 1932, 5, 8; "救國會第三十五次會議誌," 30 July 1932, 5; "救國會第三十六次常會誌," 20 August 1932, 5; "雪梨救國會第四十次會議誌," 19 November 1932, 8.

16 *Tung Wah Times*, "澳洲雪梨華僑對日救國後援會宣言," 10 October 1931, 8; "救國會電請政府迅作有效主張," 16 January 1932, 8; "救國會昨電國際調查員," 19 March 1932, 8; "救國會電告各界僑胞," 13 August 1932, 5; "救國會昨發兩要電," 27 May 1933, 5; "救國會電請西南團結禦辱," 16 September 1933, 5.

17 *Chinese Republic News*, "中華僑務委員會," 13 February 1932, 8.

Australians, as it did not provide an English translation of its Chinese title. The association's structure embraced a broader vision of democratic principles than the society, whose composition was predominantly influenced by the Kuomintang. Each of the six founding societies of the Association of Anti-Japanese Warfare Provision appointed four representatives to create a 24-member committee of six standing members and 18 executive members. The chairmanship rotated among these six standing members. The association commenced fundraising campaigns on 6 February, likewise as a response to the Shanghai Incident in 1932. Collected donations were managed by a finance committee of four members selected by the founding societies. Only if three of the four members agreed could the funds be allocated for other purposes, and donors could withdraw their subscriptions unconditionally.[18] The fundamental implementation of democratic principles partly depended on a reasonably high attendance rate at regular meetings. The association imposed a fine of 10 shillings for absence and 5 shillings for lateness (those who provided prior notification would be exempted).[19]

The first six standing members elected to the association's committee on 7 February consisted of prominent figures within Chinese Australian communities: Albert Hing for the Chamber; James Chuey for the Sze Yup Society; Charles Ng Kin for the Masons; Ping Nam (葉炳南) representing the Lin Yik Tong (聯益堂); Chen Huan (陳煥) standing for the Sydney Chinese Motivational Patriotic Association (勵誌會); and Cai Rong (蔡容) on behalf of the Hung Fook Tong (洪福堂). Yu Shun (余舜) from the Masons and Zhang Fuxiang (張富祥) from the Chamber were elected secretaries.[20] Albert Hing, James Chuey and Ping Nam formed the finance committee. While the association

---

18  *Chinese Republic News*, "戰費籌備會定期派員出發募捐," 13 February 1932, 8; *Tung Wah Times*, "烏省華僑成立拒日戰費籌備會," 12 December 1931, 8; "華僑對日戰費籌備會開始募捐," 6 February 1932, 5; "戰費籌備會組織內容," 5 March 1932, 5.

19  Committee for the Collection of Donations to Help the Struggle Against Japanese Invasion Minute Book, 1932–1937, 5, AU NBAC 111-6-1, NBAC.

20  Committee for the Collection of Donations to Help the Struggle Against Japanese Invasion Minute Book, 1932–1937, 4, AU NBAC 111-6-1, NBAC.

had been structured in the spirit of democracy, the Chamber and the Masons controlled it.

The association's support of Kuomintang China was ambiguous and ambivalent, as its distrust of Nanking was pervasive. The organisation indeed collected patriotic donations for the cause of China's fight, but the funds would not be sent to the government until an official declaration of war was made.[21] Meanwhile, donations aimed to sponsor Chinese militias volunteering to resist Japanese invasion were transmitted directly to them, bypassing the official route between Chinese Australian donors and their compatriot receivers. The association also strongly resisted any official attempts to monopolise the transfer channels. In 1933, it suspended all funds bound for China when Nanking sought to centralise all overseas donations by establishing the Central Receiving Office for Overseas Contribution (華僑愛國義捐總收款處) in Shanghai to unify agents receiving the subscriptions.[22] The association went even further in 1934 and promptly returned all funds to their respective donors, except the money for Ma Chan-shan (馬占山), realising that a declaration of war was unlikely in the short term.[23]

These actions uncovered political tension between Chinese authorities and their detractors, whose repudiation of Nanking's authority was profound. Financial support was transformed into a means to challenge China's leadership, rather than provide support to the Chinese government. What may have disturbed Nanking was not that the money failed to reach its intended destination, but that the concepts of "China" that most Chinese Australians upheld and pledged their loyalties to were not unified. As Canberra noted, the Kuomintang's influence during these mobilisations of Chinese Australian patriotism was confined to assisting rather than undertaking primary responsibility.[24]

---

21  *Tung Wah Times*, "烏省華僑成立拒日戰費籌備會," 12 December 1931, 8.
22  *Chinese Republic News*, "中央公電," 15 April 1933, 6; Committee for the Collection of Donations to Help the Struggle Against Japanese Invasion Minute Book, 1932–1937, 4–21, AU NBAC 111-6-1, NBAC.
23  *Tung Wah Times*, "雪梨戰費籌備會啟事," 7 April 1934, 5.
24  *Chinese Times*, 24 November 1941, C320, C8, 1495438, NAA.

Nevertheless, the relationship between Chinese authorities and the association was more complex than simple hostility. The Society of Chinese Residents and the consulate general more than once procured and successfully received help from the Association of Anti-Japanese Warfare Provision for Nanking's relief efforts. When the Chinese Ministry of Foreign Affairs secretly instructed Chen Wei-ping to organise a contribution of medical supplies, for example, the consul general requested and received the association's support. This collaboration did not last long, likely because it yielded few tangible results.[25]

Indeed, the relationship between the Chamber–Masons alliance and local Chinese authorities deteriorated in the years leading up to 1937. The mounting criticism of Chen Wei-ping in the *Tung Wah Times* openly challenged his prestige as the consul general and his claimed contributions to Chinese Australian wellbeing. When Chen resigned in 1936 to return to China – reportedly due to his disillusionment over defamatory attacks – the *Tung Wah Times* published no relevant coverage, and several prominent figures from the Chamber and the Masons, including Albert Hing and James Chuey, chose not to participate in the customary expressions of appreciation for Chen's service in Australia.[26] By 1937, the Association of Anti-Japanese Warfare Provision no longer trusted the Society of Chinese Residents' delivery of patriotic funds and chose instead to channel the collected funds to China through the New South Wales Chinese Residents' Refugees' Relief Fund Committee.[27]

---

25  Committee for the Collection of Donations to Help the Struggle Against Japanese Invasion Minute Book, 1932–1937, 15–17, AU NBAC 111-6-1, NBAC.
26  For the Chinese Chamber of Commerce's assertion of authority and its criticism of Chen Wei-ping, see *Tung Wah Times*, "敬頌總商會辦事啟事," 2 December 1933, 5; "總商會外交之成績," 10 August 1935, 8; "中澳商務商題," 8 February 1936, 5; "領事宜盡保僑職責," 15 August 1936, 5; Chen Wei-ping, with his secretary, Ko San Lik, sailed back to China by S.S. Tanda on 18 January 1937. See Boarding Report, 19 January 1937, SP42/1, C1937/487, 31102981, NAA.
27  Committee for the Collection of Donations to Help the Struggle Against Japanese Invasion Minute Book, 1932–1937, 25, AU NBAC 111-6-1, NBAC.

The worsening relationship between the Kuomintang and the Chamber–Masons alliance was not surprising. Apart from Chiang Kai-shek's controversial policy of "non-resistance", as already discussed in previous chapters, the most likely cause for this situation was because of the Kuomintang's internal discord; once pro-Nanking enthusiasts prevailed, the party's line shifted to hawkish. In October 1935, Wong Chih-hwa was chosen by the Chinese Ministry of Industry to study industry in Australia and was efficiently installed as the editor of the *Chinese Times* to establish valuable contacts with businesspeople in the industrial sector.[28] Wong was a faithful, enthusiastic defender of Nanking, efficiently engineering journalistic wars with the Chamber–Masons alliance in the year of his arrival. His ambition went further. In 1937, Wong attempted to manipulate intra-party affairs by endeavouring to remove D.Y. Narme from his leading position within the Australian Kuomintang. Wong slandered him for participating in the Kwangtung Movement against Nanking. D.Y. Narme physically slapped him and requested an official investigation to answer this defamation. The coup failed. Wong was removed from his office and repatriated to China, and his position was succeeded by Loh Kai-tze. The internal fragmentation directly led to reformulation of the Australian Kuomintang, marked by the establishment of the First Kuomintang Sydney Branch, which aimed to ease internal tensions and reinforce party cohesion.[29]

This is not to say that the anti-Nanking alliance was always in agreement during these political disturbances within Chinese Australian communities. Competitions between the groups over their future membership and community leadership were common. For example, the Chinese Masonic Society diligently tried to take advantage of the high circulation of the *Chinese World's News* to appeal to Chinese readers to participate in Mason-sponsored anti-Japanese campaigns.[30] This posture of acting as the leader of the anti-Japanese movement

---

28  Report from the Collector of Customs, 14 September 1936, 3103597, NAA.
29  *Chinese Republic News*, "歐陽南緊急啟事," 1 August 1936, 7; "民報編輯被撤職," 6 February 1937, 2.
30  *Chinese World's News*, "美利濱致公堂開會預告," 22 August 1936, 5, 31112332, NAA.

in Australia would attract recognition from Chinese Australians and –
alongside the blessing of Tsai Ting-kai (being a Mason and a patriotic
symbol) – encourage them to join the Masons to practise their Chinese
patriotism. By poaching their members, the Masons thus distanced
themselves from the Kuomintang as well as the Chamber of Commerce.
The Chamber–Masons alliance was precarious, and internal
disagreements were also evident within each of these groups. Upon
Chen Wei-ping's resignation, a significant number of Chinese
merchants across Sydney, Melbourne and Inverell signed petitions
urging Nanking to retain Chen. In Sydney alone, 106 individual
merchants and 40 commercial enterprises – including restaurants,
firms and shops – endorsed the appeal; among them were prominent
figures, such as Simpson Lee of the Chamber of Commerce and Charles
Ng Kin of the Masons. The farewell reception for Chen in Sydney
was attended by hundreds of guests, both Chinese and Australian,
including Deputy Prime Minister Earl Page. In Melbourne, Chen was
similarly honoured at a reception organised by nearly all the city's
Chinese merchants – reportedly more than 60 in number. Speakers,
both men and women, expressed their heartfelt appreciation for Chen's
contributions to Chinese diaspora communities in Australia.[31] His
widespread popularity at the time of his departure invites a
reconsideration of the conventional view that he was more invested in
Kuomintang affairs than in the welfare of Chinese Australians.[32]

Although many prominent Chinese Australians embraced more
inclusive views to transcend political disagreement, none possessed the
charisma or competence to heal these ruptures within the diaspora.
The hostility between Chinese authorities and anti-Nanking camps did
not begin to subside until Pao Chun-jien succeeded Chen Wei-ping in
late 1936. Part of his success can be attributed to his remarkable social
skills and strategic moves to reshape the consulate general's relationship
with diasporic Chinese elites. He accomplished this by distancing his

31 *Chinese Republic News*, "駐雪梨總領事館通告 (卅三號)," 30 March 1935, 4;
"各僑團聯名挽留陳總領事," 24 October 1936, 4; "英壬埠僑胞挽留陳總領
事," 7 November 1936, 2; "美利濱僑胞歡送陳總領事紀盛," 19 December
1936, 4; "本埠僑商公譔陳總領事盛況," 26 December 1936, 2.
32 Kuo and Brett 2013, 98.

subordinates from the politics of Chinese Australian communities and improving his office's services to both the Chinese and Australian public.[33]

## Fundraising in 1930s Melbourne

Chinese fundraising campaigns in Melbourne expanded successfully, thanks to the Chinese Citizens Society, which achieved comparatively less political bitterness between parties than Sydney Chinese organisations.[34] Indeed, the re-establishment of this society to respond to Chinese national calamity in 1931 was well received by nearly all Chinese groups despite their differing political views and backgrounds. The reopening ceremony attracted approximately 400 local Chinese and featured addresses by the Chinese consuls in Melbourne, Pao Chun-how and Lee Hong.[35] Congratulatory telegrams and gifts that hoped for Chinese Australian solidarity in China's restoration of integrity poured in from organisations, including the Victoria Chinese Chamber of Commerce, the Kuomintang's Victorian and Melbourne branches, the Society of Chinese Residents in Australia, the Melbourne Chinese Masonic Society and several traditional Chinese societies.[36]

The umbrella organisation's function, like its Sydney counterparts, upheld democratic principles. It was led by an executive committee comprising 12 members responsible for overseeing the operations of subordinate sections, including propaganda and philanthropy, and they managed to satisfy all involved. A weekly executive committee meeting was held and speakers were invited to publicise its activities. The operations of the Chinese Citizens Society in Melbourne were more transparent than societies in Sydney, as a supervisory committee was

33  *Chinese Republic News*, "駐雪梨總領事館整頓館務", "執委會委員就職宣言," 6 February 1937, 2; "總領館關懷僑況," 13 February 1937, 2; "駐雪梨總領館啓事," 20 February 1937, 4; Kuo and Brett 2013, 100.
34  Chinese Citizens Society 1932.
35  *Chinese Republic News*, "美利濱中華公會開幕紀盛," 21 November 1931, 8.
36  *Chinese Republic News*, "美利濱中華公會開幕頌詞雜誌," 28 November 1931, 8; "美利濱中華公會開幕頌詞雜誌 (續)," 5 December 1931, 8.

established to ensure the impartiality of the Chinese Citizens Society. Commissioners, selected based on their social and political networks within the member societies, were dispatched to provincial towns to publicise the society's work and collect donations from local Chinese.[37]

Melbourne Chinese fundraising campaigns resembled their Sydney compatriots in many ways. Networks established by participating societies played an indispensable role in expanding fundraising capacity and soliciting funds. Propaganda and inspection teams were installed to promote patriotism, encourage donations and inspect whether Chinese stores conformed to the decision to reject Japanese goods.[38] Differences were evident as well. The Chinese Citizens Society's fundraising web was less extensive than those in Sydney, limited to Chinese societies and stores in Melbourne and Victoria's provincial towns. In contrast, those in Sydney reached as far as Tasmania.[39] This was partly because Sydney served as the socio-economic nexus of Chinese Australian business, providing fundraisers with access to these established networks. The Society of Chinese Residents in Australia collaborated with prominent Chinese commercial enterprises, such as Wing On and Wing Sang, and established branches in Newcastle, Brisbane, Perth and provincial towns.[40] The Association of Anti-Japanese Warfare Provision allied with prosperous Chinese stores, including Sun Tuey Wah Chockson (新遂和號), Kwong Wing Chong (廣榮昌) and Yuen Tiy Tung Kee

37　*Tung Wah Times*, "中華公會會務近況," 2 April 1932, 8; "美利濱中華公會民國廿一年職員表," 7 May 1932, 5; "美利濱中華公會籌募第三次救國金勸捐隊員," 4 March 1933, 7; "通告各界僑胞限壹個月內將捐助抗日救國金掃數清繳澳洲域省美利濱中華公會通告," 2 May 1936, 5.

38　*南寧民國日報*, "澳洲美利濱華僑," 1 December 1931, 3.

39　*Chinese Republic News*, "救國會昨開特別緊急會議," 6 February 1932, 8; "戰費籌備會定期派員出發募捐," 13 February 1932, 8; *Tung Wah Times*, "華僑對日戰費籌備會開始募捐," 6 February 1932, 5; "烏修威華僑對日戰費籌備會收到捐助義軍軍費芳名列," 11 February 1933, 5; "救國會第十八次會議誌," 20 February 1932, 5; "澳洲烏修威華僑對日戰費籌備會啟事," 5 March 1932, 2; "雪梨救國會常會誌," 15 April 1933, 5.

40　Committee for the Collection of Donations to Help the Struggle Against Japanese Invasion Minute Book, 1932–1937, 17, AU NBAC 111-6-1, NBAC.

(源泰同記), expanding its branches as far as Innisfail in Queensland. Though these fundraising organisations expanded nearly nationwide to mobilise Chinese patriotism and donations for China, they were not in a position of central leadership over their branches. For instance, the Society of Chinese Residents' branches retained considerable independence in determining when and how to send their collections to China.[41]

Despite its lesser fundraising capacity, the Chinese Citizens Society was determined to avoid the bitterness that had occurred among Sydney Chinese, by strongly emphasising member parties' shared interests. An in-between approach was adopted. It pledged to send donations to Nanking only when actual fighting took place, rather than the society's as-collected delivery to Nanking and the Association of Anti-Japanese Warfare Provision's fiscal custody until an official declaration of war. If hostilities ceased or peace was maintained, the funds would be held in reserve for the "purchase of warships for national defence and the protection of overseas Chinese".[42] The arrangement offered greater flexibility in reconciling member parties' varied political views and demands. This approach similarly reflects the neutral political line and language of the Society of Chinese Residents in Australia, as previously discussed, which earned recognition from and ensured amicable relations with Chinese Australian leaders in Sydney.[43]

The Chinese Citizens Society was also more creative than their Sydney compatriots when it came to fundraising campaigns. The monotonous calls for donations in public and private settings in Sydney were overshadowed by colourful and engaging requests in Melbourne. The drama club owned by the Chinese Citizens Society was deployed to regularly stage plays with themes ranging from Chinese patriotism to romance. In fact, Chinese opera had been used for fundraising purposes since the 19th century, drawing both Chinese and

41   陳志明 1935, 144, 152.
42   *Tung Wah Times*, "美利濱華僑募集滅敵救國軍費基金宣言," 14 November 1931, 5.
43   *Chinese Republic News*, "謝啟二," 19 December 1931, 8; *Tung Wah Times*, "美利濱各界華僑捐助第一次救國金進支結束," 23 April 1932, 5.

non-Chinese audiences, before it saw a decline at the turn of the 20th century.[44] However, by the 1930s, the resurgence of Chinese patriotism revitalised this form of fundraising, making it one of the primary means of entertainment and education for audiences in Australia. Many social organisations were affiliated with drama clubs, and Chinese dramas were regularly staged in more populous Chinese Australian communities.[45] Using the commercial networks of the Chinese Citizens Society's member parties, tickets for these plays were made available in "every Chinese shop" in Melbourne.[46] Audiences were thus less likely to be bored by repetitive patriotic themes and discourses. This approach succeeded, and the shows were welcomed. In 1932, one performance attracted an audience of approximately 1,000 resident Chinese and white Australians. They cheered during a scene depicting "warriors besieging and attacking the Japanese".[47] Fundraising aside, these dramas served as patriotic education that encouraged "Chinese nationals to shoulder the responsibility of homeland salvation collectively".[48]

Even more types of entertainment joined the Melbourne roster, including Chinese calligraphy auctions and magic shows. These maximised the possibility of harvesting as many donors and donations as possible. Lee Hong once auctioned his Chinese patriotic poems written in calligraphy during a show that more than a thousand people attended, significantly boosting interest and funds. The drama tickets and auctions raised more than £200 in one night, £30 of which Lee himself contributed.[49] Lee's participation conferred official recognition of the Chinese Citizens Society's authority and reinforced the solidarity of Melbourne's Chinese Australian community. Sydney Chinese officials lauded such cohesion. Loh Kai-tze, the Nanking-assigned commissioner based at the Chinese consulate general, praised the

---

44  Williams 2021b, 166–208.
45  澳洲總支部執行委員會秘書處 1931, 172; *Manilla Express*, "Chinatown in Darwin," 11 February 1938, 2.
46  *Tung Wah Times*, "美利濱中華公時白話劇社廣告," 26 March 1932, 5.
47  *Chinese Republic News*, "演劇募捐盛況," 30 April 1932, 8.
48  *Tung Wah Times*, "美利濱中華公時白話劇社廣告," 26 March 1932, 5.
49  *Chinese Republic News*, "演劇募捐盛況," 30 April 1932, 8.

Melbourne Chinese for their unity in fundraising campaigns supporting China.[50] This further improved the society's prestige while deepening Nanking's predicament, as its authority depended on collaboration with Chinese Australian leaders.

Propaganda often aims to cultivate values and attitudes in an innate rather than imposed way.[51] Chinese Australian propaganda in fundraising campaigns, while organised by different parties for various aims, unanimously and subtly drummed identification with China into its audiences. Chinese patriotism was cultivated through a combination of nationalism and diasporic experiences. The Chinese in China were reinforced as "our brothers" and China as the "fondly remembered and missing motherland", legitimately framing patriotic subscription to China as fulfilling the audience's national obligation to support "our Chinese nation's independence in the world with freedom and equality".[52] What was simultaneously and paradoxically underplayed was their "Australianness" – part of the diasporic experience; Australia was solely described as a "foreign land" of "Westerners". Even the grammatical structures used, with commands (imperatives) and conditional (modal) verbs, helped to establish an intimacy with the homeland that transcended spatial and temporal barriers.[53]

The concept of *jia* (家, home) was central to constructing patriotic discourse that connected the diaspora Chinese to the homeland. Studies have shown that "home" inalienably links Chinese abroad and China through race, culture, history and affection, giving meaning to everyday life.[54] The *jia* has always been tightly associated with *guo*

---

50  *Tung Wah Times*, "駱介子致謝啟事," 7 January 1933, 5.

51  Kushner 2006, 25.

52  *Chinese Republic News*, "澳洲雪梨華僑抗日救國會籌募戰費宣言", "澳洲烏修威華僑對日戰費籌備會勸捐小啟," 6 February 1932, 8; "澳洲昆省皮裏士濱埠華僑對日救國後援會成立宣言," 19 March 1932, 8; *Tung Wah Times*, "烏省華僑成立拒日戰費籌備會," 12 December 1931, 8; "快郵代電," 16 April 1932, 8.

53  *Chinese Republic News*, "商量應否再繳納救國金的問答," 27 February 1932, 5; "商量應否再繳納救國金的問答 (續)," 5 March 1932, 5; "商量應否再繳納救國金的問答 (續)," 12 March 1932, 5; "商量應否再繳納救國金的問答 (續)," 19 March 1932, 5.

(國, state), making up terms like *guojia* (國家, state-home) or *jiaguo* (家國, home-state). Despite the different priorities of home or state in understanding the Chinese nation, all these terms illuminated an imagined place where families, clans, ancestral villages, cultural heritage and national identity intersected and intertwined. The concept of *jia* also extended to residences and families in Australia. Through this shared idea of *jia*, the social status of Chinese Australians and their homeland's present and future were intertwined.

Propagandists, therefore, argued for proactive attention and action for China, as "the collapse of the Chinese nation is the downfall of *jia*, and the downfall of *jia* is the end of individuals". For either Chinese at home or abroad, the demolishing of *jia* would reduce them to "the status of stateless and nationless servitude dominated by the Japanese".[55] While partly resonating with what historians have found – that diasporic Chinese connected their status in diaspora to China's international status[56] – this notion was different. It focused more on external threats to China, rather than the status of Chinese Australians within Australia. This promoted a collective identity, based around the idea of "Chinese nation first". Not only were patriotic campaigns justified, but more people were persuaded to participate.

Propaganda discourse also drew on curated glory to cement this collective identity of the Chinese nation. Such terms as *wenming guguo* (文明古國, a civilised ancient country), *liyi zhibang* (禮儀之邦, a nation of etiquette) and *baowei zongbang* (保衛宗邦, shielding the home-nation) were repeated to nurture Chinese Australian affiliation with their Chinese-ness and loyalty towards China.[57] Research has demonstrated that recipients often respond to and structure their realities on the meticulously selected features presented in propaganda

54    Davidson 2008, 30; McKeown 1999, 323.
55    *Chinese Republic News*, "澳洲雪梨華僑抗日救國會籌募戰費宣言", "澳洲烏修威華僑對日戰費籌備會勸捐小啟," 6 February 1932, 8; "西澳普扶華僑抗日救國會籌款敬告僑胞書," 12 March 1932, 8; *Tung Wah Times*, "烏省華僑成立拒日戰費籌備會," 12 December 1931, 8.
56    S. Fitzgerald 1996, 179; McKeown 1999, 326.
57    For connections between larger group identity and chosen glory and trauma, see Volkan 2005, 6.

over other possible ones.[58] By omitting unimpressive parts of the Chinese past, the propaganda adroitly directed recipients' mindsets to Chinese national interests and antagonism of the Japanese, positioning this as core to the everyday life of Chinese Australians.

Manipulation of sentiment aside, the legal position of diasporic Chinese as Chinese citizens was asserted to justify the publicised notion of "Chinese nation first" and pressured Chinese Australians to meet their national obligation. Indeed, Chinese rules of nationality prioritised parental lineage over birthplace and upheld China's claimed hold over Chinese overseas. It is no surprise to see that the patriotic organisations in Sydney and Melbourne toughly stressed that resident Chinese ought to support China militarily and financially due to their "obligation and responsibility" as "citizens of China".[59] Hence, social, political and economic stratification boundaries between Chinese Australians were blurred and replaced by a group identity of "Chinese nation" and a collective loyalty towards it.

Sociopolitical organisations of Chinese Australians were not the sole agents producing propaganda of Chinese patriotism. Concurrently, local Chinese were subject to substantial amounts of discourse, including diverse publications imported from China, such as the *Pictorial of the Jehol Fight* (熱河大戰寫真), the *Magazine of Yuguan Battle* (榆關戰事書刊), the *Young Companion* (良友畫報), the *Time Pictorial* (時代畫報), and *Current Affairs Monthly* (時事月刊). Apart from the last one, available for 5 pence each (7 pence if purchased through the consulate general), the rest were sold for 6 pence through local Chinese-language newspapers and the Chinese consulate general.[60] The prices were acceptable for the Chinese Australian majority, who could thus access updates on China's fight, albeit in the form of patriotic propaganda.[61]

---

58  Pratkanis and Aronsonn 2001, 77.
59  *Chinese Republic News*, "澳洲省域華僑募集第二次救國金宣言," 20 February 1932, 8; "商量應否再繳納救國金," 27 February 1932, 5; "商量應否再繳納救國金," 5 March, 5; "商量應否再繳納救國金," 12 March, 5; "商量應否再繳納救國金," 19 March, 5; "為促募捐款告各界僑胞書," 23 July 1932, 8; *Tung Wah Times*, "美利濱華僑募集滅敵救國軍費基金宣言," 14 November 1931, 5.

Although records detailing the total donations were lost during the 1930s,[62] surviving evidence indicates that Chinese Australian fundraising campaigns were successful due to the effectiveness of patriotic propaganda. Between 1931 and 1937, the Society of Chinese Residents in Australia and the Association of Anti-Japanese Warfare Provision in Sydney garnered approximately £6,170 and £4,636, respectively. In Melbourne, the fundraising total reached £12,138. Together with less-known collections, they contributed more than £23,255 (roughly $2,888,885 in Australia today),[63] most of which was collected between 1931 and 1933.[64] While Chinese Australian donations might not be impressive compared to their counterparts in South-East Asia and the United States, the much smaller population yielded an impressive contribution per capita. Yet, the limited proportion of total subscriptions collected between 1933 and 1937 suggest the devastating repercussions of the political divisions within Chinese Australian communities.

The success of fundraising mirrored the rise of Chinese Australian patriotism among individuals. Some Chinese residents, senior and junior, expressed their desire to return to China to offer services, including Lu Wah-yue (盧華岳), a prominent Australian Kuomintang member, and Lew Mon Ham, a young graduate from Adelaide who had studied Engineering at the School of Mines and Industries in Australia with strong academic performance.[65] These people were not all-words-and-no-deeds. Many volunteered to serve in China, sharing

---

60    A half-year subscription of *Current Affairs Monthly* cost 4 shillings, and a yearly subscription cost 7 shillings and 6 pence. See *Chinese Republic News*, "本報新到各種畫報," 13 May 1933, 8; "駐雪梨總領館啟事," 20 May 1933, 5.

61    For the wages of Chinese Australians, see Williams 2018, 122.

62    陳志明 1935, 154.

63    Based on the inflation calculator of the Reserve Bank of Australia. See https://www.rba.gov.au/calculator.

64    王光輝 2018, 61, 93.

65    陳立夫函吳鐵城轉蔣中正中國國民黨澳洲支部常委盧華岳發明電砲可抵禦飛機請准匯旅費助其回國投效並附盧華岳函, 11 November 1933, 002-080102-00079-004, AH; *Advertiser*, "Clever Chinese Student," 4 February 1933, 14.

accommodations with others from South-East Asia in cities like Kunming (昆明).[66] In this context, the Chinese diaspora in Australia was integrated into a process of politicisation in Chinese patriotism among Chinese immigrant communities worldwide.[67]

The effectiveness of the fundraising does not indicate that these campaigns faced no challenges. Registering donations in advance via subscriptions often incurred frequent defaults in payment. The campaigners had to warn those who failed to make their payments on time that their names would be publicly exposed in newspapers as a form of punishment.[68] The enthusiasm of Chinese Australians also dwindled over China's successive concessions to Japan before 1937, and some of the headlines of propaganda articles suggest Chinese Australians' unwillingness to continue contributing. Low attendance saw the frequency of regular meetings diminish over time, transitioning from weekly to monthly sessions. Eventually, they became monthly meetings due to low attendance rates, ranging from about 12 to 30 attendees.[69] Moreover, not every member of the Chinese diaspora was convinced by the propaganda, much the same as their Japanese counterparts in Australia.[70] Aware of the Kuomintang regime's corruption, doubts arose about whether the patriotic donations were adequately utilised. Leaders of the Chinese diaspora had to request that Nanking provide them with invoices of the subscriptions received to clarify the allocation of these contributions. Although the request was efficiently approved and the invoices were published in Chinese-language newspapers, distrust lingered.[71] Family interests additionally remained the priority of many Chinese Australian

---

66  Koh 2013, 81.
67  McKeown 1999, 324.
68  *Tung Wah Times*, "中華公會通告," 2 May 1936, 5.
69  *Tung Wah Times*, "救國會通告," 23 April 1932, 5; "雪梨抗日救國會第三十九次會議誌," 5 November 1932, 5; "救國會常會誌," 22 July 1933, 5; "救國會重要啟事," 30 June 1934, 5.
70  Oliver 2012, 45–6.
71  美利濱中華公會執行委員會常務委員雷宜爵呈國民政府主席蔣中正為呈報歷次匯繳救國捐款情形恭祈鑒核准予分飭各收款機關速給歷次正式收據, 9 April 1932, 001-067140-00007-020, AH.

residents; as the Sze Yup Society reported, for example, many Chinese were more concerned with the idea of *jia* (home) than *guo* (state), and were unwilling to contribute patriotic funds.[72]

## Short-lived unity for China

After Japan's all-out invasion in July 1937, the Chinese government shifted from a policy of appeasement to full-scale resistance. The total war soon evoked a myriad of concerns and anxieties within Chinese communities worldwide about the future of their homeland and compatriots. In Australia, local Chinese set their feuds aside and were much united by seeing China's definite resistance. Nanking's previous dissidents dedicated themselves to sponsoring the Kuomintang. The New South Wales Chinese National Salvation Association (紐修威華僑國難後援會) was established to coordinate leading organisations (the Chinese Chamber of Commerce, the Chinese Masonic Society and the Kuomintang) in a concerted effort to collect subscriptions. Concurrently, the Australian and South Pacific Chinese National Salvation Association (澳洲及南太平洋國難後援總會) emerged as a transnational federation. The newly formed association quickly began soliciting financial support from Chinese communities across the nation for the relief of China, successfully raising over £10,000 within three months.[73] Much of this achievement can be attributed to Consul General Pao Chun-jien's effective mobilisation of local Chinese communities and his close relationships with community leaders.[74]

To further solicit financial assistance from Chinese Australians, the Chinese National Salvation Bond Administration was established in 1937 in Australian states, headquartered at the Chinese Chamber

---

72  Committee for the Collection of Donations to Help the Struggle Against Japanese Invasion Minute Book, 1932–1937, 17, AU NBAC 111-6-1, NBAC.

73  *Chinese Republic News,* "鳥修威華僑成立國難後援會", "駐雪梨總領事館敬告全澳僑胞書," 4 September 1937, 2, 4; "紐修威華僑國難後援會啟示," 11 December 1937, 4; *Daily Mercury,* "Chinese consul," 16 July 1938, 6; *Sydney Morning Herald,* "Chinese Distress Funds," 14 October 1937, 10.

74  *Chinese Republic News,* "本埠舉行僑民國難大會," 16 October 1937, 3.

of Commerce in Sydney. The collaboration between the Chamber and Nanking leveraged the former's networks with affluent Chinese merchants and facilitated the sale and circulation of the initial issue of the bond. Each was valued at 10 Chinese yuan, totalling fifty million Chinese yuan.[75]

The *Tung Wah Times* naturally participated in the fundraising for Nanking's cause, updating readers about China's fight and promoting the sale and patriotic significance of the Chinese National Salvation Bond. It notably expanded the news space to accommodate this demand and introduced a new compositor – Jong Foo Chong – from China. Soon renowned as a distinguished writer and scholar and earning high regard from Albert Hing, Jong Foo Chong was promoted to assistant editor and later became the paper's final editor. Jong Foo Chong had been acting as editor during the serious illness of Stanley South before doubling as both the assistant editor and the compositor.[76] Chinese authorities also appreciated his talent, and he assumed the role of general secretary of the Bond Administration. To ensure his stay in Australia, Pao Chun-jien spared no effort to admit Jong Foo Chong's wife into the country for a family reunion. The extreme diligence of Pao's efforts surprised and convinced Australian authorities, who reversed their initial rejection.[77]

Support from the wealthy aside, ordinary Chinese residents were encouraged to purchase the bond to sponsor Nanking's war effort. Propaganda discourse on *jia* and *guo* to bind diasporic Chinese with their homeland was again sought in relevant publications: "Saving China is to save yourself", as one slogan put it, "and to save yourself, you should buy the National Salvation Bond".[78] The connection was extended to Chinese compatriots at home, as another advertisement proclaimed that "buying one *yuan* of the Chinese National Salvation Bond is equivalent to saving one life of our fellow countrymen."[79] The

---

75  *Chinese Republic News*, "公債條例," 20 November 1937, 8.
76  Memorandum, 28 June 1938; Jong Foo Chong, 22 June 1938; Jong Foo Chong and wife, 1940–1942, 3093972, NAA.
77  Jong Foo Chong, 2 June 1938; H.B. Cody to Boarding Inspector, 21 June 1938, 3093972, NAA.
78  *Chinese Republic News*, [Untitled], 18 December 1937, 3.
79  *Chinese Republic News*, [Untitled], 27 November 1937, 6.

authority of history was also utilised to inspire Chinese Australians to follow their predecessors and make patriotic donations.[80] A Chinese National Salvation Bond Week was established for intensive publicity, with detailed prospectuses published in newspapers.[81]

Nanking valued responses from Chinese Australians towards the government's financial solicitation and expected a favourable reaction. It commissioned two prominent Chinese Australians who were members of the Overseas Chinese Affairs Commission, Charles Yee Wing (余榮) and Ng Hung Nam (伍洪南), as official representatives to convince their fellows in Australia of the significance of purchasing the National Salvation Bond as well as to solicit donations to Chinese refugees. Upon returning to Australia, the representatives received warm welcomes from various prominent Chinese societies. They took every opportunity, such as banquets hosted by Chinese societies, to urge the bond sale as an "obligation of Chinese people" and to preach Nanking's commitment to resistance.[82] To provide further incentives, rewards based on the proportion of National Bond purchases were made available to the Chinese in Australia.[83] This strategy worked, and it was reported that the Chinese Citizens Society alone raised £25,000 (around $2,759,273 in Australia today) for Chinese war bonds.[84]

The solidarity between Chinese Australians, and between Chinese Australians and Kuomintang China, was a result of a confluence of factors. One was Nanking's shifting policy, which removed a significant point of contention that had divided Chinese Australian communities. Criticism centred on the Kuomintang's submission to the enemy was no longer tenable. Equally important was Nanking's increasing awareness of the unlikelihood of having the Chinese diaspora unified under its leadership, along with growing awareness of the urgent need for collaboration. Instead of enforcing Kuomintang ideology, as in the early

---

80  *Chinese Republic News*, "歷史上捐輸救國的故事," 4 December 1937, 7.
81  *Chinese Republic News*, "救國公債宣傳周," 20 November 1937, 8; "救國公債募集辦法," 27 November 1937, 4.
82  *Advertiser*, "Relief for Chinese refugees," 8 February 1937, 23; *Chinese Republic News*, "余伍兩氏奉派抵埠," 11 December 1937, 2.
83  *Chinese Republic News*, "購募救國公債分等獎勵辦法," 4 December 1937, 4.
84  *Telegraph*, "Impossible to exaggerate atrocities in China," 20 June 1938, 9.

1930s, a cordial relationship between Kuomintang China and Chinese Australians was emphasised across four dimensions: *jiuwang tucun* (救亡圖存, national salvation and survival), *duanlai tuanjie* (端賴團結, all rely on solidarity), *zhongcheng baoguo* (忠誠報國, patriotic loyalty to serve the country) and *yongyue shujiang* (踴躍輸將, make strenuous and diligent contributions).[85] The previous party-rule authority was replaced by patriotic discourse favouring a broader notion of "China".

The fundraising federation in Sydney was supplemented by three additional fundraising groups, each characterised by distinct approaches. The Chinese National Salvation Fund predominantly employed conventional methods for fundraising, while the New South Wales Chinese Women's Relief Fund (紐修威中國婦女慰勞會) and Young Chinese Relief Movement (澳洲雪梨青年華僑救濟會) relied heavily on social functions and concentrated their efforts on the collection of material supplies needed in China. They worked together in close collaboration to maximise fundraising capability and geographic reach. Indeed, in less than three weeks, they successfully raised about £7,000 (about $791,545 in Australia today).[86]

Also featured in Chinese fundraising efforts in the late 1930s was a notably growing collaboration between diasporic Chinese and white Australians. While only a few white Australians were seen at the memorials, plays and fundraising for Chinese patriotic campaigns throughout much of the 1930s, the situation began to change in the wake of Japan's full-scale aggression in July 1937. On Easter Saturday of 16 April 1938, more than 20,000 spectators at the Sydney Sports Ground witnessed a magnificent Chinese pageant and a spectacular fireworks display.[87] This event echoed and exceeded the numbers at a February procession to celebrate the 150th anniversary of the First Fleet's arrival.[88] It was organised by the New South Wales Chinese Residents' Refugees' Relief Fund Committee, aiming to support Chinese campaigns to aid Chinese war refugees as well as publicise

---

85  Tablet paper, 1938, 3093972, NAA.
86  *Workers' Weekly*, "Local Chinese aid victims of Japan," 9 November 1937, 4.
87  *Sydney Morning Herald*, "Chinese repeat festival," 18 April 1938, 17.
88  *Labor Daily*, "Chinese dragon seen again," 18 April 1938, 4.

their hardship. The pageant also expressed gratitude and goodwill to Australians for their sympathy towards the appeals made on behalf of the suffering Chinese populace.[89]

Much like those recently established umbrella organisations, the New South Wales Chinese Residents' Refugees' Relief Fund was more inclusive than those with similar missions in early 1930s Sydney. It was another manifestation of diaspora community solidarity that garnered unanimous support from various political camps. The fund's committee included Pao Chun-jien, Mar Leong Wah, James Chuey, Charles Ng Kin and Quan Mane.[90] What distinguished the pageant from most Chinese fundraising campaigns was its inclusion of the Australianness of diasporic Chinese alongside their Chinese heritage, a dual identity that had largely been overlooked by the traditional patriotic discourse.

The pageant commenced with an Australian marshal, G.A. Cummins, leading the procession, flanked by two Chinese assistant marshals, James Yee Tong and T. Lowe Loong. The procession featured Chinese and Australian culture: Boy Scouts and Chinese gongs. The program traversed through Chinese tales that illustrated immigrant Chinese peoples' embrace of Australian modernity alongside inheritance of Chinese tradition, including *Suwu Muyang* (蘇武牧羊, Suwu Tending the Sheep), *Wenji Guihan* (文姬歸漢, Wen Ji Returns to China), *Woxin Changdan* (臥薪嘗膽, Honour through Hardship) and *Bai Meigui* (白玫瑰, White Rose).[91]

The event engendered Chinese goodwill by fostering friendship between China and Australia. After Chinese lion dances and a 43-metre-long Chinese dragon procession, a lantern parade showcased animals and fruits unique to Australia, such as emus, sheep, koalas and kangaroos. White Australians actively organised and promoted the pageant, collaborating with their Chinese counterparts to ensure its smooth execution.[92] The pageant impressed white Australians, and it was reenacted at the Exhibition Ground in Brisbane two months later,

---

89  N.S.W. Chinese Residents' Refugees' Relief Fund Committee 1938, Foreword.
90  N.S.W. Chinese Residents' Refugees' Relief Fund Committee 1938.
91  N.S.W. Chinese Residents' Refugees' Relief Fund Committee 1938, sections 6–9.
92  N.S.W. Chinese Residents' Refugees' Relief Fund Committee 1938.

attracting "a crowd of 35,000 people". The *Courier-Mail* even featured the event on its front page.[93] The captivating event blurred traditional racial boundaries and promoted the hybrid identities of Chinese Australians, challenging nationalist Chinese and Australian perceptions centred on racial division and highlighting their complex loyalties to both countries. It was a strong demonstration of China's presence in Australia, bringing wartime China to the attention of White Australia, whose continued indifference contributed to an emboldening of Japan's aggression.

Similar efforts to unite local Chinese communities for fundraising and solidarity were also taking place beyond Sydney and Melbourne. Like their predecessors, these newly formed fundraising groups sought assistance and expanded their influence through Chinese Australian commercial networks, both locally and nationally.[94] In Queensland, the Overseas Chinese Association (華僑聯合會) was established in 1937 as a mediator for local community affairs.[95] In Darwin, the United Chinese Association was founded and continued to function into the 1940s.[96] Vibrant communication and visits between Chinese communities within Australia were common, many of which aimed to collaborate on fundraising for China's interests.[97] These organisations, hoping to unify local Chinese efforts, were cautious about their leaders and members expressing public opinions in case of causing misunderstandings. For example, the New South Wales Chinese National Salvation Association required pre-approval for any published article or public speech.[98]

Grassroots fundraising was also taking place in towns with few Chinese Australians, organised by Chinese and non-Chinese Australians working together. In Brisbane, the War Victims' Relief Fund and the Society of Friends (the Quakers) extended their call for

93   *Courier-Mail*, "Chinese pageant delights crowd of 30,000," 11 June 1938, 1; *Telegraph*, "Chinese pageant was huge success," 11 June 1938, 8.
94   *Warwick Daily News*, "Chinese war refugees," 30 August 1938, 4.
95   See *Chinese Republic News*, "啓事," 29 May 1937, 2.
96   *Northern Standard*, "Chinese picnic," 16 August 1940, 12.
97   *Morning Bulletin*, "Relief of distress in China," 12 July 1939, 8.
98   Chen Suen Yao, 16 October 1937, MLMSS 10277/Box 1X, 1JkPRroY, 9639983, NSW State Library (NSWSL), Sydney.

relief to include China.[99] The Citizens' Association of Queensland for the Relief of the Distressed in China, co-chaired by W. Richardson and Frank Yow, included local Chinese and white Australians who sent funds and supplies to China through British and American associations in Hong Kong.[100] In rural towns like Tully, Queensland, such collaboration between Chinese and white Australians became indispensable for fundraising.[101] Even donations from areas with only a small Chinese population were impressive; for instance, in Hamilton, Victoria, where only 16 Chinese families resided, donations totalled £578 from 1937 to 1939.[102] In Adelaide, resident Chinese gathered and decided to donate towards China's purchase of airplanes.[103] The uneven distribution of the Chinese population also affected how subscriptions were collected. In metropolises like Sydney and Melbourne that housed major Chinese communities, contributions from Chinese Australians were primarily sourced through regular wage deductions. In contrast, in regions with smaller or more sparsely populated Chinese communities, fundraisers depended on voluntary donations.[104]

In addition to interracial cooperation, inter-generational efforts were observed, and adults were not the sole participants in relief campaigns. They were joined by efforts made by Chinese children. Leveraging their dual identity as both Chinese and Australians, they helped stimulate interest in raising funds for China. Arranged by the Young People's Fellowship of the Church of Christ, a choir of children donned Chinese national dress and sang a Chinese "welcome song", followed by a chorus of "Beautiful China" by Presbyterian mission children at a war relief fundraising campaign held in Melbourne.[105]

Kuomintang China greatly appreciated these Chinese patriotic campaigns in 1930s Australia. One newspaper enthusiastically reported the incredible patriotic zeal in Melbourne, where local fruiters "donated

---

99  *Courier-Mail*, "Relieve distress in China," 7 December 1937, 14.
100  *Telegraph*, "Appeal for relief of distressed Chinese," 9 December 1937, 15.
101  *Townsville Daily Bulletin*, "Tully notes," 2 March 1940, 4.
102  駐各地領事館巡視轄區, 18 July 1940, 020-019999-0018, AH.
103  *Chinese Republic News*, "南省華僑籌款購飛機," 27 February 1932, 6.
104  *Daily News*, "W.A. Chinese send £1,000 for war relief," 27 August 1938, 3.
105  *Argus*, "The life of Melbourne," 13 July 1938, 8.

## PRACTICAL OPPORTUNITY TODAY TO AID ALLIES

### Lord Mayor Urges Practical Sympathy For Appeal

THE Lord Mayor (Mr. Soundy, M.H.A.) yesterday asked for the hearty co-operation and support of citizens for Allies Appeal Day, to be held in Hobart and other parts of Tasmania today.

"It is only fair and just that we should do honour to those countries allied with us in the effort to stem the advance of the aggressor," said Mr. Soundy, who is treasurer of the appeal committee. "The sacrifice made by these nations and the terrible hardships endured by the people demand our sympathy and practical help."

Appeal proceeds will aid Russian Medical Aid and Comforts, Fighting French Forces Appeal, Chinese and Greek relief funds, and funds of other Allies. Badges will be sold throughout the city, and an all-day fair will be held in the Hobart Town Hall from 10 a.m. to 5 p.m. A stall will be conducted by the Australian Broadcasting Commission at the commission's offices, and Remington Business College will hold an old clothes sale at Burn's mart. Lady Clark will pay an official visit to the fair at 3 p.m.

Soldiers will carry Allied flags, and a military band will parade the city from 1.15 p.m. to 2.15 p.m.

A concert arranged by the A.B.C. Patriotic Committee will be held in the Town Hall tomorrow night. The programme will include sketches, musical items, interpretative and national dances, and the A.B.C. Light Orchestra will participate.

Donations of money or goods for stalls may be left at the office of the secretary to the Lord Mayor, Town Hall. Donations so far are:

### HUTCHINS OLD BOYS

### School Supported

His Excellency the Governor, £15; Lady Clark, £5; Chinese community of Hobart, £151/7/; Greek residents, £35; Grand Lodge of Freemasons, £50; Chas. Davis Ltd., £25; Miss Morey, £15; collections at Blackwood and Lowe, by Mrs. G. O. Smith and others, £11/13/6; Dr. T. H. Goddard, £10/10/; the Lord Mayor and Mrs. Soundy, Harris and Marsh Pty. Ltd., Commander and Mrs. James Murray, Mr. and Mrs. Alf Davis, each £10; Dr. L. A. Triebel, Mr. W. H. Strutt, M.L.C., and Mrs. Strutt, each £5/5/; A.G., Kemp and Denning Pty. Ltd., Mrs. T. Came, each £5; donations collected by Mrs Cummings, £2/19/; Mr. T. Ellison, £2/2/; R. W. Legat, £1/1/; Ajax, Eric Cuthbertson, Mathers Domain Store, M.A.G., E.K.F., J.W. each £1; W.E., the Rev. L. A. Bowes each 10/; Mrs. Bredby, 5/; Mr. and Mrs. H.E.C., 3/; total, £487/10/6.

Details of donations from Chinese community of Hobart: Henry and Co., £15; Ah Ham and Co., Chung Man Chock, Chung Sing Wal, each £10; Peter Quong Goon, Stan Henry, each £5/5/; W. Chung Sing, G. Chung Hon, C. Howe, Wing Lee, Chung Ah Doo, Chung Gon Bros., each £5; Mei-Ling Chung Gon, £4/18/8; Ah Kong, T. Ah Gim, each £4; Sing Goon, £3/3/; Chung Ah Yet, £2/3; Chung Ah Goon, Chung Sing Woo, Quan Yot Hie, each £2/2/; Chung Pak Koon, L. T. Henry, Ah Hing, Wah Shing Yee Sing, Ah Wah, Chas. Lee Fook, W. Ah Wah, each £2; Chung Tallam, Chan Wook, Chung Doo Hoy, James Sing, J. Ah Fee, W. Long, Lew Yee, each £1/1/; Sun Sing, Kwong Yee Sun, Ah Hing, Yee Lee, Ah Sang, Fung Hing, Jack Hong, Ah Pang, Ah Tong, Chung Hong, Lee Ack, G. Soo, each £1; Mrs. Yee Sing, W. Chung Doo, anonymous, each 10/6; How Foon, Wong Chock Quong, Henry Sang, Ah Yung, Wing Shing, each 10/; Pon Ming, 6/; Win Sui, Chung Sing Ping, Tom Goon, each 5/.

Details of donations from Greek residents: Casimary Brothers, £60; G. Haros, £13; S. Casimaty, £7/10/; J. Flaskas, £5; Anonymous, £5; P. Baros, £2/10/; G. Vasilon, James Vallas, each £1.

Little Mei-ling Chung Gon made a delightful study as she presented to the Lord Mayor (Mr. Soundy M.H.A.) a cheque for £151/7/ towards Allies' Day Appeal. The amount was contributed by the Chinese community of Hobart.

Figure 4.1 Mei-ling Chung Gon presenting a cheque to Hobart Lord Mayor Mr Soundy M.H.A. (*Mercury*, "Practical opportunity today to aid Allies," 31 July 1942, 5. Mercury Historical Collection, State Library and Archives of Tasmania).

a thousand pounds" and dedicated "one-twentieth of their daily income" to regular subscriptions, with numerous individual donations ranging from £1 to £200.[106] The Chinese government specifically cited the enthusiastic patriotism of Melbourne's Chinese community when it received about $7,000 Hong Kong dollars from the executive committee members of the Chinese Citizens Society, led by Chen Mingxin (陳明新).[107] Contributions made by Chinese and white Australians in places like Launceston, Ipswich and Rockhampton were also remembered by

---

106　南寧民國日報, "澳洲美利濱華僑," 1 December 1931, 3.
107　西北文化日報, "捐匯巨款," 29 November 1938, 1.

Chinese people in China.[108] The National Salvation Bond sold well, through which reportedly around 14,000 yuan was collected in 1941 alone.[109] Chinese Australians' enthusiasm for fundraising and determination to win seemed, in the eyes of Australian press, unbreakable.[110]

Despite the collaboration and remarkable outcomes achieved through these campaigns, the Chinese Australian fundraising landscape remained polycentric and fragmented. Few inter-regional organisations were formed. The Chinese Citizens Society in Melbourne remained focused on efforts in Victoria, engaging only partial collaboration with Sydney Chinese elites. In Perth, the Chung Wah Association (中華會館) fundraised only through the Perth Chinese Relief Committee.[111] This fragmentation constrained the Chinese Australian community's collective potential and Kuomintang China's ability to secure more substantial support. While the Chinese government conceived and attempted to unify the disparate Chinese fundraising enterprises with a new federation organisation modelled on the Chinese Citizens Society in the lead-up to the Pacific War,[112] it met limited success (see Chapter 5 for further detail).

## Conclusion

Studies have shown that Chinese diasporas' shared national heritage, reinforced by mutual participation in nationalist activities, was ironically fragmented into new and hostile identities shaped by class, occupation and education.[113] This chapter adds a political perspective.

108 *Examiner*, "Appreciation from China for help for refugees," 24 August 1938, 5; *Queensland Times*, "Splendid efforts," 1 September 1938, 8; *Morning Bulletin*, "Rockhampton Chinese Refugee Appeal Committee final meeting of successful campaigns," 10 March 1939.
109 南寧民國日報, "港募債運動狂熱," 15 June 1941, 2.
110 *Shepparton Advertiser*, "Sino-Japanese War," 6 January 1939, 7.
111 Chung Wah Association, 1 May 1944, A9108, ROLL 4/13, 1609496, NAA; *Daily News*, "W.A. Chinese find £600 for war relief," 29 October 1937, 4.
112 西康民國日報, "澳洲華僑," 14 September 1941, 2.
113 McKeown 1999, 324.

Chinese Australian fundraising campaigns in Sydney and Melbourne illustrate that heterogenous patriotic missions based on divergent concepts of "China" and visions of "Chinese interests" produced little unity among diasporic Chinese. Even within each group itself, distinction was pronounced, and performances detached from political positions were not uncommon. Moreover, the role of their homeland (represented by Kuomintang China) was intertwined with political dynamics within the Chinese diaspora. It could either rupture community, as the fundraising contests in Sydney have shown, or partly heal them in the case of the National Salvation Bond and the Relief Fund. Additionally, the changing international system encouraged Chinese patriotic campaigns to focus more on the inclusiveness of Chinese Australian hybrid identities and interracial cooperation than on nationalist discourse to fundraise.

# 5
# Reformation of fundraising and political landscapes

On 20 October 1945, about 1,500 Chinese Australians gathered in Sydney under the praesidium leadership of the Kuomintang, the Chinese Chamber of Commerce and Chinese Masonic Society to celebrate China's victory over Japan. The attendees represented various newly formed associations that had emerged after China's War of Resistance broke out, including the Chinese Comforts Fund (全國慰勞總會), the Chinese Youth League, the Chinese Seamen's Union (中華海員工會) and the Chinese Women's Relief Fund. The event proceeded smoothly, with no apparent politically motivated tensions between participants. In total, the gathering raised £1,478 for the Chinese Relief Fund and presented a special booklet to the Chinese government expressing best wishes for China's bright future and admiration for Chiang Kai-shek's prestigious leadership.[1] However, this apparent harmony was superficial and concealed a deeper path marked by division.

This chapter explores the fragmented chorus of Chinese patriotism in Australia during the Second World War by examining the polycentric dynamics within Chinese Australian communities, which evolved in a nature distinct from the 1930s. Prominent organisations

---

1    袁中明 1945.

emerged, representing community members with different political, social and gender backgrounds. The first section examines the Kuomintang's persistent efforts to unify Chinese Australian fundraising institutions and how they adapted to the complex social milieu of the diaspora. The next section investigates the complex role of Chinese women in transnational relief work. The chapter then shifts to explore the financial and political initiatives of left-wing and Australian-born Chinese, shedding light on the rising leadership of younger generations. In doing so, the chapter illuminates the diverse and evolving nature of Chinese Australian patriotism and how it reshaped the broader war effort and the contours of the diaspora community.

## Donations to Kuomintang China

China became a member of the Allies during the Pacific War. A reinvigoration of Chinese Australian patriotism was also taking place alongside the forging of the Sino-Australian alliance. Kuomintang China was determined to take this opportunity to magnify propaganda, enlisting the support of Chinese Australians for their homeland. Several patriotic institutions were established to carry on the propaganda and fundraising initiatives that had emerged in the 1930s. The operations of these newcomers varied significantly, as each needed to adapt to the Chinese community it served.

Some new institutions sought collaboration with established local Chinese associations to advance their cause. This was often achieved through shared leadership, typically dominated by prominent local Chinese families. In Perth in 1943, for example, the Chinese Patriotic Society (救國會) was set up to better collect funds from the local Chinese community, whose support for Chiang Kai-shek and his government in Chungking was reportedly unanimous. This initiative resulted from cooperation between local Kuomintang and the Chung Wah Association, the most esteemed traditional Chinese society in Western Australia since its inception in 1909, and through the shared leadership of the Shem family whose involvement spanned these three prominent institutions. Alex Shem of R. Sim & Co. served as the president of the Chung Wah Association and co-president of the

Chinese Patriotic Society alongside Harold Shem.[2] Alex Shem was also the president of the Kuomintang's Perth branch, with Harold holding the treasurer's position.[3] The prestigious organisations in the city were interwoven with family networks, seemingly much less democratic than those in Sydney and Melbourne. Nevertheless, such an arrangement ensured efficiency and coherency in social mobilisation for patriotic purposes. Barely a year into its existence, the Chinese Patriotic Society raised approximately £4,778 for China (equivalent to $471,251 in Australia today).[4]

In regions with a lower Chinese population, the Kuomintang primarily conducted fundraising activities, as it was often the only organisation that survived. In South Australia, only the poorly attended Chinese Citizens' Society (中華公會) existed in Adelaide under Kit Dare's leadership. Unlike its influential cousin in Melbourne, the society failed to lead the local Chinese yet affiliated itself with the Kuomintang. This Kuomintang branch became more a social than a political organisation, with only half of its 100 members actively participating.[5] In Tasmania, the Chinese Masonic Society had ceased functioning, leaving the local Kuomintang on its own to undertake fundraising. Gin Ack, a fruiter, tobacconist and owner of G.A. Henry's shop, assumed the presidency of the Tasmanian Kuomintang, with Chung Manchork as the secretary, and actively collected funds for Chinese relief. While the monopoly that the Sydney Kuomintang had craved was realised, the Tasmanian group was depoliticised due to the dwindling and ageing Chinese community. It had a membership of just 17, including ten Chinese-born, three naturalised, and four Tasmanian-born Chinese, and no longer contributed politically, only engaging in social functions.[6] Much of the propaganda and fundraising campaigns for China relied heavily on interracial cooperation (as discussed in Chapter 4), such as the Chinese Relief Club, run by Mrs J.A. von Alwyn as

2   Chinese Community in Australia, 1944, 3051769; Associations and Societies, 1944, 1609496, NAA.
3   Kuo Ming Tang, 3 May 1944, 1609496, NAA.
4   Chinese Patriotic Society of Western Australia, 3 March 1944, 1609496, NAA.
5   Chinese Citizens' Society, 26 February 1944, 1609496, NAA.
6   Chinese Masonic Society, 3 March 1944; Chinese Societies and Organisations in Tasmania, 29 March 1944, 1609496, NAA.

president and Mrs A. Hollingsworth as patron, supported by Y.M.C.A. and prominent Chinese Australians including Alex Chen Kaw and Ann Chung Gon.[7]

Chungking did not stop trying to unify Chinese Australian fundraising enterprises. It made another attempt with the establishment of the Australian division of the Chinese Comforts Fund in Sydney in June 1944. The fund was chaired by T.Y. Lin (林子耀), Sydney manager of Easten Industries Ltd, and had the patronage of Hsu Mo (徐謨), the Chinese Minister to Australia.[8] Originating in Wuhan (武漢) in 1938 and established as a nationwide organisation in Chungking in 1939, the Chinese Comforts Fund successfully created overseas branches in various cities ranging from Bombay to Cuba, Vancouver, London and Sydney.[9] The organisation expanded efficiently in major Australian cities and rural towns, except Darwin, where local Chinese were evacuated due to the concern about Japan's invasion. Its fundraising capability was impressive, raising a total of £36,083 (approximately $3,151,037 in Australia today) within one year, approximately 84 per cent of which came from the Chinese diaspora.[10] The achievements surprised the Chungking headquarters, which expressed its appreciation for such enthusiastic and effective fundraising.[11]

The success and prominence of the Chinese Comforts Fund in Australia was built on collaboration within Chinese Australian communities. On the one hand, it solicited support not only from prestigious Chinese Australians, including D.Y. Narme and Mar Leong Wah in Sydney, Harry Fay (雷妙輝, also known as Louie Mew Fay) in Inverell and Stanley Young in Glen Innes, across metropolitan and rural areas,[12] but also from leading figures who were politically independent

---

7   *Examiner*, "Help for needy Chinese," 6 July 1938, 8.
8   *Daily Telegraph*, "Confident that China will win," 1 February 1939, 9; "Comforts Fund is Generalissimo's wish," 30 June 1944, 11.
9   全國慰勞抗戰將士委員會總會 1947, 2.
10  Chinese Comforts Fund 1945, 7.
11  *西京日報*, "豫鄂軍民協力作戰," 23 April 1945, 3; *新疆日報*, "澳洲僑胞匯款勞軍," 19 September 1945, 2.
12  Chinese Comforts Fund 1945, 10.

from the Kuomintang, such as Fred Wong (黃家權) of the left-wing Chinese Youth League and the Chinese Seamen's Union. D.Y. Narme, Mar Leong Wah and Fred Wong were all installed as vice presidents to ensure representation by multiple political parties.[13] The fund even received support for establishing a branch in Perth from well-known Chinese figures in Singapore, Tay Lian Teck and his wife Grace Tan Chow Neo, thereby reaffirming the longstanding connection between Chinese communities in Western Australia and those in South-East Asia, a relationship dating back to the colonial era.[14] More importantly, the Chinese Comforts Fund was not just a trans-political organisation, it was gender inclusive. A Chinese Women's Auxiliary Committee was set up to welcome Chinese women in areas where the fund expanded. In Sydney and Brisbane, the committees organised fundraising events, such as dances, with the assistance of renowned Chinese women from local communities.[15]

Meanwhile, the Chinese Comforts Fund cooperated with white Australians to establish branches in places with small Chinese populations. In the Tasmanian division, key positions were occupied by white Australians; Tasmanian Premier Robert Cosgrove was the patron and Anglican Bishop of Tasmania, G.F. Cranswick, was the president.[16] Although local Chinese held office positions in Perth, non-Chinese Australians filled most of them.[17] In Rockhampton, not only did Mayor H. Jeffries accept the position of patron of the fund's local branch, but Australian women from the Rockhampton District Patriotic Fund assisted the branch in selling badges and goods during campaigns.[18] The extensive interconnections with non-Chinese Australians enabled the Chinese Comforts Fund to leverage Australian newspaper networks (alongside the *Chinese Times*) to promote its visibility among the Australian public and highlight the fund's patriotic vision for China.[19]

---

13  Chinese Comforts Fund, 25 September 1944, 1609496, NAA.
14  *West Australian*, "Relief for China," 10 February 1945, 2. For the connection between Chinese people in Western Australia and South-East Asia, see Ryan 1995.
15  *Cairns Post*, "Obituary," 25 June 1945, 3; Chinese Comforts Fund 1945, 7.
16  *Mercury*, "Chinese Comforts Fund," 11 May 1945, 6.
17  *West Australian*, "Relief for China," 16 February 1945, 2.
18  *Morning Bulletin*, "Chinese Comforts Fund," 22 June 1945, 9.
19  *Barrier Daily Truth*, "Chinese Comforts Fund," 2 September 1944, 3.

Interracial collaboration was further strengthened by the Chinese fundraisers' demonstration of goodwill towards and desire to foster friendship with non-Chinese residents by contributing to Australian causes as well. In Townsville, the Chinese Comforts Fund delivered £175 to the local Red Cross and £198 at another auction sale for the same cause. These donations improved general comments about Chinese residents who were thus "honourably accepted" by the local community.[20] Likewise, during a fundraising event for Spanish children in Queensland, 62 out of 67 donors were Chinese; in another event, "everyone stood up and cheered" when a young Chinese handed the chair a donation from the "Chinese Relief Committee".[21] It was often hoped that such efforts would elicit goodwill from white Australians.[22]

Indeed, in the case of the Rockhampton Chinese Comforts Fund's successful appeal, Anglophone Australians generously offered advertising spaces in newspapers and shops and on radio for the cause of China's fundraising efforts in the area. Over 1,000 booklets were distributed and approximately £1,774 was collected within 48 days. Around 80 per cent of the donors were white Australians and 20 per cent local Chinese.[23]

Notwithstanding collaboration between local Chinese leaders and white Australians, Kuomintang China adhered to many of the fundraising and propaganda strategies used in the 1930s to sustain, if not expand, its authority and support from the Chinese community in Australia. The anniversary of the total war between China and Japan, for example, was commemorated by Chinese authorities at home and abroad. This observance served a dual purpose: it not only presented a contested narrative to Chinese dissidents in the diaspora by emphasising China's resilience and steadfast war efforts, but also reignited and reinforced loyalty towards the Kuomintang among

---

20   Chinese Comforts Fund, 28 September 1944; Edward Kwong and the Chinese Comforts Fund, 4 December 1994, 1609496, NAA.
21   *Workers' Weekly*, "62 Names were Chinese," 10 February 1939. 3; "China aids Spain," 21 February 1939, 3.
22   Papers of Marina Mar, National Library of Australia (NLA), Canberra.
23   *Morning Bulletin*, "Chinese Comforts Fund," 14 August 1945, 2.

Chinese residents and refugees. It is hard to measure how efficacious these tactics were, because the accolades reported in the news outlets under strict censorship in unoccupied China cannot always be considered reliable.[24] Yet those Kuomintang-centred strategies, including party-rule-oriented rituals, were integral to the efforts of Chinese Australian factions, like the left-wing Chinese Youth League, in consolidating their legitimacy.[25]

Persistent homeland-oriented support partly indicates that there were multiple beneficiaries beyond Chungking whom Chinese Australians felt obliged to look after. Indeed, families and relatives living at home villages in the Pearl River Delta of Kwangtung mattered to them as well. The greatest blow to those villages arrived after Japan occupied Hong Kong at the end of 1941. Traditional remittances that relied on transnational store-based systems were reduced to a trickle, and starvation became a reality for many families.[26] The Chinese diaspora in Australia had to ensure remittance flowed through new channels to reach them.

This dilemma was significantly alleviated with the establishment of a branch of the Bank of China (中國銀行) in Sydney in 1942. Founded in 1912 under the republican government, the Bank of China had expanded its operations throughout South and South-East Asia, establishing offices in cities such as Batavia, Penang and Calcutta, in addition to its branches in London, Osaka and Singapore. This expansion facilitated the transfer of money after the Japanese blockade of China's major ports from 1937 onwards. The opening of the Sydney branch was somewhat serendipitous, as Japan's efficient occupation of South-East Asia led to the closure of the bank's branches in the region and prompted officials from the Singapore office to relocate to Australia. Recognising the importance of remittances in balancing China's foreign exchange market and supporting the government's war efforts,[27] the Chinese legation in Australia seized this opportunity to

---

24  For the reportage in Free China, see 西安晚報, "撤至澳華工捐獻巨款," 2 August 1942, 1; 西京日報, "古巴澳洲捐款援華," 23 December 1943, 3; Giese 1997, 28.
25  Chinese Youth Club, 9 August 1944, 3051769, NAA.
26  Williams 2018, 63; Kuo 2018, 160–78.

establish the Sydney branch, ensuring that it could not only support its own operations but also alleviate the remittance difficulties faced by the local Chinese community. Communications between the Bank of China in Australia and the Chinese government, as well as foreign banks outside of Australia, were privileged and conducted through diplomatic channels.[28]

The Sydney branch of the Bank of China operated with dependence rather than autonomy, functioning primarily in an advisory capacity for Chinese interests while having all financial transactions monitored and supervised by the Commonwealth Bank of Australia. The branch was described as "most cooperative and fully obedient to all requirements", which pleased Canberra. The bank's Sydney office was viewed by Australian authorities as a potential foundation for postwar arrangements between China and Australia.[29] More reliant on Australian banking networks than on Chinese transnational webs of commerce,[30] the Bank of China in Australia was able to launch its remittance business efficiently. Funds remitted to China – whether in the form of bank drafts, money orders, postal notes or currency – were first processed through the Sydney office before being approved for transfer by the Commonwealth Bank's exchange control branch.[31] In Kwangtung, the Bank of China similarly became the primary wartime channel for remittances, primarily through telegraphic transfers routed via Chungking.[32] Reports indicated that these remittances successfully reached their intended recipients in China.[33]

Although remittances to home villages were re-established, sending money through the bank was not without cost. Remittances intended for household use incurred a charge of 7 shillings for airmail postage, while remittances made for the purchase of national bonds were exempt from this fee. Additionally, bank drafts and private cheques from remitters outside New South Wales were subject to a

---

27   For the value of Chinese remittances, see Gregor and Liu 2018, 58.
28   Diplomatic Bag, 16 September 1943, A989, 1943/150/11/2, 183560, NAA.
29   Bank of China, 10 June 1944, 3051769, NAA.
30   Remittances to China, 17 February 1943, F320, 1943/264, 339677, NAA.
31   Chinese, 11 August 1944, 3051769, NAA.
32   Gregor and Liu 2018, 81, 111.
33   Chinese, 11 August 1944, 3051769, NAA.

stamp tax of 2 pennies.[34] The most significant cost was typically the cable charge for the initial schedule, with the cost decreasing for subsequent transfers. For instance, a remittance of approximately £16.8 would incur a £3 charge for the first schedule, which could then be reduced to £1.5 for subsequent remittances. Applicants were advised to account for these charges when applying. As a result, it became a common practice to consolidate multiple remittances – usually three or four, each in rounded amounts – into a single schedule to reduce the cable fees. In such cases, the Bank of China assigned each beneficiary a serial number after the first remittance, which would encompass the remaining transfers under one schedule.[35] Much of these remittances were simultaneously subsidised by Chungking, whose active encouragement was apparent. From 1944, an additional 50 per cent in Chinese yuan was offered to the beneficiaries of all overseas Chinese remittances. However, this subsidy was partially offset by a 2 per cent re-transferring fee levied on all remittances from Chungking to districts in southern Kwangtung, where the home villages of many Chinese Australians were located.[36]

The financial tactics proved effective, with the average monthly remittance to China in 1943 reaching about three million yuan from Australia alone. This shift largely redirected funds from Australian banks, where remittance business had slumped from three or four applications per week to none. Although the remittance volume was substantial, individual amounts were typically small, rarely exceeding £10 to £12. This could be attributed to the presence of illicit or informal channels alongside the official ones, often facilitated by seafarers. While these alternative routes were cheaper than the official channels, they exposed senders to risks of financial loss due to potential misappropriation during transit or the possibility that the ships carrying remittances would be bombed.[37]

34  雪梨中國銀行, 1940s, Sam He's Private Collection.
35  Remittances to China, 19 March 1943; Remittances to China, 17 August 1943; Remittances to China, 17 February 1943; Sustenance Remittances in Chinese National Currency to China, 13 January 1943, 339677, NAA.
36  Bank of China, 28 December 1943, 339677, NAA.
37  Remittance of Money to China by Chinese Nationals in Australia, 10 June 1944; Transmission of Money to China, 20 July 1944, 3051769, NAA.

## Chinese women and fundraising campaigns

Traditionally narrated as a predominantly male space, Chinese Australian history has recently been re-examined with particular attention to Chinese women, recognising women's crucial roles in the longevity and continuity of the Chinese diaspora since the 19th century.[38] The population of Chinese Australian women increased significantly from 474 to 2,550 between 1901 and 1947, with many being Australian-born and residing in metropolitan areas. Their growing numbers raised Chinese Australian womens' visibility and prominence in household and community affairs, as well as national and transnational politics.[39] During China's War of Resistance, these women actively engaged in the transnational politics of the Chinese community through their own fundraising and propaganda. These female-dominated efforts diversified the sociopolitical territory and typically male leadership within Chinese Australian communities.

Before Japan started total war in China in 1937, Chinese Australian women had already been involved in philanthropic and humanitarian activities and actively participated in Chinese political affairs. They coordinated to raise funds for people in need in Australia and China, putting on dances, plays, dramas and music shows.[40] Women were also indispensable performers in Chinese patriotic enterprises, such as fundraising balls and memorial services in 1930s Sydney and Melbourne.[41] Some women actively engaged in local Kuomintang affairs, such as Chong Shue Hing (鍾少卿) and Lena Lee in Darwin, both of whom were recognised for their strenuous promotion of women's involvement in politics.[42]

---

38  Bagnall 2011; Bagnall and Martinez 2021; Gassin 2021; Kamp 2022; Khoo and Noonan 2011; Kuo 2024b; 郭美芬 2019.
39  Kamp 2022, 52–4, 79.
40  Miscellaneous, mainly relating to the import of tea and the Celebration of Confucius Birthday, 1913– 1913–1926, AU NBAC 111-2-3, NBAC; Kuo 2020; 郭美芬 2019, 97–9.
41  *Chinese Republic News*, "美利濱中華公會演劇誌盛", "雪梨華僑抗日救國會," 11 June 1932, 6.
42  陳誌明 1935, 124; J. Fitzgerald 2007, 130; Julia 2015, 252–5.

While their involvement was often seen as aligning with traditional gender roles and as supplementary to male-led campaigns, some women transcended these confines. For instance, Chong Yook Fun arrived in Australia on 31 October 1938 to join her husband, Jong Foo Chong, and was exempted from the Australian dictation test and sponsored by Albert Hing and Spence Mah Hing. Initially engaged in domestic duties, she later became associate editor of the *Tung Wah Times*, arguably the first female editor of a Chinese-language newspaper.[43] Similarly, Berenice Lum from Adelaide, daughter of Lum Yow, began composing verses at the age of 12 and published a book of poetry in Melbourne at seventeen.[44]

Despite such emerging prominence of ethnic-Chinese women, no patriotic organisations or fundraising campaigns existed under their leadership until the onset of Japan's total war with China, when these women moved beyond traditional roles as mere participants and began organising systematically for Chinese national salvation. In 1937, the New South Wales Chinese Women's Relief Fund was established, with Rose Chuey (Rose Chung Gon, also known as Mrs James Chuey) emerging as a central figure. Leveraging her extensive networks built from her decade-long presidency of the Chinese Club and the Hwa Yuen Club, she successfully recruited 80 women, both Chinese and non-Chinese.[45] A committee of 40 was formed, with Rose Chuey at the helm, and the relief fund was heralded as the "largest Chinese women's movement in Australia."[46]

A bond of sisterhood was cultivated among these women, as well as between them and their counterparts in China. This bond represented a convergence of Chinese patriotism and gender consciousness. The dire circumstances in China, coupled with the flourishing sense of Chinese nationalism, consistently drew ethnic-Chinese women into a deeper connection with the homeland of

---

43 Jong Foo Chong and wife, 1940–1942; J.R. Evan's Note, 29 October 1938; untitled file, 29 November 1939, A433, 1945/2/3557, 3093972, NAA.
44 *Advertiser*, "Adelaide author," 22 November 1932, 8.
45 *Mercury*, "The Social Round," 14 December 1938, 3.
46 Kuo 2024b, 3613; *Australian Women's Weekly*, "What women are doing," 13 November 1937, 23.

Figure 5.1 The New South Wales Chinese Women's Relief Fund Committee (NSW Chinese Women's Relief Fund Photograph and Badge, 29 October 1938. State Library of New South Wales: 9676001).

their imagination. Simultaneously, their gendered experiences, which often placed them in subordinate roles within the patriarchal hierarchy, heightened their awareness of the unique gender dimensions of Chinese nationalism. Thus, it is not surprising that Chinese Australian women were inspired by the courage of "our sister patriots" in China, as well as from Soong Mei-ling's (宋美齡) appeals to pledge their loyalty and identification with China. Through this call, they proactively integrated themselves into the nationalistic cause by forming a "band of kinship" dedicated to Chinese national salvation. It was equally unsurprising that the organisation proudly declared this as the "first occasion in history" when women of the Chinese diaspora emerged from the domestic sphere to collectively work for the salvation of their homeland. Indeed, Chinese Australian women viewed this event as an opportunity to challenge traditional gender norms, advocating for greater independence and assuming the role of spokeswomen for all "Chinese women across the entire state of New South Wales".[47]

The pivotal sense of sisterhood was most evident in the establishment of communication frameworks and support systems between the fund and its beneficiaries. On most occasions, the exchange of requested aid and returned support was managed exclusively by Chinese women in Australia and China. Shipments of relief supplies destined for Hong Kong were directed to key women-led Chinese relief organisations, such as the Chinese National Women's Association, sponsored by Chang Lo-yi (張樂怡), the National Women's Relief Association, led by Chen Suk-ying (陳淑英) and the Chinese Women's Club in Shanghai. However, the sisterhood was not blind to potential misuse of funds or mismanagement. Regular cross-verification with receiving associations was undertaken to track the whereabouts of provisions, particularly when concerns about appropriation or misconduct were raised.[48]

Notably, the concept of sisterhood transcended ethnic boundaries, extending to interracial solidarity between Chinese and non-Chinese women. The experiences of Chinese and Australian women often converged, fostering mutual encouragement and participation in Chinese fundraising initiatives. White Australian women, both from urban and rural areas within New South Wales and other states, actively assisted Chinese women by donating clothes, knitting socks for Chinese soldiers, and creating novelties for charitable fetes. In Tasmania, for instance, Mrs Denis Cossins contributed a large Christmas stocking full of gifts to Miss Ann Chung Gon for the benefit of the Chinese Relief Fund. Similarly, in Adelaide, white Australian women made substantial contributions to the local Chinese Famine Relief Fund. The generosity and collaboration of these non-Chinese women were deeply appreciated by their Chinese counterparts in Australia.[49]

---

47   Rose Ah Chuey to Soong Mei-ling, 2 October 1937; Opening speech, 19 October 1937, NSW Chinese Women's Relief Fund, 9639983, NSWSL, Sydney; 西京日報, "電蔣夫人致敬," 1 November 1937, 2.

48   Rose Chuey to T.V. Soong, 17 November 1937; Rose Chuey to C.H. Kan, 21 January 1938, NSW Chinese Women's Relief Fund, 9639983, NSWSL.

While sisterhood predominantly shaped the establishment, operation and interactions of the Chinese Women's Relief Fund with China, femininity played a central role in how Chinese Australian women expressed their patriotism. It redefined traditional household duties, transforming them into politically and culturally charged acts of solidarity with China. Women's expertise in needlework, for example, was utilised to sew and mend garments for relief efforts in China, with materials gathered from depots across New South Wales.[50] Fairs and concerts, where traditionally feminine attributes such as hospitality, empathy and solicitude were prominently displayed,[51] were also frequently organised to support the cause.[52]

The convergence of sisterhood and femininity was manifest in the everyday patriotic practices of Chinese Australian women. This fusion was particularly visible in a tribute to Soong Mei-ling. In May 1941, Chinese Australian women honoured Soong's dedication to national relief by arranging for her to receive an exquisitely embroidered afternoon tea cloth, created by Miss Maud Moynow. The cloth, made of cream linen, featured symbolic Australian flowers, including the waratah and redgum blossoms, embroidered in their natural colours at the corners. At the centre of the cloth was Soong Mei-ling's name, surrounded by the names of the committee members of the relief fund, embroidered in red and blue. Prominent ethnic-Chinese and non-Chinese figures in Australia, including former Prime Minister Billy Hughes and H.A. Donald (brother of William Donald, Chiang Kai-shek's advisor), also had their names embroidered in red silk. The cloth featured approximately 1,157 autographs, in both Chinese and English. Each signature was accompanied by a charge of 80 pence, with the proceeds directed to the Chinese Orphans' Fund. The cloth was placed in a casket crafted by an Australian veteran from fine Australian timber, and the embroidery work was contributed by Miss Nancy

---

49   *Examiner*, "Christmas stocking gives threefold joy," 13 November 1943, 8; Letters of thanks, 1937, 9639983, NSWSL.
50   *Wellington Times*, "Help sought," 23 June 1938, 3; *Daily Telegraph*, "Sydney Chinese speed up war relief work," 23 June 1938, 7.
51   Vanelli 2015.
52   *Labor Daily*, "Eastern fair," 20 November 1937, 6; program, 24 November 1937, 9639983, NSWSL.

Barrett. Before being sent to China, the cloth was publicly exhibited at the Cathay Chinese Studio in Sydney.[53]

This gift to Soong Mei-ling symbolised both intergender and interracial support from Australia. Through its public exhibition in Sydney and coverage in the media, it became a powerful tool for educating the public about Sino-Australian friendship. The display promoted the strength and voice of women, grounded in interracial sisterhood and gender solidarity. The tribute not only raised the visibility of the ties between Chinese Australians and their imagined homeland but also subtly underscored Chinese hardships and their pressing need for relief.

The fusion of femininity and sisterhood often intersected with a blend of re-Sinicisation, re-Orientalisation and Australian modernity, as ethnic-Chinese women's campaigns for China evolved and grew. Social and fundraising events, such as concerts and dances, frequently embodied an intercultural nature, merging both Chinese and Australian heritage within the diaspora community. One of the most prominent examples of this cultural confluence was the Dragon Festival Ball, which began in 1938 under the sponsorship of the Young Chinese Relief Movement. At this event, Chinese Australian women reinterpreted the dragon symbol, traditionally associated with imperial power, as a symbol of justice and prosperity, distancing it from its imperial connotations.[54] This aligns with what historians have argued: that Chinese Australians frequently demonstrated their fitness for inclusion in White Australia through re-interpretations of their Chineseness with embodiment of Western custom.[55] However, historical evidence suggests a more nuanced picture and that traditional symbolism of Chinese culture persisted. For example, Chinese women donned traditional Chinese dress, one of which was reportedly owned by the Dowager Empress of China, performed folk

---

53  *陣中日報*, "雪梨婦慰會," 19 May 1941, 2; *革命日報*, "贈送蔣夫人," 23 May 1941, 3; *西北文化日報*, "獻贈蔣夫人名貴桌毯," 6 June 1941, 2; *Sydney Morning Herald*, "From day to day in Sydney," 20 March 1940, 22; "1100 signatures embroidered on cloth," 19 December 1940, 16.
54  Kuo 2024b, 3615.
55  Lim 2012, 165.

AUTOGRAPHED supper-cloth to be presented to Madame Chiang Kai-shek, wife of the Chinese generalissimo by the N.S.W. Chinese Women's Relief Fund. It bears Australian floral emblems and autographs of more than 1000 well known State personalities.

Figure 5.2 *Daily Telegraph*, "For China's First Lady," 18 October 1940, 4. State Library of New South Wales.

Figure 5.3 The tea cloth (private collection of Gordon Mar).

dances at another celebrity entertainment staged at Sydney Town Hall in 1941, and depicted the Great Golden Dragon, a cultural symbol traditionally associated with rain, to symbolise their hopes to end the ongoing drought in China.[56]

Other elements of social events exhibited similar features. The dresses worn by ethnic-Chinese women at the Dragon Festival Ball, for instance, varied significantly. Young debutantes typically donned

---

56  *Daily Telegraph*, "Chinese to end drought," 23 November 1941, 4.

white Australian debutante dresses, while Chinese hostesses often wore traditional Chinese gowns and robes.[57] Chinese female contestants in various Australian beauty pageants, such as "Popular Girl" and "Queen of the Allies", often showcased their cultural heritage by wearing traditional Chinese dresses, particularly the cheongsam.[58] In the "Brides of East and West" mannequin parade organised by the Young Chinese Relief Movement in 1939, the Australian "bride" wore a white lace gown, complemented by a Honiton lace veil falling from a feathered headdress, while the Chinese "bride", represented by Mrs Charles Ma, wore a gold and silver satin gown embroidered in red and black, sponsored by J. Simpson Lee and Co. and Swatow Handwork Manufacturing Co.[59] Through these performances, which strategically invoked exoticism, Chinese women sought part re-Orientalisation that reminded the audience of traditional cultural and gender boundaries between Chinese and non-Chinese Australians.

However, cultural markers of Chineseness in fundraising campaigns may have played a significant role in engendering reverse assimilation, where non-Chinese Australians were drawn into Chinese culture, rather than merely Orientalising ethnic Chinese. Chinese food, for example, was central to numerous Chinese-women-led fundraising activities. As a powerful marker of cultural identity, it has been traditionally seen as a connector linking Chinese donors to China.[60] But the role of Chinese food was more complex. It was a favourite of non-Chinese donors. Chinese recipes sold at fundraising fetes were highly popular. Chinese cookery demonstrations were also well-received, with one particular demonstration taking place twice between September and October 1938 due to non-Chinese Australian enthusiasm. Hilda Young, wearing "the picturesque costume of her native land," assisted by Miss Gwen Hughes and Alison Irwin, led the presentation.[61] Chinese culture, as demarcated by food, seemed

---

57  For more about the Dragon Festival Ball, see Grace 2021.
58  Khoo and Noonan 2011, 104–6.
59  *Sydney Morning Herald*, "Unusual fashion parade," 11 May 1939, 20.
60  Khoo and Noonan 2011, 102.
61  *Sun News-Pictorial*, "Chinese cookery demonstration repeated by request," 12 August 1938, 43.

to be becoming an integral part of the everyday household of white Australians. Their interests in Chinese food further prompted promotion of Chinese cuisine by Chinese Australians in the postwar period.[62]

Equally important was the role of Western food. While the cuisine itself hardly evoked images of China's war or Chinese hardship, it was strategically employed as a means to engage a broader Anglophone Australian audience. In both 1938 and 1939, the Victorian Chinese Women's Relief Fund, established in October 1937 under the leadership of Mrs W.S. Fong, organised an "Oriental Bazaar" at Melbourne Town Hall. The event featured cookery competitions where winners were awarded "Chinese gifts", such as jade earrings for the best-decorated cake and a Chinese luncheon set for the best butter sponge.[63] This strategy capitalised on shared female experiences, particularly those rooted in domestic affairs, effectively strengthening the connection between ethnic-Chinese and white Australian women. Similar events, such as card-playing parties and tea party dances, distanced themselves from repetitive patriotic rituals and slogans, offering fresh entertainment while continually drawing funds for China's relief efforts.[64]

The complexity embedded in these diverse and often contradictory practices reflects not only a strategic flexibility aimed at maximising fundraising efforts for China and, later, Australia, but also a deep-seated ambiguity regarding diasporic identities among Chinese Australian women. As Mei-fen Kuo has argued, these women navigated new social identities as cosmopolitan minorities, grappling with the complexities of modernity.[65] However, their attempts to explore and redefine their Chineseness risked reinforcing, rather than challenging, traditional racialised perceptions of China and the diasporic Chinese in White Australia. Indeed, coverage of Melbourne's Chinese bazaars continued

---

62  For a sample of Chinese recipes after the war, see Geechoun 1948.
63  *Advertiser*, "Melbourne cooks to compete for oriental gifts," 27 January 1938, 8; *Age*, "Chinese fete for refugees," 8 July 1939, 19.
64  *Sun*, "National costumes at Chinese tea dance," 6 June 1939, 4.
65  Kuo 2024b, 3605–6.

to portray China as exotic, and the women involved as alien to the mainstream Australian experience.[66]

The diverse fundraising practices of Chinese women were notably successful. Their cultural performances at social functions captured the Australian public's imagination of "China". In 1943, one of the Dragon Festival Balls attracted over 1,350 attendees, many of whom travelled from far distances to attend. The ballroom was packed to capacity, and hundreds of ticketholders were turned away. One Australian police officer remarked that it was the largest crowd he had ever seen at a ball in his 15 years of service at the Town Hall.[67] The widespread popularity of Chinese women's philanthropic efforts also drew the attention of unscrupulous profiteers. In 1937, Pao Chun-jien warned the public about unauthorised sellers of raffle tickets in aid of the Chinese Women's Relief Fund in Sydney.[68]

The success in Sydney inspired Chinese women in other states to take similar initiatives. In addition to the Chinese Women's Relief Fund in Melbourne, which consistently expanded its fundraising activities through balls, cultural exhibitions, fairs and fetes,[69] the Western Australian Chinese Women's Refugee Helpers was established in 1938, and the Citizens' Association of Queensland organised a Chinese Lion Dance Ball in Brisbane.[70] All of these initiatives were partly modelled on the Sydney example, emphasising cultural and interracial exchanges. The impact of these efforts spilled across gender boundaries towards male-led societies who later institutionalised fundraising approaches like balls and thus enriched their own strategies.[71] The appeals made by Chinese women also reached rural areas, where they were met with enthusiastic donations of money and clothing.[72]

---

66  Chinese Bazaar, 13 June 1945, MT395/1, 97, 31647648, NAA.
67  *Truth*, "Chinese ball too popular," 27 June 1943, 14.
68  *Daily Telegraph*, "China war relief appeal," 15 October 1937, 3.
69  *Age*, "Bridge party for Chinese relief fund," 9 December 1937, 3; "Chinese relief," 8 August 1938, 3; *Argus*, "The world of women," 20 June 1939, 14.
70  *Daily News*, "W.A. Chinese send £1,000 for war relief," 27 August 1938, 3; *Telegraph*, "Chinese lion: ball to assist war orphans," 20 September 1938, 21.
71  *Daily Mirror*, "Welfare worker's diary," 23 March 1944, 10.
72  *Wellington Times*, "Help sought," 23 June 198, 3; *Horsham Times*, "Relief for China's war refugees," 8 July 1938, 1.

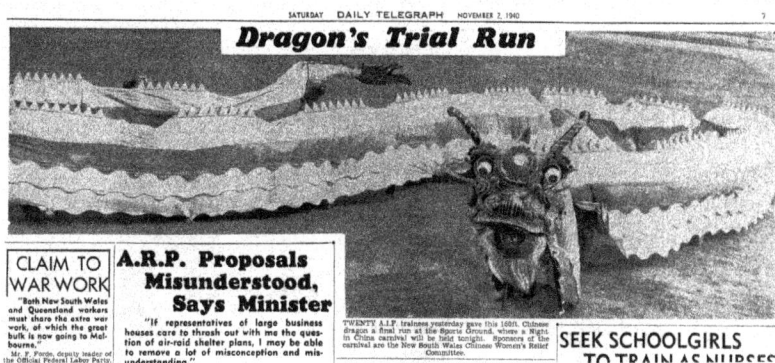

Figure 5.4 *Daily Telegraph*, "Dragon's trial run," 2 November 1940, 7. State Library of New South Wales.

Chungking appreciated the dedication of Chinese Australian women and valued the connections they forged.[73] It further consolidated the tie through direct collaboration with Chinese Australian women. In 1938, Alice Lim Kee (伍愛蓮), an Australian-born journalist and film actress in Shanghai, and Chinese American woman Elsie Lee Soong, were assigned as Chinese delegates to the International Women's Conference in Sydney. During the event, Alice read an appeal from Soong Mei-ling to the delegates, urging their support for Chinese women. Their visit was soon staged as a propaganda tour to garner support in Australia for China's cause, giving public speeches, meeting with civic bodies and socialising with prominent non-Australians to expose Japanese outrages in China and promote Chinese culture. Alice Lim Kee became a propagandist for Chungking in 1941, broadcasting on its behalf in Hong Kong. In 1943 she gave over 50 public talks in Australia to highlight ongoing Chinese modernisation and equality between the two nations, winning many hearts in Australia over to the China cause.[74]

---

73    *Sydney Morning Herald*, "Thanks from Madame Chiang Kai-shek," 30 June 1941, 4.
74    Macgregor 2021, 175–203.

In fact, support from Chinese authorities was crucial to the success of these ethnic-Chinese women. Soon after Japan's full-scale aggression in China, the Chinese consulate general realised the potential of Chinese women in supporting China's cause and actively facilitated their involvement. Rose Chuey's fund received endorsement from Editha Townsend Pao, the wife of Pao Chun-jien, who became an active patroness. Greater support also came from the Australian Kuomintang and the Chinese consulate general for the Young Chinese Relief Movement, which was initiated by Mrs L. Chang in July 1937 and later led by Mrs D.Y. Narme, months before Rose Chuey's initiative.[75] The movement made significant financial contributions to both Chinese and Australian wartime efforts, raising £4,399 between 1937 and 1942.[76] These efforts often juxtaposed Japanese atrocities in China with broader campaigns to promote China's image abroad. Recognising the importance of the Young Chinese Relief Movement, Chinese authorities granted it special status: in 1944, following Chungking's ban on unofficial receptions, it was designated the sole host of official Chinese functions in Sydney.[77]

Equally important was the inter-gender assistance that proved indispensable. White Australian men extended their sympathy to China's cause. In 1937, Messrs. G.S. Yuill & Co., who managed the Australian-Oriental Steamship Line, waived freight fees for the Chinese Women's Relief Fund in Sydney on at least two occasions within two months, saving over £20. In 1940, Greater Newcastle Council reduced the rental fee for its sports ground by £40 when the fund's "Night in China" carnival was postponed twice due to rain. Local Chinese performed ritualistic efforts to prevent the rain from hindering the event.[78] Support also came from Chinese men, including Chen Suen-yao (陳順堯) and Alex Chen Kaw who helped organise,

---

75  *Sydney Morning Herald*, "Chinese distress funds," 14 October 1937, 10.
76  *Daily Mirror*, "Local Chinese do not forget own folk," 4 January 1943, 10; *Sun*, "Who goes where," 15 August 1943, 8.
77  *Daily Mirror*, "Welfare worker's diary," 5 September 1944, 11.
78  Letter to Madame T.V. Soong, 20 November 1937, 9639983, NSWSL; *Newcastle Sun*, "Chinese Night postponed until December 7," 25 November 1940, 6; *Newcastle Morning Herald and Miners Advocate*, "£40 refund to Chinese relief fund," 19 December 1940, 8.

publicise and even sponsor the women's efforts in Sydney.[79] It was through these collaborative efforts that the relief funds led by Chinese women not only survived but remained active in the postwar period,[80] challenging the traditional assumption that Chinese female participation in relief work was solely tied to wartime exigency.[81]

Although historians have suggested that feminine sociability reconciled male-dominated contests and clashes for power,[82] women could also play an opposing role as catalysts of male conflicts. In Australia, ethnic-Chinese women were not exempt from male-centred political confrontations. The leadership of the Chinese Women's Relief Fund in Sydney was primarily derived from the spouses of leaders of the Chinese Chamber of Commerce and the Chinese Masonic Society, excluding the Australian Kuomintang. The intelligence reports of Australian authorities also indicated that Rose Chuey's fund was controlled by the Chamber–Masons alliance. The reports suggested that this prompted the Australian Kuomintang to take action to "offset" its influence by fostering the Female Chinese Salvation Association and later the New South Wales Chinese National Contribution Fund at 66A Dixon Street – both of which were run by Chinese women.[83] Interestingly, this tension was partly alleviated by the male helpers in Rose Chuey's institution, due to their connections with the Australian Kuomintang.

Despite their fundraising success, the status of Chinese women should not be overstretched. Their effective collaborative and organisational skills were heavily reliant on the power and authority of patriarchal figures within the diaspora community. Many of the female organisers were known by the names of their husbands, and their social and political positions often stemmed from the roles played by their husbands or fathers. For instance, Rose Chuey's leadership emerged

---

79   *Sun*, "Pageantry at Chinese tennis club's ball," 31 July 1938, 10; *Argus*,
     "Chinese guests," 2 August 1938, 5; Opening speech and list of men helpers,
     19 November 1937, 9639983, NSWSL.
80   *Sydney Morning Herald*, "Chinese ceremony of thanksgiving," 4 September
     1946, 6.
81   Khoo and Noonan 2011.
82   Vannelli 2015.
83   Chinese Societies in New South Wales, November 1941, 3051769, NAA.

in part from her husband's prestige.[84] On the other hand, Chinese Australian women were still largely expected to focus on household duties rather than lead public events. Chinese-language newspapers like the *Tung Wah Times* once applauded Japanese women, especially those with a modern education, for being better trained in household affairs than their Chinese counterparts.[85] When leading fundraising events, Chinese women like Mrs W. Pak Poy had to juggle these responsibilities with their household duties.[86] Chinese women's patriotism continued to be promoted in the postwar period, though the emphasis was placed on their role as mothers and cultivating children with Chinese identity and national consciousness.[87]

Notwithstanding with these limits, Chinese Australian female patriotism merged with traditional gender roles and created a form of feminine transnationalism that reinforced their connection with China. This approach diversified the link between Chinese Australians and China, traditionally framed through masculinity, emphasising devotion and sacrifice for the homeland. Instead of reinforcing women's attachment to patriarchal authority, a gender boundary was drawn to assert their subjective agency. This gender self-awareness also transcended racial boundaries between Chinese and white Australians, based on shared experiences as women in patriarchal societies. Women-led fundraising fostered a cross-cultural bond between women in China and Australia, forging a transnational female alliance in support of China's war effort. These experiences partly reconciled the intersectionality of Chinese Australian women's experiences, shaped by gendered, racialised, and class-based structures of power.[88]

---

84   James Chuey's prestige was recognised by both Chinese and non-Chinese Australians, see *Sydney Morning Herald*, "Chinese rites at funeral," 15 October 1938, 13.

85   *Tung Wah Times*, "修身明倫與婦女關系," 5 October 1935, 2.

86   *News*, "Presides on Chinese women's committee," 24 August 1943, 5.

87   袁中明 1945, 14.

88   For Chinese Australian women's intersectional experiences, see Kamp 2022.

## Left-wing Chinese patriotism

Though present in Chinese community politics in Australia,[89] Chinese leftists, including those with pro-labour leanings and advocates of communism, had not been formally organised prior to 1939. That year, Chinese seafarers who sought refuge in Australia from serving on Japan-bound ships were organised by Chinese associates of Australian leftists, namely Fred Wong, Stanley Wai (布德威) and William Jong, to establish the left-wing Chinese Youth and Dramatic Club in Sydney. The title later changed to the Chinese Youth League (also known as the Chinese Youth Club). The league published a journal called "The Voice of the Overseas Chinese" and had about 200 members, aiming to encourage Chinese youth to participate in Chinese national salvation.[90] Membership was not exclusive to Chinese people but was open to all Asian seafarers in Australia. The Chinese Youth League in Melbourne, established in 1943, also set up an Asian section to open membership to Malays, Javanese and others. But attempts at Asian inclusiveness was less well received. By May 1944, only about 83 Malays and Javanese were registered, and they, unlike Chinese members, were inactive and uninitiated into the league.[91]

The leftist Chinese movement became a formidable political force when the Chinese Youth League successfully organised stranded Chinese seafarers to start the Australian branch of the Chinese Seamen's Union in Sydney in January 1942, with assistance from white Australian leftists. While garnering recognition through their battles for fair treatments for Chinese workers, the League–Union further strengthened in the following years with the arrival of more than 2,000 Chinese seafarers working on foreign cargo and passenger vessels stranded in Australia due to the war.[92] About one-third of them subscribed to the Chinese Seamen's Union.[93] Many of them (around

---

89   J. Fitzgerald 2006.
90   Chinese Societies and Associations, 23 January 1945, 3051769, NAA.
91   H.H. Poon to Leong Kum Ling, 22 May 1944, 1609496, NAA.
92   Benton 2007, 78; Cottle 2003, 135.
93   Chinese Societies at Present Operating in New South Wales, 3 May 1944, 3051769, NAA.

**UOTA**

**NOT SO GRIM AS IT LOOKS**

**HENRY POUND,** as a Japanese officer, "tortures" Chinese peasant, Peter Cheung Ping, at the anti-Japanese pageant in Sydney Town Hall last week. Both are members of the Chinese Youth League.

Figure 5.5 The dramatic performance, "Not so grim as it looks," organised by the Chinese Youth League (*Tribute*, "Not so grim as it looks," 10 July 1945, 6. State Library of New South Wales).

800) were concentrated in Sydney.[94] The union received sustained support from its Australian counterparts throughout the war years and advocated for the economic equality of Asian seafarers at national and international levels.[95]

The rising prominence of left-wing Chinese sentiment highlighted the changing social networks and landscape of the Chinese community in Australia, reformulating what Henry Yu and Stephanie Chan describe as the "Cantonese Pacific".[96] Most Chinese seamen stranded in Australia were not Cantonese but from Chekiang (浙江) and Hainan (海南) and they tended to establish enclaves. In Brisbane, for example, Chinese seafarers from Shanghai (上海) and Ningpo (寧波) coalesced as a distinct group and set themselves apart from local Chinese.[97] A seaman once affiliated with Ching Hung Bong (青紅幫) in Shanghai even garnered prestige and later became a leader among those from Shanghai, Chekiang and Kiangsu (江蘇), acting as their spokesperson.[98]

The Hainanese group seemed to be the most populous among these seafarers and preferred to remain politically independent from Cantonese-dominated Chinese Australian communities. Small in numbers in the early 1930s, Chinese seamen of Hainanese descent who worked on ships operating between Australia and East Asia had already sought to detach from the Australian Kuomintang, and Chen Chih-ming, editor of the *Chinese Times*, had to persuade them to stay.[99] As their population increased in subsequent years, these seafarers established the Hainan Club at 58 Dixon Street in Sydney, close to the League. It boasted approximately 150 to 200 members dispersed across Sydney, Melbourne and Brisbane. Under Hing Yet Kong's leadership, it served the dual purpose of providing recreation and study. Regular English–Chinese and Chinese–English classes, conducted on Mondays, Wednesdays and Fridays, were facilitated by a teacher appointed by

---

94   Chinese Seamen's Union, 3 May 1944, 1609496, NAA.
95   Benton 2007, 78–80.
96   Yu and Chan 2017.
97   Chinese Community in Australia, 1944, 3051769, NAA.
98   J.C.G. Kevin to J.R. de Chazal, 14 December 1944, 1609510, NAA.
99   陳志明 1935, 52, 92.

the Chinese consulate general to instruct in Mandarin. These classes were purportedly utilised to attract non-Chinese overseas students.[100] Cantonese and Hainanese operas were often staged to raise funds for China. Perhaps because these non-Cantonese seamen hoped to return to China after the war,[101] their societies showed little interest in setting long-term objectives.

The League–Union's considerable influence translated into significant strength to rally financial support for not just China but Australia. They soon proved themselves the cornerstone of many fundraising campaigns. Tactics to attract donors resembled those adopted by Melbourne Chinese in the 1930s, emphasising public interaction with potential subscribers more than compelling individual donors to be locked into donating through registration. Social functions – including Chinese opera shows, dances and grand concert parties and auctions – were commonly held to interest Chinese and Australians in different age groups. These events often centred on patriotism in didactic tone, instances of Japanese outrages, heroic Chinese resistance and the obligation of diasporic Chinese to support China. Some performances were based on interracial collaboration between Chinese leftists and white Australians, such as the "Lady Precious Stream" (王寶釧) staged throughout Australia.[102] Interestingly, Chinese authorities saw the potential of these patriotic movements and endorsed them as appeals for greater Chinese–Australian intercultural exchange while promoting the narrative of China's heroic resistance of Japan's invasion.[103] The League–Union's endeavours were profitable, claiming to have raised £30,000 for China's war effort. Their donations to Australia's war effort were also generous. In 1943, a single campaign in Brisbane raised £776

---

100 Chinese Societies and Associations, 23 January 1945; Chinese Organisations, 1 February 1945; from Chuang Ya-ko to the Minister of Overseas Department, 25 January 1945, 3051769, NAA.
101 Cottle 2003, 144.
102 Chinese Youth and Dramatic Club, 2 May 1944, 6 June 1944, 1609496, NAA; *Daily Mirror*, "Chinese seamen as actors," 23 July 1942, 2; *Tribune*, "Australian Chinese united in tribute," 8 July 1943, 4; *Queensland Times*, "Chinese play," 9 October 1943, 2.
103 Liu 1942.

for the Australian Red Cross.[104] This success was impossible without intensive but smooth collaboration between Chinese leftists, and little evidence suggests internal conflicts.[105]

However, the funds collected for China may not have been entirely handed over to Chungking. Historians have found that portions of such funds found their way to the Chinese Communist Party through remittance networks of overseas Chinese.[106] It is highly probable that a comparable distribution occurred within the Australian context, as a newly established committee, spearheaded by Fred Wong and the Australian communist Mrs R. Whitfield, emerged with the primary objective of subscribing funds for Soong Ching-ling (宋慶齡) – the wife of Sun Yat-sen and by then a sympathiser with Chinese communists – through London to China. This coincided with a report that the Australian Security Service received from the Kuomintang that the claimed funds collected by left-wing Chinese did not reach their intended destination and were purportedly diverted to the Chinese Communist Party.[107] Although there remained the possibility that fundraisers may have appropriated funds for personal use,[108] this coincidence suggests a less visible channel linking the Chinese leftists in Australia to the Chinese Communist Party in China.

What made them a thorn in Chungking's side was not only the reported missing donations but also their anti-Kuomintang propaganda. During the Pacific War, the League–Union remained independent from Kuomintang messaging about China's warfront, staying in close contact with left-wing news agents in China.[109] It was no surprise that updates on the Kuomintang's inefficiency in the war, limited military successes and jaw-dropping governmental corruption were often highlighted. The Chinese leftists then initiated a less noticeable but intensive propaganda campaign against Chiang Kai-shek. Particularly outspoken among the League–Union members

---

104  *Telegraph*, "Chinese give £776 to Red Cross," 31 December 1943, 4.
105  Chinese Youth Club, 4 February 1944, 1609496, NAA.
106  Benton and Liu 2018, 110, 141.
107  Chinese Seamen's Union, 1947, 3051769; Australian Branch of Chinese Seamen's Union, 1945, 1668197, NAA.
108  Espionage, 19 January 1944, 821337, NAA.
109  New South Wales Security and Censorship, Undated, 1495438, NAA.

Figure 5.6 Kwok Muk, a Chinese seaman, and his Pennant of Patriotism (*Courier-Mail*, "Chinese help countrymen," 11 October 1943, 3. State Library of Queensland).

was Stanley Wai, whose close affiliation with Australian communist leaders meant he was perceived as a left-wing Chinese leader who influenced Sydney, Melbourne and Brisbane communities.[110] Wai and Tsui Chang-hsi (徐昌熙) of Cathay Café orchestrated a "hit-and-run" anti-Kuomintang press agent, Tai Chung (大眾, the mass) Publishing Co. The agent operated secretly, without official registration with Australian authorities. A Gestetner machine within the local Chinese Youth League in Brisbane printed out pamphlets before subsequent delivery to Sydney's Nanking Café, owned by Charles Ng Kin of the Chinese Masonic Society, through undisclosed channels to be distributed along with other Chinese-language publications. The Chinese seamen were the primary readership known by then.[111]

Stanley Wai aimed to publish and distribute monthly anti-Kuomintang propaganda pamphlets, denouncing Chiang Kai-shek's passive resistance approach to "save the party" over efforts to "save the country", and promoting left-wing, if not communist, ideologies and news from China and America. Their left-wing publicity appeared to demonstrate such evident sympathy towards Chinese communists that both the Australian Kuomintang and Australian Security Service identified the League-Union alliance as explicitly "communist."[112] On the other hand, the Sino-Soviet relationship was actively promoted by left-leaning Chinese Australians. A film evening was organised and featured Soviet films including *Inside Fighting China, Russians and Us* and *This is the Enemy*. It was marked by an appreciation of the "firm bonds of friendship and cooperation" between "the Chinese and the Soviet peoples", upon which a "democratic China" would be built postwar. The event drew audiences of 300 to 500 and received approximately £107 in donations for the film producers.[113] These initiatives came as little surprise, given that many members

---

110 Chinese Seamen's Union, 1947, 3051769; Australian Branch of the Chinese Seamen's Union, January 1942, 1668197, NAA.
111 Chinese Pamphlets and Publications, 1945; Chinese Societies and Organisations, 25 January 1945, 22 February 1945, 3051769; Australian Branch of the Chinese Seamen's Union, January 1942, 1668197, NAA.
112 Chinese Nationalist Party to Overseas Department of Central Executive Committee, 9 December 1942, 3051769; Chinese communities in Australia, 1948, 1668197, NAA.

expressed clear sympathy for Chinese communists, and several of their leaders were affiliated with communist parties in Australia and China.[114] By 1949, these Kuomintang opponents openly celebrated the establishment of the People's Republic of China.[115]

The League–Union's promotion of communism and opposition to Chungking drew the ire of the Kuomintang in Australia, who pressured Canberra to suppress the League–Union's propaganda and supply intelligence information regarding their activities. The move to seek Canberra's collaboration implied that the Australian Kuomintang's authority within the Chinese diaspora was still limited, despite the rising prestige of Chungking. Part of the Kuomintang's inability to effectively manage those dissidents stemmed from the political settings of Chinese bureaus. It was beyond the Australian Kuomintang's purview to discipline diasporic Chinese organisations, which usually fell under the supervision of the Department for Social Affairs of the Executive Yuan.[116] Nevertheless, the prevailing sentiments among the Second World War Allies in favour of Russia and the vibrant left-wing movements in Australia contributed to Canberra's reluctance to take action on behalf of their Kuomintang ally. The Australian Security Service explicitly stated that they had "no intention of taking any action in stamping out" political activities opposing the Kuomintang and had "no function" to "inform opposing foreign political factions of the activities" of one side or the other.[117]

Unable to obtain Canberra's endorsement, Chinese authorities had to counter these challenges independently. One of the measures was to restrain the expansion and dilute the influence of left-wing Chinese by forming a federation association that included the Chinese Youth League and Chinese Seamen's Union. As such, Chinese authorities hoped to influence those leftists through balancing them with other

113 Chinese Youth and Dramatic Club, 2 May 1944; Chinese Youth Club, 4 February 1944; Chinese Aid League, February 1945, 1609496, NAA.
114 Cottle 2003, 140.
115 Maurice Leong interviewed by Diana Giese, Chinese Australian Oral History Partnership Collection (East Malvern, 2 June 2000), NLA.
116 Chinese Nationalist Party to Overseas Department of Central Executive Committee, 9 December 1942, 3051769, NAA.
117 Chinese Pamphlets and Publications, May 1945, 3051769, NAA.

member societies. An example of this attempt occurred in Brisbane, where local Chinese were divided among families and political groups.[118] Aided by Hsu Mo and Tuan Mao-lan (who was the then Chinese consul general), the honorary Chinese consul in Queensland, Chen Tso Mu, organised the Federation of Chinese Associations in Brisbane (僑團聯合會) under Tsui Chang-hsi's chairmanship to unify major Chinese societies in the area, including the Chinese Youth League, Chinese Seamen's Union, Chinese Patriotic Society and Teo Sia Musical Club. Twenty committee members, representing Chinese born both in Australia and in China, were elected from representatives of these participating societies and pledged to be loyal to Kuomintang China. The arrangement thus restrained the voice of Chinese leftists and limited the power of Tsui Chang-hsi, as any decision required the majority's favour.

Some 400 to 500 Chinese attended the foundation of the federation at a meeting hall at 248A George Street, Brisbane, which was adorned with Chinese national and Kuomintang party flags and Sun Yat-sen's portrait. Accentuating the Kuomintang authority, the federation focused on common interests shared by member societies rather than Chinese political affairs, including ceremony organisation, Australian-born Chinese education, suppression of gambling and smoking, and promotion of Sino-Australian relations. Hsu Mo believed that law-biding behaviour of local Chinese would benefit the Sino-Australian relationship.[119] The meticulous attention that Chinese leftists paid to China's war effort was hoped to be directed to diaspora community affairs and preclude their potential criticism of and endeavours to turn the federation into another left-wing platform. But these efforts were thwarted when no unity was realised among Brisbane Chinese after the federation's less-than-successful attempts to garner their unanimous cooperation on community affairs.[120]

Despite the Chinese Youth League and Chinese Seamen's Union constantly advancing left-wing views, their political contentions about

---

118  Ling 2001, 72.
119  United Brisbane Chinese Council, 2 October 1944; Summary, 26 June 1944, 1609509, NAA.
120  Report, 1944, 3051769, NAA.

and actual connections to Chinese authorities were inconsistent. The political disagreement did not stop Chinese leftists from associating with the Kuomintang's advocates, joining pro-China Australian groups and inviting Chinese officials and their Australian supporters to lecture local Chinese.[121] Some Chinese dramas they staged also reinforced the Kuomintang's authority and leadership.[122] But the largest paradox was the union's diligent efforts to procure recognition from the Chinese government that it simultaneously condemned. Obtaining legal status from Chungking would be considered an acknowledgement of the League–Union's authority and contentions against China's official line. It could also be seen as Chungking's compromise in the face of political rivals. All such applications were thus rejected.[123] Most opposition to the union's attempts emanated from Australian Kuomintang and Chinese consuls who apprised the Kuomintang's Overseas Department about the League–Union's left-wing orientation and aversion to Chungking.[124] The insistence on precluding the union's request did not last long. Chungking ultimately gave it recognition to relieve Chinese consulates in Australia, already burdened with the overwhelming workload of war-related exigencies. It was considered cost-effective to have Chinese seamen's affairs delegated to their union.[125] The arrangement was a beneficial compromise for Chungking, as the move lessened the workload of local officials while demarcating a political boundary with the leftists and easing the tension.

Left-wing Chinese patriotism towards China enriched what Drew Cottle has termed "proletarian patriotism", marked by devotion to the Australian war effort on terms according to union values and equality.[126] But their articulation of Chinese patriotism was even more

---

121 *Courier-Mail*, "Chinese help countrymen," 11 October 1943, 3; Chinese Youth and Dramatic Club, 2 May 1944; Harry Poon to Leong Kum Ling, 22 May 1944, 1609496, NAA.
122 *Daily Telegraph*, "Chinese actors in historical play," 17 May 1943, 3.
123 Chinese Seamen's Union, 1947, 3051769, NAA.
124 Chinese Nationalist Party to Overseas Department of Central Executive Committee, 9 December 1942; Chuang Ya-ko to the Minister of Overseas Department, 25 January 1945, 3051769, NAA.
125 Chinese Seamen's Union, 1947, 3051769, NAA.
126 Cottle 2003, 148.

complex – grounded in vague, flexible and sometimes contradictory allegiances to several parties. Together with their diverse identities beyond Cantonese heritage and broad connections with left-wing white communities, Chinese leftists reformulated the social landscape and complicated political dynamics within Chinese Australian communities.

## Australian-born Chinese leadership

In December 1931, a senior member of the Chinese community in Australia expressed deep concern about Australian-born Chinese people's "patriotic loyalty" towards China. He urged Australian-born Chinese not to become Japan's "subjugated slaves" by being indifferent to its aggression on the pretext of being Australian.[127] Interestingly, the *Sydney Morning Herald* journalist Terry Southwell-Keely observed that the ties of Australian-born Chinese to China "remain unbroken".[128] Writing on the Chinese community in Darwin, journalist Ernestine Hill described Australian-born Chinese as "Chinese-Australians" with "dual nationality", who appreciated Australia's advantages over China yet maintained "a deep love of their native earth".[129] Others told another story of the Australian-born Chinese in Darwin who upheld an Australian outlook and felt unbothered when their fireworks for new year celebrations were banned.[130] These depictions suggest that Australian-born Chinese were characterised more by a sense of in-betweenness than by a fixed nationalist identity. The anti-Fascist wars in China, Europe, and later the Pacific exacerbated this identity confusion while also intensifying their search for self-definition, a process mirrored in the efforts of local-born Chinese women engaged in wartime fundraising and propaganda campaigns for China. These developments underscored the growing prominence of

---

127 *Chinese Republic News*, "告澳洲青年華僑," 26 December 1931, 5.
128 *Sydney Morning Herald*, "Chinatown in Darwin," 5 February 1938, 7.
129 *Advertiser*, "Aliens in Australia," 13 April 1935, 16.
130 *Telegraph*, "Darwin curbs Chinese new year celebrations with fireworks," 27 January 1938, 13.

Australian-born Chinese in both diasporic community affairs and the broader Sino-Australian relationship. Although their numbers in various social and political associations were limited, Australian-born Chinese often occupied leading positions within them. Alex Shem, who was locally born, led the Chung Wah Association, of which only 4 per cent of the membership was composed of local-born Chinese.[131]

During China's War of Resistance, Australian-born Chinese played a pivotal role in leading fundraising initiatives. Just a year after the Mukden Incident, Mee How Ah Mouy founded the Young Chinese League in Melbourne. Lauded by the Australian press as a sign of "progress", the league encouraged local-born Chinese to engage with social, political and scientific questions while maintaining a non-political stance.[132] It combined social activities with patriotic objectives. In 1938, the league organised the first all-Chinese debutante ball in Australia, with proceeds devoted to supporting China,[133] thereby adding a male-led counterpart to similar fundraising events spearheaded by Chinese women in Sydney.

One of the most important contributions made by Australian-born Chinese to China's cause was the interracial connection they facilitated between Chinese Australians and Anglophone Australians. Their bilingualism and hybrid identities enabled them to access broader social networks that were often inaccessible to Chinese immigrants. These interracial friendships and alliances were fostered through active participation in Australian social and political affairs. Many Australian-born Chinese served in both Chinese and non-Chinese organisations, advocating for the causes of both their homelands, including the Australian Communist Party.[134] Rural Australia was also connected to Asia through diaspora networks, business practices and financial sponsorship by Australian-born Chinese merchants. These merchants connected rural Chinese communities to transnational politics and also established goodwill with prominent

---

131  Chung Wah Association, 1 May 1944, 1609496, NAA.
132  *Herald*, "Young Chinese League," 14 November 1932, 10.
133  *Age*, "Young Chinese League," 12 September 1938, 4.
134  *Daily Mirror*, "Welfare worker's diary," 8 February 1945, 16; Chinese community in Victoria, 10 February 1944, A373, 8774, 65573, NAA.

Australian politicians.[135] Figures such as Harry Fay, the proprietor of Hong Yuen & Co (逢源公司) in Inverell, New South Wales, were therefore highly regarded by Chinese authorities, and their connections often passed down to their successors in the consular ranks.[136]

In their engagement with Chinese patriotic campaigns, Australian-born Chinese increasingly developed a keen awareness of their unique position in bridging connections to China. On one hand, their assertive actions in launching Chinese patriotic institutions resonated with local-born Chinese in regions beyond major metropolitan areas. In Rockhampton, for instance, 17-year-old H. Forday led a group of young Chinese, assisted by white Australians, to form a "Chinese Youth Movement", while also serving as joint secretary of the local Chinese Refugee Relief Committee. The movement was active both locally and in Brisbane, where they raised £1,200 in supplies to be sent to China.[137]

On the other hand, their patriotic efforts brought Australian-born Chinese into closer contact with one another than ever before. Correspondence regarding national salvation promoted a shared sense of patriotism and solidarity, while personal visits facilitated mobility and further strengthened these ties. This dynamic contributed to the formation of a patriotic sense of community among Australian-born Chinese, transcending geographic and cultural boundaries. Charles Fong of Rockhampton, for example, was kept informed of the "vigorous" developments in Chinese patriotism by his counterpart Arthur Leedow from the Young Chinese Relief Movement in Sydney. Fong not only pledged his loyalty to China but also sought to inspire a broader loyalty among "China- and Australia-born" Chinese. He even planned a tour across Australia to "unify younger Australian Chinese".[138]

---

135  *Chinese Republic News*, "燕卑炉埠侨胞成立救国会," 28 August 1937, 2; Correspondence between William Scully and Harry Fay, 1941–1942, Papers of Marina Mar, NLA; Kuo 2024a.

136  Harry Fay to Pao Chun-jien, 6 December 1941, Papers of Marina Mar, NLA.

137  *Morning Bulletin*, "Good responses to Chinese appeal," 22 January 1938, 8.

138  *Morning Bulletin*, "Affairs in China," 20 January 1939, 7; "Has given service to government of China," 8 June 1939, 9.

The growing sense of identification and rising political awareness among Australian-born Chinese, fostered through patriotic endeavours, led to the emergence of community leadership grounded in their shared experiences. In 1941, the Australian Chinese Association of NSW (中澳協會) was established to pursue both social and political objectives. It received strong support from Chinese authorities and the Australian Kuomintang. Patrons included Hsu Mo, while Jock Young Wai (周元吉), the eldest son of John Young Wai (周容威) – the first Presbyterian minister of Chinese descent in Australia, a staunch republican, and a key figure in political and business circles – led the association. The association dedicated itself to the wellbeing and solidarity of Chinese Australians, the improvement of Sino-Australian relations and the promotion of patriotic efforts for China. The organisation, which was male-exclusive, had around 50 Australian-born Chinese members, drawn from both urban and rural areas, including Inverell and Killarney. Most members were younger generations of Kuomintang supporters. An entry fee of 10 shillings and 6 pence was required, along with an annual subscription fee of the same amount.[139]

The Australian Chinese Association of NSW partly modelled itself on the prominent societies of the 1930s and strived to have its voice heard and foster close connections among its peers. It started the *Australian Chinese Association News* as the association's mouthpiece, held monthly meetings and hosted a dinner showcasing Chinese food every three months. This newly formed group soon captured the attention of political parties and enjoyed an increase in membership to 120 by 1944.[140] Prestigious people from the most prominent Chinese organisations frequented recreational events that the Australian Chinese Association of NSW organised, including D.Y. Narme, Albert Hing and Yee Ben. Chinese authorities also sought the organisation's cooperation to assist with their propaganda in Australia. Its library kept

---

139 Australian Chinese Association of NSW, November 1941; Australian Chinese Association of NSW, 1944, 3051769; Australian Chinese Association of NSW, 3 May 1944, 1609496, NAA; *Sun*, "Chinese association celebrates at ball," 9 November 1941, 9.

140 *Daily Mirror*, "Welfare worker's diary," 23 March 1944, 10.

such propaganda pamphlets as *Inside Wartime China* and *Introducing China*, alongside regular circulars containing up-to-the-minute news from China that members could read or borrow. Some members, like Clement Chung, engaged actively in Chinese propaganda efforts and compiled circulars issued two or three times a week. Jock Young Wai furthered this collaboration by heading the Australian branch of the People's Diplomatic Association (國民外交協會), established in 1944 as part of Chungking's propaganda efforts and which assigned Alice Lim Kee to Australia to strengthen Sino-Australian connections and create "a body of public opinion" opposing the White Australia policy.[141]

Multiple factors drove the Australian Chinese Association of NSW's popularity, one of which was its alignment with the shared agenda of Chinese Australian parties on ethnic equality and promoting patriotic campaigns. It hoped to challenge the White Australia policy by introducing more Chinese immigrants after the war, citing the growing number of intermarriages between Chinese and non-Chinese Australians.[142] Australian-born Chinese philanthropy for China's relief constantly foregrounded their Chinese heritage, which was pleasing to Chinese authorities and residents.[143] While largely backed by Chinese authorities, the association was openminded and accepted members from the Kuomintang's critics. Its members also established close cooperation with the white Australian community. The vice president, William J. Lee, worked for the Australian Security Service as an interpreter and doubled as the legal adviser for the Chinese Seamen's Union. Member Charles Fong, who had enthusiastically pledged his staunch loyalty to China, began his career in 1940 as the "official Chinese censor" in Darwin after his lavish wedding banquet.[144] Other

---

141 People's Diplomatic Association, 21 March 1944, 1609496; *Australian Chinese Association News*, April 1944, 3051769; The Third Annual Report of Financial Statements, 31 August 1944, 1609510, NAA; 新疆日報, "加強中澳友誼," 8 April 1944, 2.

142 Australian Chinese Association of NSW, 3 May 1944, 1609496, NAA.

143 *Australian Chinese Association News*, April 1944, 3051769, NAA; Correspondence between C.J. Pao and Harry Fay, 1940–1941; Correspondence between M.L. Tuan and Harry Fay 1942–1945, Papers of Marina Mar, NLA.

members, including Eric Hon, Harry Fay and William Liu, attended the first function of the Australia–China Association organised by pro-china white Australians (see Chapter 7).[145] While membership was restricted to men, the association valued inter-gender sociability and initiated a social and fundraising ball called "Ladies Night", to which members were encouraged to invite female companions.[146] The Australian Chinese Association thus played a conciliatory role within the diaspora and coordinated efforts between ethnic Chinese and their Australian sympathisers in support of China's cause.

But the rising influence of Australian-born Chinese sometimes intensified relations within the Chinese diaspora by challenging the leadership of the more senior Chinese. Their hybrid and fluid identity struggled between "home Australia" and "imagined China" and often held a more complex vision and response to multiple loyalties than older Chinese. One such example occurred in June 1943 at the Townsville branch of the National Salvation Society (救國會, initially formed in 1937). Senior Chinese and many wealthy merchants controlled the branch. Ma Kong was the chairman, alongside members like Mar Fan, James Leong and Henry Lum Mow. Their leadership received wholehearted support from the local Kuomintang.[147]

A dispute over wartime rice rationing arose between the "progressive polity of the youth" and the "traditional reverence for elders." It caused a split among Townsville Chinese and resulted in the removal of several Australian-born and senior Chinese members from the branch, including Harry Sunn – Henry Lum Mow's English secretary and assistant – and Ma Kong.[148] The situation worsened, and Chen Tso Mu (the general manager of Pagoda Handwork Manufacturing Company and the honorary Chinese consul in

144 *Northern Standard*, "Marriage of prominent citizens," 2 July 1940, 6.
145 The Third Annual Report of Financial Statements, 31 August 1944, 1609510, NAA.
146 The Third Annual Report of Financial Statements, 31 August 1944, 1609510, NAA.
147 Chinese Nationalist Salvation Association, 5 April 1944; Chinese societies in Townsville, 25 September 1944, 1609496, NAA.
148 Chinese Nationalist Salvation Association, 5 April 1944; Young Chinese Friendship League, 5 September 1944, 1609496, NAA.

Queensland) had to intervene to ensure no disruption in Chinese solidarity and patriotic campaigns. Interestingly, Chen sided with the Australian-born youth, encouraging them to have their association "take bold moves for their progressive policy" despite opposition by older Chinese. They rejected Chen's suggestion of using "league" in their association's title to denote political duty but preferred "club" to depoliticise their social gatherings. In August 1944, the Townsville Chinese Youth Club (湯士威爐埠青友社) was established, which senior reformists like Ma Kong joined.[149]

Official support aside, the founding of the club was made possible in part by the geo-cultural diversity and political vacuum within Queensland's Chinese communities, as well as the social vibrancy of the Chinese population in Townsville. Alongside those from Chekiang, Kiangsu, and the Pearl River Delta region of Kwangtung, there was a notable rise in the population and influence of Teochew (潮汕) speakers from eastern Kwangtung. Prominent Teochew merchants assumed critical roles in supporting China's wartime efforts and managing Chinese Australian affairs: T.Y. Lin served as chairman of the Chinese Comforts Fund[150] and Chen Tso Mu was appointed honorary Chinese consul.[151]The Teochew community also established the Chiao Sheng Music Club in Brisbane to promote their communal interests.

At the same time, no single social or political organisation within Queensland's Chinese communities held enough dominance to monopolise socio-political influence or suppress dissents. Chungking's advocates in Sydney exerted limited influence in the region, evident not only in the failed attempt to establish a Federation of Chinese Associations in Brisbane but also in the rise of local leftist movements. These movements reshaped the ideological orientation of organisations such as the local Kuomintang and the National Salvation Society, pushing them in a more left-leaning direction. The National Salvation Society, for instance, was reportedly sponsored by Soong Ching-ling and upheld more open anti-Japanese hostility than Chungking's line (though little evidence suggests an intimate connection with politically

---

149  Young Chinese Friendship League, 5 September 1944, 1609496, NAA.
150  *Telegraph*, "Bride on board," 6 May 1932, 2.
151  Under Secretary to F. Strahan, 17 January 1944, 594816, NAA.

similar relief organisations in China). Moreover, the Chinese in Townsville seemed more dynamic than their counterparts in the rest of Queensland. Within six months of its inception, for example, the local branch of the Chinese Comforts Fund contributed about £3,400 of the total £22,000 from the state.[152] These dynamics enabled Australian-born Chinese to assume more leadership roles in Queensland.

Interestingly, the Townsville Chinese Youth Club's aim of depoliticisation was partnered with a symbolic emphasis on the Kuomintang's authority. Its opening ceremony on 22 October 1944 consisted of such rituals as singing the Chinese national anthem, reading Sun Yat-sen's "Three Principles of the People", formal bows to Sun's portrait, a three-minute silence, speeches by Philip Leong and white Australian guest speakers, and an informal dance and supper.[153] But their aim was not to foreground Kuomintang authority but rather to legitimise Chinese Australians' sociopolitical presence and stabilise their complex identity, because affirming China's authority justified local-born Chinese people's presence in White Australia. This ostensible paradox illuminated the younger generation's efforts to negotiate between multiple loyalties and identities to locate their transnationality in White Australia.

Thus, the Townsville Chinese Youth Club sought to instil solidarity among young Chinese and pride in their heritage, especially for those who "despise their Chinese origin". Meanwhile, it hoped to build understanding between resident Chinese and white Australians, establishing study groups for Chinese and English language learning, swimming parties on Sundays, a table tennis group hosting regular competitions, and regular dancing classes taught by Miss Ah Moon in the basement of her home on Thursday or Saturday nights (which was opposed by senior Chinese). White Australians were more than welcome to join in their events, for many Chinese boys and girls preferred the company of their white Australian peers.[154] This inclusiveness, despite senior Chinese opposition,

---

152 Chinese Comforts Fund, 28 September 1944, 1609496, NAA.
153 Townsville Chinese Youth Club, 1944, 1609496, NAA.
154 Young Chinese Friendship League, 5 September 1944, 1609496, NAA.

highlighted young Australian-born Chinese self-awareness and practice of their complex identity: based on notions of transnationality, interraciality and intergenerationality. This hybridity defied traditional sociopolitical exclusion between White Australia and the Chinese diaspora. But members also faced many challenges, including exceptional language hurdles. Though mostly Australian-born, many members found it difficult to communicate fluently during meetings, as some were monolingual and expressed less optimism about the club's prospects.[155]

The divisions within Townsville Chinese did not cause ruptures as devastating as those in 1930s Sydney, thanks to the former's tightly intertwined family connections and personal networks. They wove the Townsville Chinese Youth Club, the National Salvation Society and the Chinese Comforts Fund's Townsville branches into social webs that strengthened the Chinese community's capacity to accommodate disagreements. The three societies shared members from the Lum Mow family: Henry Lum Mow served as the Townsville Chinese Comforts Fund's treasurer and continued as the National Salvation Society's secretary after the rice ration dispute (despite the opposition of some senior Chinese); Thomas Lum Mow (Henry's brother) acted as the Townsville Chinese Youth Club's president. Wong Foo Yuen, a 22-year-old recent immigrant from China, worked as the executive, the senior executive and the Chinese secretary in the three organisations respectively. While he supported the conservatives in the dispute, his proficiency in Chinese and calligraphy was rare in a small city like Townsville. Edward Kwong also served in the three societies as secretary. Miss Ah Moon, the club's English secretary, was the de facto wife of William Chun Tie, who chaired the local Chinese Comforts Fund branch and was reputed to be the wealthiest Chinese individual in Townsville: in early 1944, he alone made donations of £650 to the National Salvation Society.[156]

---

155  Young Chinese Friendship League, 5 September 1944, 1609496, NAA.
156  Chinese Nationalist Salvation Association, 5 April 1944; Chinese Societies in Townsville, 25 September 1944, 1609496, NAA. See Chung King Café, 821337, NAA.

The rising leadership of Australian-born Chinese coincides with the intensification of the Pacific War, when China and Australia became allies, allowing them to bridge their dual identity and practise their patriotism to both homelands. Studies have explored their endeavours in various forms of Australian and Chinese war efforts.[157]

Nevertheless, the Australian government and white citizens never stopped suspecting the loyalty of Chinese Australians during the war and placed them under close surveillance.

Expressions of dissatisfaction – such as criticism of the limited Allied support for China or sceptical views on the "fighting prowess" of the British and Australians – were often dismissed as the voices of "malcontents", with those who shared such concerns subjected to monitoring.[158] Chinese cultural symbols that were inconsistent with Australian modernity, such as outside labels of fireworks imported from Hong Kong that depicted a partially bare-chested Buddha, were regarded as "offensiveness", "obscene" and "objectionable".[159]

Ironically, the intelligence collected was frequently imprecise, misleading and even contradictory, exemplified by blanket assertions like "all Kuomintang members are supporters of China".[160] Officials' limited understanding of Chinese Australian communities and their complex ties to both China and Australia severely constrained their ability to discern credible information from reports provided by informants and censors operating within a politically fragmented diaspora.

In contrast to such suspicion and exclusion, the contributions of Chinese Australians were met with enthusiastic acclaim from their counterparts in China. However, much of this recognition was filtered through a Kuomintang-oriented nationalist lens, reinforcing Chiang Kai-shek's elevated status as the legitimate leader of the Chinese people.[161] Both homelands of Chinese Australians at the time and in

---

157 Loh 1989, 13–14, 26; Kennedy 2015, Khoo and Noonan 2011, 104–5.
158 Chinese Societies Operating in New South Wales, 3 May 1944, 3051769, NAA.
159 Fireworks of Chinese Origin, 20 January 1937, A425, 1937/3924, 66114, NAA.
160 Chinese Societies Operating in New South Wales, 3 May 1944, 3051769, NAA.

subsequent years offered little acknowledgement of their complex in-between identities and their transnational expressions of patriotism.

While new leadership emerged within Chinese Australian communities, the fragmentation of traditional authority deepened. Leaders of the three prestigious associations in Sydney – D.Y. Narme, Albert Hing and Yee Ben – "always appear[ed] to be at loggerheads with each other". Yee Ben, who once ostensibly supported Chiang Kai-shek but opposed him privately, had less power than the other two among the diaspora.

Ill feelings intensified during Loh Kai-tze's tour of Australia in 1941.[162] Within the Kuomintang, internal power struggles and rivalries were evident, particularly between Mar Leong Wah and D.Y. Narme, each leading factions antagonistic to the other. Narme was reportedly unpopular among the "loyal Chinese", whereas Mar Leong Wah was said to wield "considerable influence" and was regarded as "probably more trustworthy". Similar divisions were evident within organisations such as the Chinese Chamber of Commerce and the Chinese Masonic Society, with their Newcastle branches expressing strong support for Chiang Kai-shek. The Chinese Citizens Society also experienced internal divisions over Chinese affairs, though personal relationships among members generally remained amicable.[163]

These political and organisational frictions were further complicated by social and regional differences between Chinese Australian communities. In Darwin, Hakka-speaking Chinese often remained socially distant from their Cantonese counterparts, and local Chinese Masons reportedly preferred not to mingle with the broader community. Meanwhile, evacuees from Darwin found the Chinese community in Adelaide less welcoming than expected, while Adelaide Chinese maintained active social connections with Chinese in Melbourne through organised events.[164] In other words, the emergence

---

161 福建日報, "勝利為日已近," 27 February 1941, 2; 西京日報, "澳洲華僑礦工," 19 July 1942, 2; 西北文化日報, "盛贊我領袖," 19 July 1942, 1.

162 Chinese Societies in New South Wales, November 1941, 3051769, NAA.

163 Chinese Societies Operating in New South Wales, 3 May 1944, 3051769; Chinese Masonic Society, Chinese Chamber of Commerce, 3 May 1944; Chinese Citizens Society, 4 February 1944, 1609496, NAA.

of leaders from diverse gender, sociopolitical, and generational backgrounds further complicated the already fragmented Chinese Australian communities, making them more divided yet also more diverse than before.

## Conclusion

This chapter delves into the complexity of Chinese Australian patriotism between 1937 and 1945 through four case studies. It uncovers how social and political diversity, as well as gender and generational consciousness, shaped diasporic Chinese patriotic and propaganda campaigns that essentially reorganised social networks and political landscapes within the Chinese Australian community. This process caused the multi-polarisation of diaspora Chinese community leadership and further internal divisions. It contradicts what historians have argued, that Chinese Australians were united after the official outbreak of China's War of Resistance against Japan in 1937.[165] Nevertheless, organisations successfully mobilised resident Chinese of different gender, generational and political backgrounds to participate in China's war effort and established cross-community exchange and collaboration between ethnic Chinese and non-Chinese Australians. The complexity and multiplicity of Chinese Australian patriotism, through which loyalties and identities were reformulated, adds a historical dimension to recent discussions on "Chineseness", a concept that continues to shape identities of long-settled Chinese Australians today.[166] What Chinese Australians might not expect is that the multi-polarisation of community leadership undermined the intended impact of Chinese propaganda directed at White Australia.

---

164 *Mail*, "Adelaide's Chinese aren't friendly," 27 December 1941, 5; Ray Chin interviewed by Diana Giese, Post-War Chinese Australians Oral History Project (Darwin, 22 December 1996); Charles Tsang See-Kee interviewed by Diana Giese, Post-War Chinese Australians Oral History Project (Darwin, 4 January 1993); William Fong interviewed by Diana Giese, Post-War Chinese Australians Oral History Project (Darwin, 8 December 1992), NLA.

165 S. Fitzgerald 1996, 136.

166 For more on the discussion of "Chineseness", see Ngan 2008, 76.

# 6
# Sino-Japanese propaganda contest in Australia

In 1938, *Smith's Weekly* published an article that reminded Australian readers about the imperative necessity of vigilance against the Japanese and Chinese propaganda campaigns in Australia that were "designed to mould Australian public opinion on foreign affairs" and repress views of "Australian daily newspapers". The publication, however, demonstrated confidence in the Australian populace's discernment, stating that "Australians can work it out for themselves."[1] But the reality starkly contradicted the newspaper's optimistic outlook, and a significant contingent of Australian journalists and the press played the role of de facto cheerleaders for Japan, actively disseminating messages from Japan's propaganda apparatus.

This article was a reminder of the expansive Sino-Japanese propaganda rivalry in Australia and its compelling influence between 1931 and 1941. Although geographically and psychologically distant from the Sino-Japanese hostility, the military clash in North-East Asia was paralleled by a propaganda showdown that unfolded in Australia and engaged the Australian public to a degree underplayed by accepted wisdom. Not only were overseas residents of both sides mobilised, but white Australians also participated. The intensity of the propaganda competition to garner Australian sympathy illustrated the complex

---

1    *Smith's Weekly*, "Thousands a year to influence us," 16 July 1938, 3.

political dynamics within Asian Australian communities and between them and White Australia. It also uncovered the deep-seated connections between Australia and North-East Asian politics.

## Japanese propaganda in Australia

Japanese propaganda in Australia was much more centralised than their multifaceted but loosely organised Chinese competitors, with the Japanese consulate general in Sydney playing a pivotal role. It was a transmitter of Tokyo's propaganda policy and a hub for intelligence collection and distribution, and the consul general was believed to be "the most important channel", harbouring intelligence officers receiving funds and instructions.[2] Indeed, the Japanese consulate general relentlessly disseminated misleading information to justify Japan's aggression and pin responsibility for the war on China since their clash began in September 1931. Kojiro Inoue, the consul general, denigrated Nanking for the destruction of "a portion of the Southern Manchuria Railway" that caused the confrontation between Chinese and Japanese troops.[3] His successor, Kuramatsu Murai, consistently legitimised the aggression as a righteous mission to correct political chaos and restore social order for the Chinese people, whose government was fragmented.[4] The narrative positioning of the Japanese as responsible guardians protecting inferior Chinese was one of the key motifs in Japan's propaganda.[5]

This propaganda found receptive audiences in Australia who accepted it at face value. Leading politicians seeking to conciliate Japan, such as John Latham (who served as the Attorney-General, Minister for External Affairs, and later as the Chief Justice of the High Court in 1934), supported the view that the Sino-Japanese war was due to Nanking's violation of treaties that initiated anti-Japanese boycotts.[6]

---

2   Japanese Organisations in Sydney, C320, J208, 3047929, NAA.
3   *Daily Telegraph*, "Why Mukden was occupied," 22 September 1931, 7.
4   *Sun*, "Japanese consul's view," 20 April 1933, 17.
5   Kushner 2006, 122.
6   Frei 1991, 125.

Broader public opinion also favoured Tokyo. The Japanese occupation of Manchuria faced little scepticism from Australian newspapers, some of whom even believed "Manchuria is not strictly an integral part of China".[7] As historians have demonstrated, these papers unanimously upheld that British and American interests were best served by acknowledging Japan's claim to Manchuria.[8]

This Japanese propaganda and Australian opinion received bitter criticism from Chinese Australians. William Gock Young, the chairman of the Society of Chinese Residents in Australia – the most active "spearhead" of Chinese propaganda[9] – deconstructed Japanese propaganda by exemplifying the "disorganisation" and "disorder" of Japan caused by the conflicts between their militarist faction and civilian government officials.[10] He also challenged Australia's endorsement of Japan's claim to Manchuria, equating Manchuria being "an integral part" of China to the Northern Territory in Australia.[11] The society's secretary, Chen Suen-yao, reiterated that China was "united" under a "strong" government and resisted Japanese aggression alongside unanimous support from Chinese overseas.[12] Meanwhile, not all Australians were convinced by pro-Japan views. As a lecturer at the University of Melbourne and later a prominent official within the Australian Department of Information, William Macmahon Ball likewise criticised the Australian press for embracing parochialism. He urged Australians to view the world through a more global rather than exclusively "Australian lens".[13]

The general Australian attitude favouring appeasement of the Japanese lasted from 1931 to 1937 and put the Chinese perspective at a disadvantage, sustained by a concurrence of factors. There was widespread favouritism towards Japan due to admiration of its successful Westernisation in social, economic and military areas. Even

---

7   *Sydney Morning Herald*, "The Far East," 8 September 1932, 8.
8   Murray 2004, 107.
9   Confidential Report, 31 August 1934, 176185, NAA.
10   *Newcastle Morning Herald and Miners' Advocate*, "Reply to Japanese consul-general," 3 April 1933, 4.
11   W. Liu 1932, 17.
12   *Townsville Daily Bulletin*, "The trouble in China," 18 September 1937, 10.
13   Macmahon Ball 1938, 16, 27.

before Japan's victory over Russia in 1905, some Australians already held the country in high esteem.[14] This positive perception persisted into the 1930s, with Japan being featured in Australian newspapers and the country itself being dubbed "the English of the East".[15]

The admiration starkly contrasted with grim Australian perceptions of China, where backward alienness was the pervasive view.[16] Unfavourable accounts appeared frequently in Australian newspapers and travel writings.[17] Some triggered protests from Chen Chih-ming, who countered their reports of China's anarchy with a list of murders and robberies in Sydney and scathing remarks comparing the dire living conditions of Australian workers to Chinese beggars.[18] Chen Wei-ping also wrote pointed letters to John Latham (then head of the 1934 Australian Eastern Mission to visit China), accusing him that his "brief visit in the East is very strongly biased". Chen criticised Latham's claim that "Japan has no territorial ambitions" and "only want[s] trade", and condemned his condescending posture toward the Chinese, whom he "lectured" while they merely "listened". This, Chen noted, stood in sharp contrast to Latham's visit to Japan, where the Japanese did most of the talking and Latham appeared merely to "voice their opinions". The situation became so dire that some Chinese Australian leaders, including Albert Hing, had to publicly distance themselves from the statements, with Chen ultimately withdrawing his remarks as well.[19] Echoing Chen's perspective, resident Chinese criticised the vilification of Chinese people in Australian films and novels, which often cast them as threats to Australian women.[20]

---

14  Foxall 1903, 63–4.
15  Jones 2001, 134; *Advertiser*, "Japan and the League of Nations," 5 September 1934, 8.
16  Strahan 1996, 19.
17  *Daily Telegraph*, "China today," 28 June 1934, 6; *Newcastle Morning Herald and Miners' Advocate*, "China today," 14 July 1936, 5; Mitchell 1939.
18  *Chinese Republic News*, "西報言論荒謬," 7 July 1934, 3; "狂妄記者密勒," 14 July 1934, 2; Chen Wei-ping to John Latham, 15 August 1934, A981, FAR 3, 176185, NAA.
19  John Latham to Joseph Lyons, 12 September 1934, CP103/19, 20, 362177, NAA.
20  *Brisbane Courier*, "Letters to the editor," 12 October 1932, 3.

The distinct perceptions of China and Japan were not helped by the underdeveloped state of Australian journalism during the 1930s. There was a shortage of qualified Australian correspondents stationed in China, and news sources had to rely on local newspapers that were under the influence of Japanese propaganda and European journalists whose understanding of the war was superficial and who inadvertently parroted anti-Chinese propaganda.[21] The reports Australian journalists produced frequently echoed Japanese propaganda that frustrated Chinese authorities. Chen Wei-ping complained that the Australian public "could not be expected to know the [Japanese] irritation tactics".[22] He appealed to them and their government to assess the war from the perspective of Japan's actions rather than rhetoric, after which "the misunderstandings are self-explanatory".[23]

Moreover, Australia's limited independence in international affairs constrained its ability to take initiative in investigating Japanese aggression in China. Commercial interests in maintaining trade relations with Japan were prioritised over political engagement with China's War of Resistance, reflecting a broader failure to appreciate the war's complexity beyond economic considerations. Knowledge of the belligerents was described as "extremely lacking", and diplomatic responses were shaped by a narrow, business-focused perspective.[24] Faith in the sustaining power of collective security – particularly through Britain – remained strong.[25] Although a few intellectuals advocated for a foreign policy less beholden to commercial interests and British influence, and called for a deeper understanding of Australia's Asian neighbours,[26] these calls translated into limited action, most notably the appointment of trade commissioners to China and Japan in 1935.[27]

However, China's suffering found genuine sympathisers among Australian radicals, leftists and unionists in the late 1930s. As historians

---

21   Murray 2004, 28–31, 35–6, 42, 94, 106; O'Connor 2010, 297.
22   W. Liu 1931, 3, 8.
23   Chen 1934, 29.
24   Philips 1933, 29, 34, 40; Ross 1933, 82; 1934, 63, 65; Walker 2019, 93.
25   Jones 2001, 135; Waters 2001, 96; Watt 1933, 100–1.
26   Melbourne 1932, 39; 1935, 26–7; Moore 1932, 40–1.
27   Schedvin 2008, 44–60.

have noted, much of this solidarity stemmed from their transnational labourism shaped by anti-colonial movements in China.[28] While expressions of support began as early as 1932 – when approximately 200 Australian communists protested Japanese aggression outside the Japanese consulate general[29] – widespread mobilisation across Australia did not materialise until Japan launched a full-scale war against China in 1937. The ensuing protests, primarily led by leftist, unionist and feminist groups, petitioned the federal government to boycott Japanese goods in response to "the ruthless murders of the peaceful Chinese." These actions offered a sharp rebuke to Japanese militarism, paired with a compelling display of compassion for its Chinese victims. On 12 October 1937 alone, approximately "50,000 leaflets" promoting the boycott were reportedly distributed in New South Wales.[30] The campaign was enthusiastically welcomed by Chinese elites and officials, who had initiated similar boycott efforts in earlier years. Now revitalised, these initiatives encouraged local Chinese participation and called for action from Australian authorities.[31]

But the boycott initiative failed to gain universal support. In Melbourne, for example, several large firms reported minimal effects.[32] It was partly due to intense pressure from Tokyo. Both the Japanese consulate general and the Japanese Chamber of Commerce in Sydney and Melbourne – established in June and July of 1933[33] – voiced their strong opposition, threatening that such protest "might lead to the destruction of the friendly relations" between Australia and Japan.[34]

28   Loy-Wilson 2011.
29   *Chinese Republic News*, "本埠共黨反對戰爭之大巡行," 6 August 1932, 6.
30   Chinese–Japanese Dispute, 14 October 1937, A461, K420/1 Part 1, 97419, NAA; *Macleay Argus*, "Labor to boycott Japanese goods," 1 October 1937, 5; *Warialda Standard and Northern Districts' Advertiser*, "Boycott of Japanese goods," 4 October 1937, 6; *Workers' Weekly*, "Here's how! Boycott Japanese goods," 19 November 1937, 9.
31   *Sydney Morning Herald*, "Chinese Chamber of Commerce," 2 October 1937, 18; *Newcastle Sun*, "Protest meeting on Sunday," 12 October 1937, 2.
32   Ward 1937, 5.
33   *Glen Innes Examiner*, "Eastern trade," 10 June 1933, 1; *Daily Telegraph*, "In two cities," 4 July 1933, 9.

Both Japanese groups continued to rehash the discourse to elevate Japan as a protector of the Chinese and deconstruct the boycott's legitimacy.[35] Notably, the two organisations were different from their Chinese counterparts in nature, in that they received subsidies and were led by local Japanese authorities to accommodate leading members from Japanese consular and diasporic communities and loyal white Australians.[36] Essentially, Japanese Australian organisations conveyed Tokyo's voice, not that of the diaspora.

Meanwhile, the responsibility for the boycott was blamed on China, with claims that Chinese propaganda misled Australians into protesting.[37] A similar opinion was expressed by leading Japanese figures in Japan: that "poisoned sources" of Chinese propaganda caused Australia's perceived "unfriendly feeling", alongside reiteration of Japan having "no territorial ambitions" and requests to have Australia safeguard mutual Japan–Australia interests.[38] These warnings appeared effective, and concerns about potential Japanese retaliation surfaced in Australia. For example, the *News* in Adelaide cautioned South Australian protesters of the ramifications on Australian trade with Japan and potentially severe repercussions, advising them to "walk warily" while waiting for Canberra's answer to appeals for boycotts.[39] Some Australians expressed genuine concern that the boycott might provoke war between Japan and Australia.[40]

However, the boycott proved more successful in eroding Australian indifference than in impacting Japan's economic interests in the country. Anti-Japanese sentiment and pro-Chinese sympathy were stirred. As Andrew Melville Pooley captured in his 1937 play, *History*

---

34  *Age*, "Friendly relations threatened," 5 October 1937, 12; Chinese–Japanese Dispute, 19 October 1937, 97419, NAA.
35  Japanese Chamber of Commerce Sydney and Melbourne 1937a; 1937b; 1937c.
36  Llewelyn 2019, 31–2.
37  *Sydney Morning Herald*, "Japanese consul's statement," 4 October 1937, 9.
38  *Examiner*, "Relations with Japan," 19 November 1937, 6; Japanese Chamber of Commerce Sydney and Melbourne 1937b; Chinese–Japanese Dispute, 15 November 1937, 97419, NAA.
39  *News*, "Boycott of Japanese goods," 7 October 1937, 10.
40  *Courier-Mail*, "Letters to the editor," 14 March 1938, 4.

*Unrolls*, "If the Japanese win now, they'll have lost. If the Chinese lose now, they'll win".[41] Letters flooding Australian newspapers vehemently condemned Japanese brutality, called for action to halt Japan's aggression, and expressed heartfelt sympathy for Chinese suffering, urging support for China's plight.[42] One reader, with the penname "DISGUSTED", even expressed his anger at Australian women continuing to buy Japanese silk and asking "when will the sex learn to put the fashion plate last and common humanity first?"[43] Meanwhile, others predicted China's eventual victory, admired its heroic resistance and foresaw a hopeful resurgence.[44] Despite some who still sought to placate Japan, there was a general consensus that Japan's atrocities should be stopped.[45] Humanitarian aid was collected by the Australian Red Cross Society and sent to China in response to a request from the People's Foreign Relations Association of China.[46] The value of the supplies was substantial, with one shipment alone worth approximately £12,000 (about $1,189,224 in Australia today).[47] Canberra did not oppose these efforts, seemingly seeking to balance public sympathy without provoking Japan through non-governmental actions.[48] During the Pacific War, munitions were included in the aid as China and Australia formed an alliance.[49] Simultaneously, public interest in China grew, with Chinese Australians interviewed in newspapers emphasising China's modernisation, advanced by national resistance to Japanese aggression.[50]

41  Application for the registration of copyright in a dramatic work, 8 October 1937, A1336, 30454, 3547142, NAA.
42  *Advocate*, "China and Japan," 29 January 1938, 8; *Argus*, "To the editor of the Argus," 2 October 1937, 3; *Courier-Mail*, "China Relief Fund," 3 November 1937, 12; *Methodist*, "The Japanese atrocities," 2 October 1937, 11; *Sunshine Advocate*, "To the editor," 4 October 1940, 2; *Telegraph*, "Letters to the editor," 1 July 1937, 14; *Wiluna Miner*, "Letters to the editor," 16 September 1938, 5.
43  *Argus*, "Japanese atrocities," 25 February 1938, 8.
44  Phillips 1941, 19; Goss 1941, 6; Wilkie 1941, 9–10; Wilson 1937, 14.
45  *Methodist*, "Letters to the editor," 16 October 1937, 7.
46  Provision of Medical Relief in China, 1941, MP508/1, 282/704/56, 3362894, NAA.
47  外人捐贈藥品醫具書籍, 1941, 020-011903-0001, AH.
48  Joseph Lyons to A.B. Parry, 2 December 1938, 97420, NAA.
49  澳大利亞供我軍火, 1943, 020-011503-0004, AH.

Scholarly studies have revealed that the Nanking Massacre marked a turning point in Australian indifference towards China, catalysing a surge of sympathy for the Chinese nation.[51] What remains less explored, however, is that the revelations of the massacre were, in part, the result of China's international propaganda to obtain Australian and worldwide sympathy, as discussed in the following section and Chapter 7; another part derived from the testimonies of those who had witnessed the outrages and now journeyed to Australia. On her way to Victoria, R.H. Mathews from the China Inland Mission in Shanghai told the *Telegraph* a "horrible story" of the "atrocities" perpetrated by Japanese soldiers in Nanking.[52] Similar accounts of outrages soon found their way to urban and rural Australian newspapers.[53]

The shift in Australian public opinion, coupled with the government's decision to ban the planned Japanese development of iron ore deposits at Yampi Sound, disturbed Japanese officials and propagandists,[54] who prompted a heightened effort to counteract the situation. While continually reusing the discourse that described Japan as a custodian of the Chinese nation,[55] the Japanese propaganda also presented a less menacing image of Japan. In particular, the expanding influence of communism in China was exploited to position Tokyo as a collaborator with Australia and Britain to curb the proliferation of Chinese communists. It was claimed that the "only effective bulwark in the East against the rampancy of Bolshevik influence" was Japan, whose actions in China were to eradicate "destructive ideas and influences

50  *Examiner*, "My native land," 22 December 1937, 7; *Horsham Times*, "War-torn China," 12 July 1938, 10; *Sun*, "Atrocities in China," 28 January 1938, 5; *Sydney Mail*, "Women's work in the Chinese war," 4 May 1938, 22; *West Australian*, "Modern Chinese girl," 5 May 1938, 7.
51  Strahan 1996, 19, 22.
52  *Telegraph*, "Impossible to exaggerate atrocities in China," 20 June 1938, 9.
53  *Canberra Times*, "Chinese buy Japanese scalps," 3 January 1939, 2; *Herald*, "Atrocities in China alleged," 28 August 1938, 5; *Newcastle Sun*, "Atrocities in China," 28 August 1937, 1; *Sun*, "Atrocities in China: prey on women," 28 January 1938, 5; *Workers' Weekly*, "Japanese atrocities in North China," 19 April 1938, 3.
54  For the banning of iron ore, see Lee 2020, 96–112.
55  Association of Far Eastern Affairs 1938a, 1; 1938b, 2; 1938d, 3–4; *Smith's Weekly*, "Thousands a year to influence us," 16 July 1938, 3.

imbued with communism", thereby safeguarding the interests of both Japan and the West.[56] Tokyo thus established itself as a friend and not a threat to Australia and the British empire. This notion was echoed by conservative Australian newspapers and continued to be reiterated during the Pacific War to attempt to persuade Australia to capitulate.[57]

Moreover, unfavourable Australian sentiment towards Japan antagonised local Japanese nationalists and provoked their engagement in Japanese propaganda and integration into Japan's war effort. Many nationalist Japanese Australians ardently believed in the righteousness of their homeland's expansion, making rather audacious responses to the mounting opposition. For example, Kijiro Miyake wrote to the Association of Far Eastern Affairs affiliated with the Japanese chambers for cultural and political affairs, arguing that Japan was "compelled to take actions in self-defence" because of threats to Tokyo's vital rights and interests that included securing China as a market for its products and a source of its raw materials during a period of "economic nationalism".[58] Hideo Kanamaru cautioned waterside workers striking at Port Kembla in 1938 that their actions were "hazardous", as it was Australia's loss to ban pig iron export to Japan, which could quickly obtain the material from other countries.[59] Pride in the might of the Japanese state apparatus to withstand "any emergency" without collapse and confidence in Japan's unwavering commitment to occupying China were stressed to caution Australians against provoking Japan.[60] This air of assertiveness was partly fuelled by Australia's apprehension of a potential Japanese invasion.[61] The paradoxical narratives of Japanese propaganda resonated with a sense of a stick-and-carrot policy.

The participation of Japanese Australians and their demonstration of homeland-oriented nationalism indicated a successful mobilisation initiated by Tokyo. Diasporic Japanese networks were deployed to expand and intensify Japan's propaganda campaigns. Association of

---

56  Association of Far Eastern Affairs 1938d, 3; Kanamaru 1939b, 13.
57  Meo 1968, 101; Murray 2004, 76.
58  Association of Far Eastern Affairs 1939b; Miyake 1939b, 5–6.
59  Kanamaru 1939, 12.
60  Association of Far Eastern Affairs 1938c, 1, 3–4, 8; Sale 1939, 1, 4; Association of Far Eastern Affairs 1939a.
61  Frei 1991, 180–2.

Far Eastern Affairs members were coordinated to produce relevant booklets and articles.[62] Those whose positions intersected with the Australian community, such as laundry workers, were valued by Japanese authorities and used as focal points for intelligence gathering through their networks with white Australians.[63]

While existing scholarship has suggested Australian newspaper journalists were susceptible to Japanese propaganda,[64] there were exceptions. Several voices questioned the veracity of Japanese propaganda and supported China. The credibility of such articles as "Dawn of a new era in China", "The financial and economic position in Japan", and "Why the fighting in Shanghai" was doubted and labelled as "Japanese propaganda". Sceptics severely condemned the Rape of Nanking as "the worst example of beastliness and brutality that the present world has ever seen". They denounced Japan's ambition to dominate Asia, pressuring Japanese propagandists to uncover "what is transpiring and what is being concealed from the public".[65] A few leftist and communist newspapers even pressed for more support for Chinese resistance. Calling for public support for China and severe sanctions against Japan, the *Worker Star* featured front-page praise of Chinese people as valiant defenders who prevented Australia from being "drawn into a bloody holocaust".[66]

## Chinese propaganda contested

Contrary to the Japanese centralisation of propaganda in Australia, the Chinese campaigns were established jointly on a collaboration between Kuomintang China and Chinese diaspora leaders. This was not only because Nanking enjoyed limited prestige among local Chinese, but also because its propaganda policy was vague and apparatus

---

62  Association of Far Eastern Affairs, 9 September 1938, C320, J194, 3047904, NAA.
63  Llewelyn 2019, 27–8.
64  Murray 2004, 104.
65  *Goulburn Evening Penny Post*, "Propaganda," 30 August 1938, 4; *Illawarra Mercury*, "Japanese propaganda," 14 January 1938, 8.
66  *Workers Star*, "Chinese attack aids Australia," 28 April 1939, 1.

disorganised, compelling local Chinese authorities to maximise their agency and procure support from both their advocates and opponents in the diaspora. Those Chinese Australians disagreeing with Nanking's policy also found it necessary to seek official authority in their delivery of propaganda for white Australians. It formed a contrasting experience to the Chinese propaganda in America, which centred much on Chinese governmental performance.[67]

Counteractions were pursued simultaneously by local Chinese authorities and diasporic Chinese, similar to the Japanese in Australia. Officials such as Chen Wei-ping in Sydney and Pao Chun-how in Melbourne elucidated Nanking's "civilised" stance and Japanese ambition "engineered" to occupy China through Australian newspapers and radios.[68] Chinese Australian organisations churned out propaganda publications staunchly denying what Tokyo claimed about the war. For example, the Society of Chinese Residents in Australia and the Chinese Citizens Society reorganised themselves as propaganda agencies that published at least five booklets in the early 1930s. Each of them had a circulation of no less than 1,000 copies. Notable among them were *China and the Trouble in Manchuria* (at least 20,000 copies circulated), *Japanese Invasion of Shanghai: A record of facts* (more than 1,000 copies), *The Sino-Japanese Question Relating to China's Three Eastern Provinces (Manchuria)* (at least 2,000 copies), a booklet on Japanese atrocities and expansion in Manchuria (at least 2,000 copies), and a memorial volume concerning the Mukden Incident.[69] Many of these booklets were also dispatched to China and read there;[70] future prime minister John Curtin read one of the booklets by William Liu and felt sympathy towards Chinese hardship.[71] The divided

---

67 Akio 2010, 40–47.
68 *Western Champion*, "China," 28 September 1931, 2; *Chinese Republic News*, "保領事對外宣傳日人之橫蠻," 7 November 1931, 8.
69 Chinese Citizens Society 1932; Society of Chinese Residents in Australia 1933b; *Tung Wah Times*, "快郵代電," 14 November 1931, 5; "救國會第廿七次常會議案誌," 7 May 1932, 5; "救國會第三十七次常會誌," 17 September 1932, 5; "雪梨抗日救國會第三十九次會議誌," 5 November 1932, 5; "救國會常會誌," 21 October 1933, 5.
70 Greene 2005, 98.
71 John Curtin to W.J. Scully, 1 December 1937, Papers of Marina Mar, NLA.

Chinese-language newspapers found cooperation where their interests intersected as propaganda conduits.[72] One of the regular motifs in the propaganda was the unanimous opposition from Chinese officials and community leaders to Japanese aggression. Japanese ambition to subjugate China and the Far East as Tokyo's "field for exploitation", as Chen and Liu illustrated, was described as "a history of so-called incidents" that Australians ought not to trust in "double-faced and insincere" Japanese diplomacy, while Australian policy of appeasement was seen in these terms: "the compromise of today will be the weakness of tomorrow".[73] Evidence was put forwards to cement their arguments, including proof of Japanese atrocities towards the Chinese and the Lytton Report produced in 1931 after the League of Nations investigated the Mukden Incident. To make their allegations more compelling, they were supplemented by news excerpts and editorials from Australian newspapers including the *Sydney Morning Herald*, *Daily Telegraph* and *Sydney Sun*. Articles authored by renowned figures, such as Edgar Snow, a famous American journalist, and Stanley Bruce, the former Australian prime minister, were also featured.[74]

The cultivation of a robust Sino-Australian trading relationship was also promoted. Studies have shown that China–Australia trade, especially in wool, played a crucial role in Chinese industrialisation and gained political importance during the Chinese nation-building process.[75] During the war, trade took on increasing diplomatic and financial significance. Australia–Japan relations were primarily based on commercial interests. Japan represented the third-largest destination for Australian exports (especially wool) and was pivotal to Australia's weathering the economic depression of the 1920s and 30s as well.[76] The total value of Japan–Australia trade in the first four years of the 1930s amounted to £62,705,479, whereas trade with China only reached

---

72  *Chinese Republic News*, "澳洲雪梨華僑對日救國後援會通告," 7 November 1931, 8.
73  Chen 1934, 8, 30, 31; Liu, 1931.
74  Liu 1931; Society of Chinese Residents in Australia 1933b.
75  Gibson and Ville 2019.
76  Frei 1991, 123; Jones 2001, 134.

£16,645,043.[77] To disentangle Canberra from this link meant a transfer of its commercial interests from Japan to China. Since Japan profited from "third country trade which existed between Australia and China",[78] William Liu argued for mutually beneficial trade between China and Australia, in which China was the "ultimate customer" and Australia "should get a good share".[79] Realisation of Liu's vision would also alleviate China's unfavourable trade position with Australia. In 1935, Australia exported goods valued at £15,430,172 to China, but imported items were worth only £1,214,871.[80] The imbalance hindered the commercial expansion of Chinese Australian merchants and exacerbated the deteriorating financial condition of the Chinese government. Liu bitterly called this trade "not even a small reciprocity", while perceiving a fair reciprocation as a manifestation of "practical goodwill".[81]

Chinese propaganda extended beyond just defences, accusations and appeals to foster a better Australian understanding of China. The writers, such as Chen Wei-ping and William Liu, knew that the unfavourable Australian perception of the Chinese nation fed their placatory attitude towards Japanese aggression, and encouraged Chinese propagandists to promote China's image in the form of cultural exchanges. Chen Wei-ping collaborated with Chinese community leaders and interested Australians in 1932 to launch the annual George Ernest Morrison Lecture in Canberra. In his well-received inaugural lecture, Chen argued that cultural exchange had the potential to unite the sentiments and thoughts of people in both countries.[82] The lecture series by distinguished speakers from China and Australia seemed to target Australian elites rather than the public, securing the attendance of senior government figures like James Scullin (former prime minister), Robert Menzies (then prime minister), William Hodgson (secretary of the Department of External Affairs) and Richard Casey

---

77  *Official Year Book of the Commonwealth of Australia, 1935*, 255–7.
78  Purcell 1981, 122.
79  Liu 1931, 38; 1932, 7.
80  *Official Year Book of the Commonwealth of Australia, 1935*, 255–7.
81  Liu 1932, 6.
82  *Tung Wah Times*, "澳人亦敬睡獅耶," 11 June 1932, 8.

(assistant Treasurer). The lectures addressed themes such as China–Australia goodwill and Chinese modernisation.[83]

However, while resonating strongly with Chinese Australians,[84] all these propaganda efforts captured a limited Australian audience. While some speeches by leading Chinese figures concluded with "tremendous ovation", and Australians reportedly sought information about the situation in Manchuria,[85] the majority was less interested. Few mentions of the distributed booklets surfaced in Australian newspapers, although one left-wing paper published Chen Wei-ping's critique.[86] Many Australians dismissed Japan's invasion, as it focused on expansionism to the north not the south, which would have more likely endangered Australia. Some even "wish Japan well in her expansion".[87] The influence of Japanese propaganda on politicians was too apparent. The Minister for External Affairs, George Pearce, assured Japan that "the Manchurian problem had nothing to do with Australia".[88]

Chinese propagandists also underestimated how strong the Japan–Australia tie was. Researchers suggest Australian woolgrowers staunchly defended Japanese interests, for a withdrawal of Japanese buyers could imperil the fragile upward mobility of Australian wool prices.[89] Even during Australia–Japan trading disputes, efforts to protect the Australian industry from the threat of low-priced Japanese products found little sympathy.[90] Meanwhile, the points made on the Chinese market's value to Australian commodities were taken as exaggerated. Ian Clunies Ross concluded that "much of the demand is potential only and without immediate significance for Australia".[91]

---

83  Australian Institute of Anatomy 1932; 1933; 1934; 1935; 1936; 1937; 1938; 1939; 1940; 1941. For more about the lectures, see Siam 2015, 27–8.
84  *Chinese Republic News*, "各僑團聯名挽留陳總領事," 24 October 1936, 4.
85  Society of Chinese Residents in Australia 1933b, 2; *Wellington Times*, "The problem of Orient," 13 February 1933, 3.
86  *Australian Worker*, "Manchuria or Manchukuo?," 14 November 1934, 11.
87  *Argus*, "Japan's good will to Australia," 7 September 1935, 25.
88  Frei 1991, 179.
89  Tsokhas 1989, 447.
90  Jones 2001, 153.
91  Clunies Ross 1936, 264, 276.

Australian views shifted towards favouring China in the late 1930s. Chinese propaganda turned out to be much better received than earlier. Propaganda published by a new group of Chinese officials, including Pao Chun-jien and Tsao Wen-yen (曹文彥), was applauded as "remarkable" and insightful, and left Australians with no excuse for "failing to realise the facts" about China and for "disputing" the "significance" of China "for the world in general and Australia in particular".[92] This change in public allegiance was caused by successful Chinese propaganda, which intensified its narratives in the milieu of the escalating China–Japan war and Australia entering the Second World War.

Given convincing evidence of the Nanking Massacre and, thereby, wider sympathy for China in Australian communities, Chinese propagandists sought to achieve broader ends. Their criticisms of Japan were now linked to the outrages it perpetuated on not only the Chinese people but its culture and were openly transformed into blunt denunciations of Japanese authorities in Australia for their "diplomacy of deception".[93] Also emphasised was wartime Chinese resilience, highlighting that such tenacity precluded Kuomintang China from collapse under the leadership of Chiang Kai-shek, whose commitment to resist Japan and modernise China was unwavering.[94] Many of these efforts expanded Chungking's instructions in order to harvest international sympathy and dispel scepticism of China's ability to survive,[95] further enlightening Australian understanding of Chinese people and the value of Chinese culture beyond unfavourable stereotypes.

---

92  *Advertiser*, "China of yesterday and today," 4 October 1941, 10; *Mercury*, "Relations with China," 10 March 1938, 14; Secretary of the Department of the Interior to the Chinese consul general, 27 November 1936; Memorandum, 14 February 1942, SP42/1, C1936/7875, 31102871, SP42/1, C1936/7734, 31102850; Secretary of the Department of the Interior to the Chinese consul general, 30 June 1937, SP42/1, C1937/4628, 31103385, NAA.

93  Pao 1938, 60–1; Tsao 1941, 117–19.

94  Tsao 1941, 20, 48–9, 54–5, 60–5.

95  中宣部國宣處工作報告, 1939–1945, 718(4)-239, 中國第二歷史檔案館 (SHAC), 南京.

Moreover, Chinese propaganda expanded its previous focus on establishing reciprocal China–Australia trade and now pressed for social and political equality. Aware of Australian sensitivity to this agenda, many of the propaganda writings were periphrastic and euphemistic to avoid confrontation and resistance from readers. Compliments about aspects of Australia and Australian contributions to the Chinese nation supported the accounts of authors like Pao Chun-jien and Tsao Wen-yen, in which an idea of "New China" was emphasised. Chinese national "rebirth" was realised not through an entire break from passive "Old China" but a continuity. The "best elements" of traditional China that nourished national traits, including peacefulness, resilience and recuperativeness, would be at the forefront of proactive Chinese modernisation.[96] The propaganda writings often drew on moments of glory in Chinese history and were couched in doctrines of Confucianism and Taoism, embodying continuity between "Old and New China".[97] In doing so, Chinese propaganda hoped to bridge Chinese traditions with modernity to justify that the Chinese nation was not antithetical to progress but rather capable of evolving alongside it. In other words, heritage and modernity could be merged and mutually reinforcing rather than mutually exclusive.

The concept of "New China" and the sense of "New Chinese" implied a reformulated Australian mindset regarding Chinese inferiority, relocating China and Chinese people in a system recognised by modern principles of equality. The argument was further developed in two aspects: the shared spirit of peace-loving and democracy between the two nations in contrast to "autocratic" Japan;[98] and the intersected security interests between both states, in which the significance of China's survival to Australia's safety was underscored by the previous alarm of Japan's potential invasion.[99] Work was also done to dismiss any perception that China was a threat to Australia, encouraging non-Chinese Australians to embrace racial equality. The

---

96  Pao 1938, 15, 25, 30, 33, 41, 49–50, 55; Tsao 1940, 17–19; Australian Institute of Anatomy 1937, 81.
97  Tsao 1941, 16, 20, 27, 49, 60, 130; 1940.
98  Pao 1938, 8, 24, 27.
99  Tsao 1941, 38, 40, 58–9, 80.

Australian racist discourse, which suggested that Chinese immigrants "would not be absorbed", was smartly used to illustrate the unlikelihood that a small Chinese Australian population in the milieu of racial exclusion would despoil Australian national homogeneity. China was not concerned with the naturalisation of immigrant Chinese, whose enormous contribution to Australia was also noted.[100]

The Chinese propaganda was clear that it expected Australia to grant Chinese migrants with fair rights and support China's war effort against Japan. However, in communicating this expectation, Pao Chun-jien and his colleagues were tactful in approach. Pao ostensibly did not challenge Australian "national homogeneity" and the "general principle of exclusion".[101] While mainly focusing on racial equality for those already living in Australia, this strategy was more practical than seeking wider changes to Australian immigration restrictions, and it was likely to be tolerated by the Australian public – if not accepted – so as not to backfire. Although these descriptions risk re-Orientalising Chinese as obedient and passive, Chinese authorities projected a strikingly assertive counter-narrative towards Chinese Australians that urged them to uplift their position by advocating for the "abolition of immigration and trade regulations".[102] This rhetorical manoeuvre, skilfully positioned in the interstices of competing narratives, echoed a literary strategy familiar to contemporary Chinese immigrant writers: crafting messages pliable enough to resonate across diverse readerships.[103]

Where Chinese authorities fell short, particularly in addressing the experiences of Chinese Australians, diasporic leaders such as William Liu and Choy Hing (蔡興) stepped in. Through initiatives like the Chinese Australasian Association (中澳僑務協進會), they amplified diasporic voices, forging alliances with "other Chinese bodies" and leveraging platforms such as the Morrison Lecture in Canberra to press

---

100  Pao 1938, 7, 10, 22, 24.
101  Pao 1938, 6, 8.
102  *Chinese Times* to the Overseas Department, 24 November 1941, C320, C8, 1495438, NAA.
103  For the literary strategy of contemporary Chinese immigrant writers, see Yin 2000, 174.

for racial equality. Their outreach extended further still, maintaining correspondence with influential propagandists like Oon Guan-neng (溫源寧) and even entertaining hopes of securing a visit from William Donald, the renowned Australian journalist working as the advisor for Chiang Kai-shek and his wife, to deepen China–Australia ties.[104] These propaganda efforts were echoed not only by official authorities and prominent elites but also by less conspicuous agents. Charles Fong from Rockhampton informed local newspapers in 1939 of Japan's widening ambitions under its "New Order in Asia" and exposed atrocities such as the use of poison gas in China.[105] Yet, the carefully curated image of a modernising China – diligently promoted by propagandists – faced resistance not only from Japanese voices and their sympathisers but from within the Chinese community itself. In a letter to the *Telegraph*, one anonymous Chinese reader dismissed praise for China penned by white Australians, asserting instead that the country was "the most conservative" in the world, rife with an endemic "'squeeze' from top to bottom."[106]

## Australian participation in the competition

Having the support of white Australians was significant to both Japanese and Chinese propagandists, as it would improve either group's credibility. Given the general favouritism towards Japan in the early 1930s, it seemed straightforward for Japanese propaganda to secure Australian supporters using personal charisma, strong voices and extensive experience shaping public opinion. Among them was Frederic Cutlack, a key journalist from the *Sydney Morning Herald* who joined the Goodwill Mission led by John Latham to the Far East and toured Manchuria in 1934. Cutlack's writings often portrayed him as favouring Japan's invasion over China's suffering. He defended Japanese

---

104 Choy Hing to Harry Foll, 27 March 1941; William Liu to Frederick Stewart, 12 May 1941; William Liu to Harry Foll, 23 June 1941, A433, 1941/2/1444, 3091095, NAA.
105 *Morning Bulletin*, "The new order in China," 3 April 1939, 8.
106 Letters to the editor, 26 October 1935, 12.

military expansionism by rejecting Nanking's sovereignty over China and criticising the League of Nations' arbitration that favoured China's territorial claims.[107] Cutlack was also actively engaged in public speaking, urging Australians to support Japan and presenting the Japanese claim to and occupation of China as natural: the Japanese invasion was an understandable response to "a debatable land forever near her shore".[108]

Jacqui Murray has shown that Cutlack was part of the Japanese propaganda apparatus whose local agents in Australia secretly sponsored him. *The Manchurian Arena*, produced from this discreetly arranged financial backing after his trip to China in 1934, was a book about this sponsorship.[109] The publication essentially echoed Japanese propaganda that portrayed Tokyo's military actions as a mission to liberate the Chinese people: "disorder and banditry" in Manchuria was "intolerable to the Japanese".[110] Cutlack's position as a well-known journalist and experience touring China and Japan made his argument convincing to some Australian newspapers and thus brought them under the influence of Japanese propaganda. Considering that "anything from his pen deserves attention", the *Advertiser*, for example, deemed *The Manchurian Arena* "invaluable" for anyone seeking to understand the ongoing Sino-Japanese tension.[111]

Frederic Cutlack was not the only individual funded by Japan for propaganda purposes. Historians have identified that journalists from major daily newspapers, including the *Daily Telegraph*, *Empire Gazette* and *Sunday Sun*, were paid around £5 to £10 per month to contribute articles with pro-Japan views, especially in response to criticism over Japan's expansion in China. Renowned intellectuals sympathetic to Japan, such as Ian Clunies Ross, were also appreciated by the Japanese consulate general in Australia.[112] Cutlack's narrative of Chinese inferiority and inability to self-rectify was also not the lone discourse

107 *Sydney Morning Herald*, "The Manchurian arena," 7 August 1934, 8.
108 *Sydney Morning Herald*, "The Japanese question of aggression," 31 August 1934, 10.
109 Murray 2004, 66, 109.
110 Cutlack 1934, 15.
111 *Advertiser*, "Japan and the League of Nations," 15 September 1934, 8.
112 Llewelyn 2019, 24–5.

adopted by Japan's Australian advocates. Some blurred Australian–Japanese racial boundaries and characterised them as sharing a familiar spirit of democracy while othering China as "not democratic".[113] Although these propaganda efforts provoked considerable protests from Chinese authorities and leaders in Australia, Canberra largely accommodated them, dismissing the criticisms from the Chinese community.[114]

Deploying white Australians for Japan's voice was not a tactic used by Japanese authorities alone. The Chinese side took a similar approach by reaching out to agents such as A.M. Pooley (radio speaker and editor of *Current Problems*) and *Smith's Weekly*.[115] In 1932, S. Lautenschlager was commissioned by the Society of Chinese Residents in Australia to condemn Japan's justification for its invasion and to call for international interference.[116] But the most active among those commissioned was John Sleeman in 1933. Sleeman was a journalist too, but less famous than Cutlack. He wrote *White China*, a book on Chinese sponsorship. Like Cutlack's, the book mainly echoed Chinese propaganda that addressed condemnation of the Japanese invasion, China–Australia commercial reciprocity, and relaxation of the White Australia policy for non-threatening Chinese immigrants. It also warned Australians not to be complacent, as the Manchurian crisis could become a broader clash in the Pacific.[117]

The propaganda apparatus of different parties in the Chinese community in Australia operated at full effect to publicise *White China*. The book was advertised in Chinese-language newspapers and available in nearly all Chinese shops and newspaper offices. Chinese residents were encouraged to buy copies for their Australian friends to influence Australian attitudes regarding immigration policy.[118] The Society of Chinese Residents in Australia purchased several hundred copies for

---

113 Labour Supporter 1937, 3, 7, 13.
114 Correspondence between Mar Leong Wah and John Latham, 24–31 August 1934, 176185, NAA.
115 Confidential Report, 31 August 1934, 176185, NAA.
116 Lautenschlager 1932.
117 Sleeman 1933, 27, 38, 44, 223, 238, 281–2.
118 *Chinese Republic News*, "劉光福敬告旅澳僑胞," 5 August 1933, 6; *Tung Wah Times*, "介紹新書," 11 February 1933, 5.

distribution to Australian institutions such as libraries and universities as well as legislators, hoping to capture the attention of those influencing Australia's policies. The book was circulated across Australia and the Pacific, reaching the Chinese in China, Batavia, Hawaii and Hong Kong. Their expectations of the book's propaganda effect were high, and the society considered it to be the most influential work in shaping Australia's perception of the Chinese nation.[119] Whether it was the most effective is unknown, but it was the most widely read book about China at the time.[120]

But the impressive quantity and scope of the book's circulation did not equate to significant efficacy. *White China* reaped numerous reviews from small Australian newspapers including *Labor Call*, *Mirror* and *Labor Daily*.[121] Their readership and influence were likewise small.[122] One of the reasons for the book's lukewarm response may be its hazardous organisation and unreadable language. One paper commented that *White China* was "slovenly stuff" composed in a "flamboyant style" and a "welter of words".[123] Furthermore, similar themes had already appeared in Chinese propaganda books and in research reports by white Australians, such as Alexander Melbourne, commissioned by Queensland Premier Arthur Moore in 1932, so Sleeman's writing did not seem original.[124]

John Sleeman's involvement cannot be attributed simply to a sense of allegiance to Chinese propaganda efforts. His meticulous registration of the book's copyright suggested he anticipated commercial profits and sought to protect them.[125] The sales strategy, based on a buy-now-pay-later approach, aimed to create the perception (if not the reality) of popularity before securing profits. Self-published for

---

119 Society of Chinese Residents in Australia 1933a, 3–7, 13–15.
120 S. Fitzgerald 1996, 128.
121 *Labor Call*, "White China: an Austral-Asian sensation," 13 April 1933, 14; *Labor Daily*, "Latest work on China: a new book with a 'kick'," 14 January 1933, 9; *Mirror*, "J.H.C. Sleeman's book: a window into the Orient," 11 February 1933, 13.
122 Macmahon Ball 1938, 10.
123 *Daily Standard*, "'White China' tells a tragic story," 11 February 1933, 4.
124 Melbourne 1932, 68, 70, 77.
125 Copyright registration, A1336, 23441, 3506297, NAA.

the benefit of the Chinese Australian community, Sleeman reportedly invested hundreds of pounds in printing. The strategy proved effective. However, what neither the author nor the Chinese elites who commissioned him anticipated was the widespread arrears in payments for the book. William Liu was forced to repeatedly call on buyers to settle their outstanding balances, charging an additional 5 shillings per copy, or return the book, in an effort to "repay kindness with kindness" and prevent Sleeman from falling into financial ruin.[126] Liu's repetitive appeals implied that Sleeman's financial venture proved much less successful than expected. He was then reluctant to take another risk with the Chinese Australian community.

While less successful in attracting Australian readers, the work for China's benefit ironically caught the Japanese consul general's attention. John Sleeman was invited to conduct propaganda on Japan's behalf, which he accepted in 1936. He then promoted a better Japan–Australia trading relationship and downplayed Japanese militarism in China.[127] Sleeman's predicament and shift in allegiance highlight the significant impact that a lack of financial support can have in the battle of propaganda.

Despite this experience, Chinese Australian elites persisted in their efforts and reached out to more Anglophone Australians following the production of *White China*. White Australian intellectuals, whose attitudes towards China and understanding of the war's nature aligned with support for China, topped the bucket list for Chinese Australian elites.[128] Among these candidates was C.H. Currey, who appeared to have a certain camaraderie with Chinese Australian elites. He attended one of the aforementioned Chinese memorial services alongside Sleeman, and his speeches echoed a tone of admiration for China. In his 25-minute broadcast on radio station 2BL Sydney in October 1933,[129] Currey lauded the Kuomintang's crucial role in China's modernisation and highlighted the diligence and talent of overseas Chinese, noting their influence in the Pacific regions where they resided.[130] While

---

126  *Tung Wah Times*, "劉光福敬告旅澳僑胞書," 12 August 1933, 5.
127  Loy-Wilson 2009, 8–10.
128  *Tung Wah Times*, "救國會常會誌," 21 October 1933, 5.
129  *Sydney Morning Herald*, "Broadcasting," 17 October 1933, 5.

Currey's praise pleased the Chinese community, its effectiveness was questionable, and even risked backfiring. His accolades, while intended to foster goodwill, instead rubbed many Anglo-Australians the wrong way, unsettling them by the very qualities of overseas Chinese that he had praised.

When China's War of Resistance intensified in the late 1930s, so did the efforts to deploy white Australian allies in the propaganda competition. Compared with China's ineffective propaganda, Japanese authorities established a well-organised propaganda network of white Australians – the Publicist Publishing Company and its journal, *Publicist* – to amplify their message and thus integrate them into Tokyo's overseas propaganda webs. The company was registered in Sydney in 1936 by William John Miles, a staunch supporter of the fascist Australia First Movement; in fact, the *Publicist* caught the police's attention for its explicit support of Japan, Italy and Germany. The company also operated a bookshop on Elizabeth Street in Sydney, using the same name as the journal. It became a distribution centre for propaganda materials imported from Japan, including *Japan's Problems*, published by the Japan Pacific Association in Tokyo.[131] The most prominent writer hired was Percy Stephenson – a graduate of the University of Oxford – who authored several pamphlets and articles supplied to the Japanese consulate general for distribution. Some of his writings were attributed to a Japanese pseudonym, "Myles Cheguin". Australian police believed Stephenson received £500 per year from the Japanese government for his propaganda work.[132]

Partially funded by the Japanese Chamber of Commerce,[133] the *Publicist* itself was distributed by Gordon & Gotch at a circulation of 1,500 copies per month. But Australian authorities estimated that an additional 2,000 copies were distributed directly to subscribers and through direct sales.[134] Like its Chinese counterparts, the *Publicist* was

---

130 *Chinese Republic News*, "茄萊博士在無線電台演講," 11 November 1931, 5; "茄萊博士在無線電台演講," 18 November 1933, 5; "Outlook in the Pacific: China," 2 December 1933, 8.
131 *Japan's Problems*, 30 March 1939, A981, CHIN 41, 173502, NAA.
132 W.J. Keefe's report, 27 July 1939, 173502, NAA.
133 Llewelyn 2019, 26.

disseminated beyond Australia to the "Japanese Society" in Suva through Japanese transnational networks in the Pacific, alongside a supply of anti-Chinese propaganda leaflets.[135] While existing scholarship has described this journal's pro-Japanese stance as mild,[136] a detailed examination reveals a quite different picture: that it essentially echoed the intense anti-Chinese propaganda and condemnation of anti-Japanese boycotts in Australia.[137]

In addition to expanding propaganda networks, Tokyo manoeuvred in channels that were less visible in order to influence white Australians and transform them into inadvertent propaganda conduits. One of these strategies was to regulate tourism, which successfully manipulated Australian travellers to view Japan favourably. Andrew Elliott has observed that officials from the Japan Tourist Bureau, South Manchuria Railway Company and other agencies accompanied these travellers, shaping their itineraries and interpreting what they saw. Australians were guided along routes orchestrated by the Japanese government to present Japanese modernity and strength while obfuscating Japanese militarism in China. The subjects and locations travellers could photograph were censored. These arrangements shaped the travel writings of Australian visitors to Japan, cultivating a sense of detachment that portrayed the war as a natural and inevitable cycle of disasters in China and presented it as a localised and distant event.[138] Travelogues were formulated to parrot official Japanese narratives, some of which were authored by the famous (Frank Clune, for example) and enjoyed great popularity.[139]

Although Chinese propagandists were at no advantage, some ramifications of their contest with Japan unexpectedly aided them. The involvement of white Australians in each propaganda apparatus and network primarily resulted in making public responses to the war more complex. The general opinion was divided so that even those

---

134 Memorandum for the Secretary of the Department of External Affairs, 12 April 1938, 173502, NAA.
135 Untitled report, 22 March 1938, 97419, NAA.
136 Hornadge 1976, 98–9.
137 *Publicist*, 1938–1939, 173502, NAA.
138 Elliott 2019, 121, 124–7, 129–30, 134–5.
139 Clune 1939; 1941.

who initially aimed to maintain neutrality in discussions about the war found it increasingly difficult. For example, the Australian Institute of International Affairs, a major institution engaged in the study of Australian external affairs, and the *Austral-Asiatic Bulletin* published in 1937 intended to remain neutral and focus on ascertaining the facts and summarising evidence, as well as presenting viewpoints related to China's War of Resistance.[140] This mechanism allowed the war to be told and retold through different perspectives at national and transnational levels, uncovering facts and interpretations suppressed in Japanese propaganda. It was not uncommon to see views in favour of Japan encountering opposition from those supporting China.[141] Despite echoing what the Chinese and Japanese campaigned for, the *Austral-Asiatic Bulletin* provided a relatively fair platform where the Chinese voice repressed by the pro-Japanese milieu and by the powerful Japanese propaganda machine was better heard.[142]

With the 1930s coming to an end, increasing attention to China's War of Resistance sparked national debates among Australian intellectuals. In 1939, two contributors to the *Austral-Asiatic Bulletin* argued whether Australians were sufficiently sympathetic to and supportive of China. One, with the penname "Uranus", believed that Australian sympathy for China was not particularly apparent. Rupert Lockwood, an Australian correspondent for Reuters who had travelled widely in China, retorted that there was deep and consistent sympathy among Australians for the suffering of China and the Chinese.[143] Their argument was an indication of an increasing division emerging between white Australians. Indeed, an even more intensive propaganda competition unfolded between white Australians supporting either China or Japan. Pro-Tokyo journalists again parroted Japanese propaganda, but more loudly, to justify Japan's invasion on the grounds of Chinese inferiority and warn Australia to maintain its

---

140  Introducing the *Austral-Asiatic Bulletin*, *Austral-Asiatic Bulletin* 1, no. 1 (1937): 1; Retrospect and prospect, *Austral-Asiatic Bulletin* 6, no. 4 (1946).
141  Burton 1937, 7–8; Chen 1938, 8.
142  Taronga 1937, 26; The war in China and its consequences, *Austral-Asiatic Bulletin* 1, no. 4 (1937): 4.
143  Uranus 1938–39, 10; Lockwood 1938–39, 9.

friendship with Japan. "All nations may theoretically be born equal", argued Hugh Millington, but they "do not always remain equal".[144] Many of his works were printed in Sydney and funded by Japanese authorities, companies and socio-commercial organisations. Their voices were joined by the Japanese puppet regime in Nanking, headed by Wang Ching-wei, who even directed their propaganda at local Chinese to secure their pro-Japan support.[145] This caught Canberra's attention and led to the censorship of publications sent from the Central Cables Agency in Nanking to the *Chinese Times* in Australia and included censorship of pro-German and anti-British motifs to prevent further propaganda from infiltrating Australia.[146]

Meanwhile, white Australians supporting China were better organised than ever. For example, the Australian headquarters (established in 1936) of the International Peace Campaign (founded in Brussels in 1935) saw an efficient expansion of state councils throughout the country, except in the Northern Territory and South Australia. One of their core missions was "upholding China's struggle for independence and freedom", articulated clearly in their common program. In addition to their protests to the Australian government for further actions in favour of China and to facilitate Alice Lim Kee and Elsie Lee Soong's propaganda tour in Australia,[147] they requested that the Chinese branch assign an influential figure to Australia to promote their anti-Japanese efforts and support China's nation-building.[148] Whether this request was fulfilled is unknown, but the Australian branches busied themselves with receiving and circulating propaganda materials, such as *China To-Day*, from their Chinese counterparts

---

144 Millington 1939, 9–10, 13–14; 1938; *Newcastle Sun*, "Australian author on China war," 14 January 1939, 4.
145 Millington 1939; A373, 1652, 65352; Association of Far Eastern Affairs, C320, J194, 3047904, NAA.
146 Publication in Chinese, 1 August 1940, SP106/1, PC295, 317787; Japanese Espionage, 4 November 1941, C320, C16, 1495444; T. Elink Schuurman to Minister for External Affairs, A981, JAP 22, 177402, NAA.
147 F. O'Sullivan to Joseph Lyons, 8 November 1937; A.C. Duncan to J.A. Lyons, 19 February 1938, 97419, NAA.
148 國際反侵略運動大會中國分會工作報告, November 1939, 718(4)-368; 國際反侵略運動大會中國分會工作報告, 1939–1940, 718(4)-371, SHAC.

whose commissions came directly from the Chinese government (as Chapter 7 uncovers).[149] There was deep appreciation from the Chinese for the support and ongoing exchanges of propaganda materials between the Australian and Chinese divisions of the International Peace Campaign.[150]

The Victorian League for Peace and Democracy also imported war films produced by Chinese propagandists, such as *Chinese War Songs*, *Nanking Capture* and *Bombing of Canton*, and from the United States, *China Strikes Back*. These films vividly depicted Japanese outrages against Chinese soldiers and civilians – including shootings, bayonetings and torture – while also showcasing China's resolute and proactive resistance, including the efforts of communist troops like the Eighth Route Army (八路軍). These films were scheduled to be screened at the Assembly Hall in Melbourne. However, the effort was thwarted by Australian authorities. Some films were censored without explanation, with *Nanking Capture* banned outright, and *Bombing of Canton* heavily cut, stripping it of its continuity and "most telling argument". This sparked vigorous protests, with many accusing the censors of "objectively" aiding Japanese aggression.[151]

The growing attention to China's War of Resistance, marked by large-scale protests,[152] also catalysed a shift in the intellectual landscape regarding Australia's role in East Asian politics. By the late 1930s, views that had once been muffled – those advocating for an Australian voice on the war – found a growing chorus of supporters. These individuals recognised the perilous risks of a policy of isolationism in a rapidly changing Asia. Canberra, it was argued, could no longer afford to cling to the outdated "dullness" of islander thinking, tethered exclusively to British perspectives. The world, it seemed, had moved on. Australia's future, the new rhetoric held, would no longer lie in Europe but in the Pacific, and the sooner it embraced this reality, the better.[153]

---

149  國際反侵略運動大會工作報告, December 1939, 718(4)-371, SHAC.
150  國際反侵略運動大會中國分會工作報告, March 1940, 718(4)-371, SHAC.
151  Censored Chinese Films, 18 October 1938, 97420, NAA.
152  Australian League for Peace and Democracy, 3 November 1939, 97420, NAA.
153  Eggleston 1936, 7, 10; Wilson 1937, 22.

There were those, of course, who favoured a cautious yet proactive engagement with East Asian affairs – an approach that sought to balance Japan's aggression without severing ties with China.[154] Meanwhile, the general public, ever keen to join the intellectual fray, voiced their opinions in letters to newspapers, urging their compatriots to "awaken to the fact" that China's War of Resistance was no mere distant conflict, but one that would shape Australia's future in profound ways.[155] These approaches, urgent yet reasoned, encouraged a paradigm shift, redirecting Australia's gaze from its comfortable, European-centric worldview towards the complex, volatile dynamics of the Pacific. For these political thinkers, to ignore these immediate dangers was to risk falling behind in a world no longer shaped by British influence.

Australia's response to China's War of Resistance was certainly not the only outcome of the fierce Chinese–Japanese propaganda contest; it also had a noticeable impact on interracial relations. Although open confrontations were rare, tensions simmered beneath the surface. In 1936, for instance, the Japanese consulate's official emblem was stolen by a group of Chinese and white Australians as a symbolic protest against Japanese militarism. The theft of the insignia caused considerable consternation for Kuramatsu Murai, the Japanese consul general, who remained disturbed by the incident until it was returned through the channel of the *Daily Telegraph*.[156] The protesters, undeterred by the theft's backlash, claimed to have formed a secret society months earlier, a group consisting of 26 members, half of whom were white Australians and half local Chinese. The aim of this clandestine alliance was clear: to oppose Japanese aggression and militarism, a cause that seemed to transcend ethnic lines, if only for a fleeting moment in the heat of the international conflict.[157]

---

154 The war in China and its consequences, *Austral-Asiatic Bulletin* 1, no. 4 (1937): 5; Mac Abbott to Joseph Lyons, 2 March 1939, 97420, NAA; Drysdale 1987.
155 *Argus*, "To the editor of the Argus," 8 October 1937, 13.
156 *Daily Telegraph*, "Consular emblem returned," 30 May 1936, 1.
157 *News*, "Strange story behind removal of Japanese insignia," 30 May 1936, 3.

Within the Asian communities, the relationship between diasporic Chinese and Japanese became increasingly strained. In the aftermath of the Mukden Incident, even the Broome Chinese, who stood to lose much in their business dealings, severed ties with the Japanese.[158] Prominent Chinese figures like D.Y. Narme distanced themselves from Japanese officials, making it clear that they were unwilling to be in contact.[159] Those perceived as having pro-Japanese sympathies, like Diamond Kwong Sang – an unofficial consular representative in Brisbane – faced social exclusion, barred from participating in Chinese organisations due to their suspected loyalties.

However, interracial interactions were not always marked by confrontation, particularly in the realm of intimate relationships. Frank Yow, a prominent figure within the Brisbane Chinese community and a staunch supporter of communist ideals and anti-Japanese boycotts, married a Japanese woman who, by contrast, "had a Japanese outlook" and was known to frequent Japanese stores.[160] This nuanced experience was not unique to Australia but was shared across many other destinations of the Chinese diaspora, including the United States. K. Scott Wong has acknowledged that, while some local Chinese in the United States treated Japanese Americans with coldness and actively participated in the implicit denigration of Japanese American loyalty, many Chinese Americans refused to engage in such behaviour.[161] Meanwhile, Xiao-huang Yin has suggested that "any holdover" from the historical enmity between China and Japan had little impact on relations between the two groups in American society.[162] This points to a rich yet diverse social fabric underlying the ethnic relationships among Asian minorities in societies of largely Anglo-Saxon heritage.

Despite monitoring the evolving situation on the Sino-Japanese battlefront,[163] the Australian government continued to placate Japan's

---

158  陳志明 1935, 95.
159  Assistance by the Chinese community, 3 April 1942, 3051769, NAA.
160  Chinese Societies in Queensland, 25 October 1941, C320, C17, 314820, NAA.
161  Wong 2005, 34, 80.
162  Yin 2000, 133.
163  Chinese and Japanese Newspapers and Periodicals Ordered, A981, PUB 76, 180484, NAA.

expansionist ambitions. In 1940, it urged Britain to comply with Japan's request to close the Burma Road, even at the expense of Chinese security.[164] John Curtin, then leader of the Labor Opposition, sought to cultivate a personal relationship with Japan in the hope of preventing the outbreak of war in the Pacific.[165] Meanwhile, surveillance was placed on all Japanese merchants and their commercial activities in Australia, but this did little to curtail their friendships with Australians or impede Japanese propaganda efforts until the Pacific War erupted.[166]

Although sympathy and support for China grew among some white Australians, the tangible contributions to longstanding Chinese fundraising campaigns remained meagre throughout the 1930s. Donations were so sparse that even a modest increase in generosity prompted Chinese Australian journalists to exclaim over the "generosity" and reflect on how "Australian Chinese should repay their friendship".[167] It was clear that despite the rise in sympathy, racial barriers remained stubbornly intact, shaping the pace and extent of meaningful support.

## Conclusion

The Japan–China propaganda contest in Australia was intense, with both sides leveraging their diasporic networks. Japan's propaganda was well-organised and highly centralised, while China's was fragmented but strategically collaborative. This rivalry was not merely about the legitimacy of Japanese aggression but also reflected each side's broader ambitions: Japan sought to sustain Australia's goodwill and China pushed for racial and national equality. However, the contest was never a straightforward duel between the two countries, but was instead constantly complicated by the Australian public's proactive participation in the propaganda war. This involvement also integrated Australia into

---

164  Frei 1991, 179.
165  Lee and Lowe 2023, 46–7.
166  Oliver 2010, 213; 2012, 45–6; Association of Far Eastern Affairs, 14 January 1943, C320, J194, 3047904, NAA.
167  *Chinese Republic News*, "趙氏昆季圓桌捐資," 11 September 1937, 2.

the seemingly distant geopolitical shifts of North-East Asia, prompting Australians to reconsider their identity and position within a changing international landscape. The complex and often fraught relationships between diasporic Chinese and Japanese communities, their heritage and residing homelands complicate the accepted notion that has simplified Australia's response into general friendliness towards Japan and indifference towards China.[168]

---

168  Oliver 2012.

# 7

# State-directed wartime propaganda

On 18 March 1941, Masatoshi Akiyama, the Japanese consul general in Sydney, lodged a complaint with Australian military intelligence, alleging that his correspondence had been intercepted by Chinese seamen working aboard steamers plying the route between Australia and the East. During the interview, Akiyama, visibly agitated, claimed that Chinese residents were organised into "Communist cells", receiving both pamphlets and direct encouragement from Chungking. He further insisted that the Chinese consulate general in Sydney was a "centre of intrigue", a hotbed of subversive activities that, in his view, should have no place in Australia. Despite his impassioned allegations, Australian authorities dismissed the incident as a matter of "little importance" and after Akiyama's departure, the issue was allowed to languish.[1] Yet, even in its dismissal, the complaint offered a window into the potential undercurrent of state-directed Chinese propaganda activity within the country.

This chapter traces the trajectory of official Chinese propaganda in Australia during China's War of Resistance against Japan. While early efforts before 1941 were shrouded in secrecy and operated at a modest level, leaving Chinese representatives in Australia a notable degree of

---

1  Japanese Consular Mail and Chinese Censorship, 20 March 1941, MP729/6, 10/401/345, 391203, NAA.

autonomy (as discussed in previous chapters), official propaganda was by no means absent. Rather, it moved in the shadows, subtly shaping the Chinese initiatives and their Australian audience. Following the outbreak of the Pacific War, however, official Chinese propaganda became increasingly prominent in Australia. Far from existing in isolation, it became interwoven with the initiatives already underway by Chinese officials and community leaders, while institutionalising and professionalising the propaganda webs already embedded in social and political networks. Meanwhile, the expansion of the propaganda apparatus saw the rise of pro-China lobbies and notable involvement of white Australians. Together, they wove an intricate, an ever-thickening web of influence.

## "Whispering" Chinese propaganda

As previous chapters have shown, the Kuomintang's branches and Chinese consulates in Australia were initially responsible for conducting propaganda. This was mainly because of China's fragmentation in international propaganda apparatus. It was not until 1937 that China's international propaganda efforts were truly centralised in order to counter the all-out Japanese aggression by appealing for intervention from powerful nations. Their answers were cautious: the United Kingdom offered little assistance while the United States and Soviet Union provided financial support but refrained from declaring war.[2] International propaganda became more necessary for China when the war settled into a protracted stalemate from 1938 onwards, marked by the invader's pyrrhic and limited victory and the invaded eking out survival.[3]

In September 1937, the Fifth Board of the Military Affairs Commission (軍事委員會第五部) was established to oversee all international propaganda activity and was later reorganised into the International Department (國際宣傳處) to further this end. The new

---

2   Mitter 2013, 214.
3   J. Taylor 2009, 160.

department comprised four offices in six sections and was staffed by 150 people.[4] It believed that propaganda was essential for China to obtain international justice, empathy and interference,[5] and that China's campaigns should be presented as credible while avoiding the public's scepticism of official propaganda by erasing "all traces of propaganda".[6] Australia appeared less significant in the spectrum of Chinese propaganda than the United States and Britain. Chinese propaganda designers believed Australia was terrified of Japan and too "solicitous of its trade" to side with China.[7]

However, Australia was not excluded from China's propaganda targeting. Recognising the potential value of galvanising public support, China sought to sway the Australian populace, hoping their influence could pressure the Australian government into adopting a neutral line towards China's War of Resistance against Japan, if not as far as favouring China. Much of the Chinese propaganda disseminated in Australia was channelled through the collaborative efforts of non-official organisations in both China and Australia. This strategy aimed to mask the official nature of the propaganda, ensuring it did not provoke public concern. As Chapter 6 highlights, the exchange of propaganda materials between the Chinese and Australian offices of the International Peace Campaign exemplifies this approach. In addition to appealing to white Australians, Chinese Australians were also enlisted to aid these efforts. Propaganda booklets, such as *China To-Day*, were circulated by the China Society in Sydney, furthering the cause.[8] For Chinese authorities in Australia, the use of materials from non-governmental organisations was a strategic choice, as it helped deflect suspicion of official interference. For instance, the publicity leaflets distributed by Pao Chun-jien to Australian officials were published by such non-official institutions as the Council of

4    Wei 2017, 185–93; 沈劍虹 1989, 75.
5    國宣處工作報告, 1939–1945, 718(4)-239, SHAC.
6    Wei 2017, 187.
7    Tong 1950, 92.
8    China Society in Australia 1939.

International Affairs in Nanking,[9] thus lending an air of independence to the efforts.

Interestingly, white Australians played both a significant role in promoting Chinese propaganda within Australia and in extending its international reach. A striking exemplar is Harold Timperley, a Bunbury, Western Australia-born journalist. Beyond his pivotal role in helping establish Chinese propaganda offices in Britain and the United States,[10] Timperley was instrumental in cultivating widespread sympathy for China across the English-speaking world through his harrowing exposé of the Rape of Nanking. Notably, Timperley's contribution was not entirely self-initiated but originating from a proposal by Hollington Tong (董顯光), the Vice Minister of the Ministry of Information leading China's propaganda. He proposed that Timperley collect and publish evidence of the Japanese atrocities during the Rape of Nanking with no acknowledgement of official support. Timperley welcomed the offer and produced the groundbreaking book *What War Means* months later.[11] The book, both meticulously documented and powerfully conveyed, became a sensation that transformed raw Japanese atrocity into compelling advocacy. It was republished twice that year and translated into multiple languages under the supervision of the International Department. The book also reached Australia, being distributed for free without interference from Australian authorities.[12] For his contribution, Timperley was paid 30,000 Chinese yuan.[13] Tong considered him "doubly valuable" to China's propaganda abroad.[14]

To reach wider audiences, the propaganda was also delivered via radio broadcasting that reinforced the themes communicated through written materials. Like Japanese radio propaganda,[15] Chinese

---

9    Information Bulletin, 18 August 1937, 97419, NAA.
10   Akio 2010, 43; Tong 2005, 108–9.
11   曾虛白 1988, 201.
12   Censored Chinese Films, 17 October 1938, A425, C1939/1513, 63562, NAA.
13   國宣處工作報告, 1939–1945, 718(4)-239; 中宣部國宣處關於田伯烈所著《外人目睹中之日軍暴行》往來函件, 1938–1939, 718(4)-250, SHAC.
14   Tong 1950, 21.
15   Ryō 1983, 331.

propaganda broadcast from radio stations in Hankow (漢口) and Chungking blended political messages with entertaining programs (like Western music and Chinese opera) in up to 13 languages and dialects, including English, Mandarin and Cantonese.[16] This approach helped conceal the propaganda's aims and increase its popularity among listeners. The consistency of propaganda content also served a strategic purpose: it avoided confusing audiences with divergent narratives tailored to different backgrounds, a practice that risked undermining credibility and diminishing the impact of the message. This was a lesson learned the hard way by Radio Australia, a wartime propaganda broadcaster, which discovered that inconsistent treatment of news across audiences could become a serious impediment to its effectiveness.[17]

The radio propaganda was well received, at least among Chinese Australians, although only a small proportion of the Australian population were regular listeners.[18] The International Department received letters of encouragement from listeners abroad, including from Australia and New Zealand.[19] Members of the Chinese diaspora were loyal listeners of China's broadcasting and were enthusiastic about identifying anti-Chungking programs. For instance, in 1939, C.P. Zhang wrote to Chiang Kai-shek to report a Cantonese-speaking program that he and his contemporaries believed to be a channel for Japanese propaganda. He also affirmed his unwavering loyalty to China.[20]

The organisers of the radio propaganda campaign considered it effective, instructing the International Department to continue and expand the effort. The latter convinced the Australian Broadcasting Commission to relay Chungking's programs in the 1940s.[21] Programs

---

16 國宣處工作報告, 1939–1945, 718(4)-239; 國際廣播節目, 1 April 1940, 718(4)-419, SHAC.
17 Hodge 1992, 102.
18 Meo 1968, 166.
19 本處辦理國際廣播經過報告, 1939, 718(4)-334; 侍二處致國宣處, 18 August 1939, 718(4)-367, SHAC.
20 侍二處致國宣處, 18 August 1939, 718(4)-367, SHAC.
21 Exchange of Broadcasts with XGOY China, 1942, MP272/2, NN, 451233, NAA.

specifically designed for Australian audiences were aired once a week, twice a week in Britain and daily in the United States.[22] The Australian Broadcasting Commission also aired its own programs about various facets of Chinese society.[23]

Foreigners in China, particularly journalists, were not only seen as targets of Chinese propaganda but conduits for its dissemination. Their involvement lent an air of impartiality, bolstering the credibility of the message while obscuring its official origins. The outbreak of the all-out war in China acted as catalyst, prompting Western journalists to flock to China to report on the unfolding conflict and inadvertently to carry China's propaganda to the outside world.[24] Hollington Tong valued the role of correspondents in bridging and interpreting China to the outside world as his "number one task".[25] He highlighted that "moving and impressing foreigners with sincerity" was indispensable to obtaining their trust.[26] In Chungking, a Press Hotel was built to provide journalists with better accommodations and to facilitate their exchange of information with Chinese officials.[27] Selwyn Speight from the *Sydney Morning Herald* recalled living "like a prince" there by 1940s Chinese standards.[28]

Opportunities to have face-to-face conversations with Chinese leaders were also provided for foreign journalists. Rex Warren from the *Herald* in Melbourne was among the correspondents invited to a reception held by Chiang Kai-shek and his wife, Soong Mei-ling.[29] Warren was even offered the rare privilege of meeting the couple privately.[30] Partly touched by the friendliness and hospitality, Warren's

22  國宣處工作計劃, 1939–1944, 718(5)-10, SHAC.
23  Aid Our Chinese Allies, 5 April 1942, MT395/1, 148, 31647699; Appeal for Hostel for Chinese Seamen, 24 May 1942, MT359/1, 192, 31534643, NAA.
24  Elliott 2019, 118.
25  Tong 2005, 39.
26  Tong 1950, 126; 國宣處工作報告, 1939–1945, 718(4)-239; 國宣處工作計劃, 1942, 718(4)-311, SHAC.
27  Tong 1950, 117; Eggleston to Minister of External Affairs, 1944, A989, 1944/554/7/1, 184465, NAA.
28  Selwyn Speight to Jo, 6 April 1943, Papers of Selwyn Speight, 1940–1979, MS 6633, Box 1, NLA.
29  *Herald*, "China's spirit hardens," 2 August 1938, 11.

reports spoke highly of the Chinese people's dauntless resistance and unyielding spirit.[31] Invitations were similarly extended to Australian correspondents from the *Daily Telegraph* and *Pix*, ensuring a steady stream of visits to China. Delicate arrangements were also made for Australian officials in China. Chinese officials who specialised in Australian affairs, including Loh Kai-tze, were hand-picked to host members of the Australian legation in Chungking.[32] All these efforts were designed to create a favourable impression for foreign visitors and secure their support for China's international propaganda. Meanwhile, these ongoing visits were strategically woven into broader Chinese efforts to appeal to strong powers, especially the United States, to remind them of China's indispensable position in the war and press for more substantive support.[33]

Impressing foreign visitors with hospitality and sincerity aside, Chungking strategically manipulated its information channels for propaganda purposes. Propaganda-oriented narratives often monopolised news sources, and Chinese authorities supervised visitors' itineraries. Upon their arrival, foreign correspondents were supplied with Kuomintang's propaganda publications for their reference.[34] R.T. Olson from *Pix* went to Chungking to take war photographs and had to adhere to a detailed schedule supplied by the International Department. Officials were sent to supervise his activities, learn his photographic skills and determine his attitude towards China.[35] His photographs, while expected to appear natural, were subtly aligned with propaganda narratives to mask overt signs of manipulation.[36] Indeed, Olson's trip delivered photos illustrating constructive

30  *Advertiser*, "China's message to Australia," 27 November 1937, 23; *Herald*, "Mme. Chiang talks to us," 14 January 1938, 6.
31  *Advertiser*, "War leaves Chinese still unbowed," 11 January 1939, 18; *Mercury*, "China's unchanging purpose," 14 January 1939, 6; *Sun*, "China's morale now bomb-proof," 10 January 1939, 4.
32  巢坤霖工作報告 1943–1944, 718(4)-323; 關於加強聯系外賓計劃 1942–1945, 718(5)-63, SHAC.
33  張克明與沈嵐 2000, 28.
34  國宣處工作報告 1939–1945, 718(4)-239; 1942, 718(4)-321, SHAC.
35  國宣處工作報告 1939–1945, 718(4)-239, SHAC.
36  張克明與沈嵐 2001, 44–5.

Sino-Australian relations, China's hardship and survival efforts.[37] The photos then received a double-check in the department-supplied printing service to ensure they served China's propaganda purpose. Likewise, Selwyn Speight's visit to the Changteh (常德) battlefront in 1944 as a press corps member had a similar outcome. The trip was not held until China secured a final victory there, ensuring the corps witnessed Chungking's success in overwhelming the enemies, not the terrible price China had paid to achieve it.[38] In both cases, the tactics were effective. Frederic Eggleston, the Australian Minister to China, was convinced Olson's photographs would be sensational in Australia,[39] and Hollington Tong claimed the corps returned with a good impression of China's military competence.[40]

The flow of information to overseas readers was also being manipulated. The International Department reiterated the importance of ensuring the content of the news dispatched abroad was "acceptable".[41] This coincides with what historians have called China's reclamation of national communication sovereignty through increased censorship. In addition to Hollington Tong's department, where a three-tiered censorship system was introduced in 1940 to replace his earlier, more relaxed approach, both the Executive Yuan and the Military Affairs Commission maintained their own censorship agencies, creating an increasingly dense apparatus of information control.[42] This tightening of control inevitably affected Australian correspondents in China. Selwyn Speight's report on the Changteh front, for instance, was subjected to close scrutiny, with censors redacting content deemed unfavourable to China.[43] Frustrated by the constraints, Speight confided in his family, lamenting the difficulty of

---

37  國宣處工作計劃, 1941–1946, 718(4)-319, SHAC.
38  董顯光致蔣介石, 13 December 1943, 718(5)-88, SHAC.
39  Diary of Eggleston, Papers of Frederic William Eggleston, 1911–1954, MS 423, Box 2, 3, NLA.
40  董顯光致蔣介石, 1943, 718(5)-90, SHAC.
41  中宣部工作報告, 1942, 718(4)-311; 國宣處工作計劃, 1939–1944, 718(5)-10; 國宣處工作報告, 1939–1945, 718(4)-239, SHAC.
42  China, 2 April 1943, SP109/3, 343/08, 266558, NAA; Wei 2017, 224.
43  外記者湘北戰績觀察團電訊選擇, 1944, 718(4)-346, SHAC.

reporting truthfully under such heavy-handed censorship.[44] Australian diplomats also noted the tightening censorship to conceal unpleasant facts and construct a positive image of the Kuomintang that effectively compelled foreign visitors to align with the official view.[45] Those who did not comply risked punitive measures, including the removal of their government-issued press cards.[46] Tong once sought to ease the censorship of journalists but was refused by Kuomintang leadership.[47]

Much of China's "whispering" propaganda aimed to appeal to the Australian public for their sympathy and support during China's War of Resistance. Exposure to Japanese atrocities and the wartime hardship of the Chinese people was the most effective way to fulfil this objective. Timperley's *What War Means* illustrated Japanese atrocities committed in occupied China, particularly Nanking. Near-constantly highlighting the details of the "barbarously cruel" Japanese treatment of the Chinese, the author "cannot recommend everyone without a strong stomach to read" about these "unbelievable" horrors. The portrayal of Japanese brutality made the case to a wide readership for the interference of the major powers in the Japanese invasion.[48]

The depiction of Japanese cruelty was also used to emphasise the resilience of the Chinese people and government in the face of Japanese aggression, showcasing their determination to prevail in the war. While revealing themes similar to Timperley's work, *China To-Day* illustrated the active Chinese participation in the Kuomintang war effort that contributed to establishing a "New China". This included spontaneous donations from different social strata, sensitive treatment of the wounded, and proud displays of the troops of the Kuomintang and the Chinese Communist Party.[49] By accentuating Chinese solidarity under the Kuomintang's leadership, the booklet foregrounded the party's legitimate rule amid ongoing political rivalry

---

44  Family Correspondence, 1943–1956; Selwyn Speight to His Mother, 1942–1944, Papers of Selwyn Speight, NLA.
45  Waller 1990, 15; Eggleston to the Ministry of Foreign Affairs, 1944, A989, 1944/554/7/1, 184465, NAA.
46  隨軍記者暫行辦法, 1940–1944, 718(4)-231, SHAC.
47  軍事委員會致國宣處, 28 June 1944, 718(5)-11, SHAC.
48  Timperley 1938, 13–144.
49  China Society in Australia 1939, 1, 8–23.

with Chinese communists. It emphasised China's national resilience and solidarity in the face of calamity as a means to inspire confidence and attract meaningful support from leading powers. At the same time, it challenged entrenched Western stereotypes of the Chinese as weak or passive by projecting a new image of proactive heroism, one that asserted not only China's strength but its parity with the West in both courage and civilisation.

The effectiveness of the centralisation of China's official propaganda efforts, together with the initiatives of Chinese officials and community leaders (explored in Chapter 6), in garnering sympathy and support for China was particularly evident in Australia, where newspapers extensively and sympathetically reported on the Japanese atrocities in Nanking, often citing Harold Timperley's work.[50] Expressions of admiration for China's heroic resistance and the "unconquerable" spirit of its people flowed from Australia in numerous letters addressed to Chiang Kai-shek.[51]

## Overt propaganda in the Pacific War

The outbreak of the Pacific War essentially reshaped the framework of the Chinese official propaganda in Australia. Chungking recognised the need for further campaigns to gain support from Australia, a crucial member of the British empire, but felt neglected by London's inattention to the Pacific front. Australia was also an essential centre for Allied intelligence and warfare operations, and a base for American troops under the command of Douglas MacArthur.[52] Successful propaganda in Australia would encourage greater involvement by Britain and the United States on the Pacific front. These conditions thus encouraged China to amplify its voice in Australia through professionalising and institutionalising local Chinese propaganda that had previously been shouldered by Chinese officials and community leaders. In 1942, the International Department started paying

---

50  *Sun*, "Appalling scenes in Nanking," 12 July 1938, 5.
51  侍二處致國宣處, 12 July 1939, 718(4)-367, SHAC.
52  Ball 1978, 300; Hodge 1992, 103; Watt 1967, 54.

particular attention to Australia and cabled Harold Timperley to open a propaganda office in Melbourne.[53] This development was accepted by Chungking as part of strengthening Chinese propaganda towards the United States, India and Australia.[54]

The Melbourne office, established in July 1942, was essential in the Kuomintang's propaganda efforts in Australia. It was staffed by three members (paid 750 yuan per month for salary and another 750 yuan office allowance) and received generous funding from Chungking, with an annual budget of 18,000 yuan in 1942 (second to those in the United States that received 42,000 yuan) and 24,000 yuan in 1943, which was equal to the sums allocated to the British and Indian offices, and twice the funding allocated to the Canadian one.[55] The Chinese consulate general in Sydney was also instructed to cooperate with the Melbourne office, with consular officials doubling as propaganda commissioners. Their duty was to "supply propaganda materials to the targeted public; establish amicable connections with local presses, cultural communities and non-governmental bodies; unify and lead local Chinese propagandists; keep an eye on local perceptions about China". The annual budget for the commissioners was USD$120, lower than those in Britain and the United States (USD$150) but on par with those in France, Germany and Canada, and higher than those in Manila and Singapore (USD$100).[56] A similar mission was given to the Chinese legation headed by Hsu Mo, established in Canberra in 1941.[57] These official propaganda settings indicate that Australia was no longer seen as peripheral but significant to Chungking's strategic calculations.

Transnational networks of the International Department played a crucial part in transmitting propaganda from Chungking to Melbourne. Such content was first broadcast from Chungking to Ventura in Southern California, where it was received, recorded and transcribed before being distributed via wireless cables and posts to

53  曾虛白致中宣部, 1937–1946, 718(4)-343, SHAC.
54  中宣部工作報告, 1942, 718(4)-311, SHAC.
55  中宣部工作報告, 1942, 718(5)-44; 國宣處工作計劃, 1939–1944, 718(5)-10; 中宣部國宣處特別經常費支出計算書, 1942–1944, 718(5)-9, SHAC.
56  設置駐外重要使領館宣傳特派員, 1939–1944, 718(5)-12, SHAC.
57  曾虛白致中宣部, 1937–1946, 718(4)-343, SHAC.

other overseas branches of the International Department.[58] Similarly, photographs used for propaganda were sent to the New York office before being disseminated abroad, and many were exhibited to the public in targeted countries. The department claimed that these photographic shows elicited positive responses.[59] The photographs were supplied to the *Sun* and *Pix* in Australia and *Women* in New Zealand, often under the guise of Kuangguang Studio (鄺光照相室) or through American presses to their Australian counterparts.[60]

However, the Chinese government was far from satisfied with the performance of the Melbourne office. Despite Timperley's extensive background in propaganda and the institutional support he received from Chinese officials, Hollington Tong deemed his work underwhelming and criticised the lack of transparency in his expense reporting.[61] Indeed, Timperley's engagement with the Australian Broadcasting Commission to promote China–Australia goodwill seems derivative, largely echoing initiatives already undertaken by Chinese propagandists in the 1930s.[62] His reports to Chungking offer little new insight, reiterating familiar points such as the potential for China to become a future market for Australian wool.[63]

Further doubts about his effectiveness were fuelled by perceptions that Timperley had strayed from his primary responsibilities. In 1942, instead of focusing squarely on Chinese propaganda, he authored *Australia and the Australians*,[64] a book aimed at strengthening ties between Australia and the United States – an endeavour only loosely aligned with Chungking's objectives. His lacklustre performance may also have been coloured by a strained relationship with Chungking that predated his appointment, casting a long shadow over his tenure from the outset. Timperley had unsuccessfully tried to obtain the position of adviser to the Chiangs, which William Donald had resigned from in

---

58 Daugherty 1942, 81.
59 國宣處工作報告, 1939–1945, 718(4)-239, SHAC.
60 國宣處工作報告, 1939–1940, 718(4)-262; 1939–1945, 718(4)-239, SHAC.
61 Wei 2017, 236.
62 For Timperley's propaganda narrative, see Gardener 2024, 68–70.
63 張克明與沈嵐 2001a, 28.
64 Timperley 1942.

1941, and he had barely hidden his eagerness to leave China.[65] In 1943, he was dismissed from his post in Melbourne.

Timperley's removal also arose from a broader shift in Chungking's international propaganda policy. By 1943, propaganda agents openly campaigned among the Allies, so hiding official provenance was of little significance.[66] As the Pacific War intensified, Tong sought to strengthen China's propaganda presence in Australia, recognising the strategic importance of both Chinese and non-Chinese Australian networks in amplifying China's message. Particular emphasis was placed on the role of the Chinese diaspora, whose involvement in publishing books, journals and pictorials allowed propaganda to be tailored to local sensibilities while promoting a favourable image of China.[67]

In this evolving context, it was believed that a qualified Chinese representative would better serve China's interests. Accordingly, Tong appointed Chau Kun-lin (巢坤霖) to succeed Timperley and reform the Melbourne office.[68] Chau was a carefully chosen candidate. Born in Sunwui (新會) of Kwangtung in 1885, he had been educated by Australians in Hong Kong and later graduated from Durham University and the University of London. Fluent in English, Mandarin and Cantonese, as well as having experience as chief postal and cable censor in 1939, Chau was well suited to the role of propagandist.[69]

Unlike Timperley, whose reliance on his Australian identity and on-again, off-again popularity with Chinese authorities limited his reach, Chau Kun-lin maximised the effectiveness of Chinese propaganda by embedding his operations within a triad of networks: official Chinese channels, diasporic Chinese communities and anglophone Australian circles. His trilingual fluency was complemented by an affable, erudite personality, marked by generosity towards the diaspora and warm hospitality extended to both Chinese and non-Chinese Australians.[70]

65 Tong 2005, 131.
66 曾虛白 1988, 323.
67 國宣處工作計劃, 1939–1944, 718(5)-10, SHAC.
68 國宣處工作計劃, 1939–1944, 718(5)-10, SHAC.
69 Chau 1945, 41.
70 For his personality, see 柳存仁 2002, 172–8.

In 1944, Chau strategically relocated the office from Melbourne to Sydney to capitalise on the city's denser Chinese diaspora and improve reach. Australian-born Chinese such as Gladys Shem (daughter of Harold Shem from Perth) were recruited as editorial staff responsible for overseeing all published materials.[71] Chau's network-building extended well beyond urban centres; his travels reached from Sydney and Melbourne to regional towns like Rockhampton and Ingham, where he typically delivered three speeches per stop to strengthen community ties and mobilise support.[72] Chau integrated seamlessly into local communities, appearing at cultural functions such as the Dragon Festival Ball as an active participant rather than an emissary.[73] His base in Sydney also facilitated closer collaboration with the Chinese consulate general, the local Kuomintang leadership and the Chinese legation in Canberra – networks that became vital conduits for his propaganda initiatives.[74] Chau's outreach extended to non-Chinese Australians as well, including members of Allied authorities based in Australia, with whom he cultivated cordial relations to enhance the credibility and reach of Chinese propaganda.[75] In this way, the Sydney office under Chau's stewardship evolved into the de facto centre of Chinese propaganda in Australia, coordinating efforts across official, diasporic and Australian lines to amplify China's wartime message with precision and purpose.

In 1944 alone, the Sydney office distributed more than 50,000 booklets alongside newsletters and a biweekly journal – each issue comprising approximately 310 copies.[76] In addition to numerous articles published in Australian periodicals, Chau Kun-lin delivered over 50 public addresses in support of China, both in person and over

---

71  *West Australian*, "Woman's realm," 1 September 1945, 10.
72  巢坤霖工作報告, 1943–1944, 718(4)-323, SHAC; The visit of Prof. K.L. Chau, 1944–1945, A8911, 316, 822102, NAA.
73  *Truth*, "The jottings of a lady about town," 3 June 1945, 29.
74  "He informs Australians about China", *Pix* no. 9 (1945): 3; Expenditure on Behalf of the Republic of China, 16 October 1944, A989, 1944/150/11/5, 183562, NAA.
75  巢坤霖工作報告, 1943–1944, 718(4)-323, SHAC.
76  中宣部致國宣處, 1942, 718(4)-311; 巢坤霖工作報告, 1943–1944, 718(4)-323, SHAC.

the Australian Broadcasting Commission airwaves, at the invitation of a wide range of bodies including the Australian Ministry of Commerce and the American military stationed in Australia.[77] Following Hollington Tong's directive to foster Australian interest in Chinese culture and society, a small library was established in Sydney, stocked with books on Chinese life, history and language.[78]

Chau's efforts were not only prolific but diplomatically astute. His sustained rapport with Australian authorities brought tangible rewards. In 1943, Wilfred Burchett, a correspondent for the Sydney *Daily Telegraph* who sympathised with Chinese communists,[79] intended to publish an article criticising the Kuomintang's incompetence and crediting the communists with most of the anti-Japanese victories. This article caught the attention of the Australian authorities, who promptly informed Chau and censored it. Burchett was also prohibited from broadcasting talks on similar themes. Chau and Hollington Tong appreciated this quick response.[80]

While Timperley and Chau advanced Chinese propaganda efforts in Australia, Chungking's broader propaganda strategy was undergoing a significant recalibration that was keen to project a more favourable image of the Chinese government and its wartime contributions. This was because Kuomintang China faced mounting criticism regarding its state-building efforts and military performance. Some within the Allies questioned whether China was a credible partner for democracies.[81] Meanwhile, Japanese propaganda persistently sought to delegitimise the Chungking regime on the international stage.[82] By 1942, Chinese authorities realised that continued emphasis on Japanese atrocities risked eroding China's moral capital and undermining the morale of its allies. Western governments, including those of the United States, Britain and Australia, warned Chungking that graphic reports of

---

77  國宣處工作報告, 1939–1945, 718(4)-239, SHAC.
78  國宣處工作進度報告, 1944, 718(4)-239, SHAC; Tong 2005, 129.
79  Knightley 1986, 3–12.
80  中澳關系及澳大利亞政情, 1944, 020-011502-0001, AH.
81  Knorr 2015, 169; Mitter 2013, 298, 312.
82  Ministry of External Affairs to Australian Legation in Chungking, 30 March 1942, A981, JAP 131, 177551, NAA.

Japanese brutality, especially against Westerners, were generating public unease at home. They recommended that only the most egregious cases be publicised.[83] Even Zeng Xubai (曾虛白), head of the International Department, conceded that constant exposure of Japanese outrages had begun to damage the prestige of the Kuomintang government itself.[84]

Chungking's recalibration was swift. It reformulated around three imperatives: to "reverse the Western stereotype of China"; to "secure the Kuomintang's hard-won international standing"; and to "counter overseas criticism of China".[85] More than a defensive gesture, this shift marked a bold attempt to claim a rightful seat at the table of international affairs from which China had long been excluded. China was now portrayed as a modernising nation in a bid to justify the Kuomintang's uneasy prominence among the Allied powers – a status that far outstripped China's actual strength. As Hollington Tong asserted, it had become urgent to elevate China's position as an equal among the leading nations.[86]

The results were pronounced and profound. Chinese journalists, long reluctant to portray their fallen compatriots as helpless victims, welcomed this rhetorical pivot.[87] Their support contributed to a dramatic reduction in the coverage of Japanese atrocities, while even official maps began to downplay the extent of Japanese occupation.[88] In propaganda distributed across Australia, depictions of Japanese brutality were now a whisper where once they were a roar.[89] Instead, publications highlighted China's pursuit of modernisation: political democratisation, economic stability, military effectiveness, social reform and growing international camaraderie with Australia and the major Allied powers.[90]

---

83  中宣部致國宣處, 1942, 718(4)-311, SHAC.
84  曾虛白 1988, 233.
85  國宣處工作報告, 1939–1945, 718(4)-239, SHAC.
86  Tong 1950, 159.
87  Coble 2015, 57–8.
88  Australian Legation to China to Australian Department of External Affairs, 18 March 1943, A989, 1943/540/3, 184430, NAA.
89  Chinese Ministry of Information 1944, 27; 1945d, 78; Timperley 1942.

Much of what Chungking now emphasised had already been anticipated by farsighted Chinese diplomats and diaspora elites in Australia. Yet what marked this new phase was a heightened focus on racial equality, not merely through mild overtures but as a key plank of propaganda. Following the repeal of America's Chinese Exclusion Act in 1943, China took aim at Australia's own "egoistic" White Australia policy.[91] No longer cloaked in euphemism, Chinese officials decried it as a contradiction of democratic values and "an echo of Hitler's parrot cry of racial supremacy". The word "white", they argued, should be struck from the national vocabulary, especially in light of China's indispensable role in shielding Australia from Japanese aggression. The accepted Chinese inferiority was also actively renegotiated. Propaganda drew parallels between Chinese and Australians, celebrating shared commitments to knowledge, culture and global citizenship. Chinese Australians were praised for their "truly cosmopolitan outlook", an asset attributed to their bilingualism and ability to bridge cultural divides. Canberra's anxieties about a "Chinese influx" were rebutted with assurances: China had neither the ambition nor the capacity for expansion due to the immense demands of postwar reconstruction.[92]

Juxtaposed with China's external projection as a "New China" was an increasingly uneasy accommodation of internal rivalry between the Kuomintang and Chinese Communist Party. The growing international sympathy for the communists put Chungking into an awkward bind that threatened the Kuomintang's prestige and legitimacy. This sympathy had its roots in solid ground. Historians have found that Chinese communists showed a remarkable ability to rise to shifting

---

90  國宣處工作報告, 1939–1945, 718(4)-239, SHAC; Chao 1944, 4–10, 39; Chinese Ministry of Information 1944, 21; 1945a, 20–2, 38, 42–6, 48–51; 1944b, 4–5; 1945c, 21; 1945d, 6–7, 40–6, 74–5; Taylor 1944, 15; Prof. Chau's Mission: Cultivating Friendship with China," Pix 13, no. 11 (1944): 15-17; China Information Bulletin, 29 August 1945, M1130, 61, 31415719, NAA; 中澳貿易, 17 August 1944, 020-991100-0182, AH.
91  澳洲華僑狀況, April 1945, 008-010602-00019-001, AH.
92  Chinese Migration and Overseas Chinese, 1943–1944, A989, 1944/554/7/1, 184465, NAA; Chinese Ministry of Information 1944, 18, 29, 46–7; 1945d, 28; *Maitland Mercury*, "Letters to the editor," 23 May 1944, 2; "Prof. Chau's Mission: Cultivating Friendship with China," *Pix* 13, no. 11 (1944): 16–17.

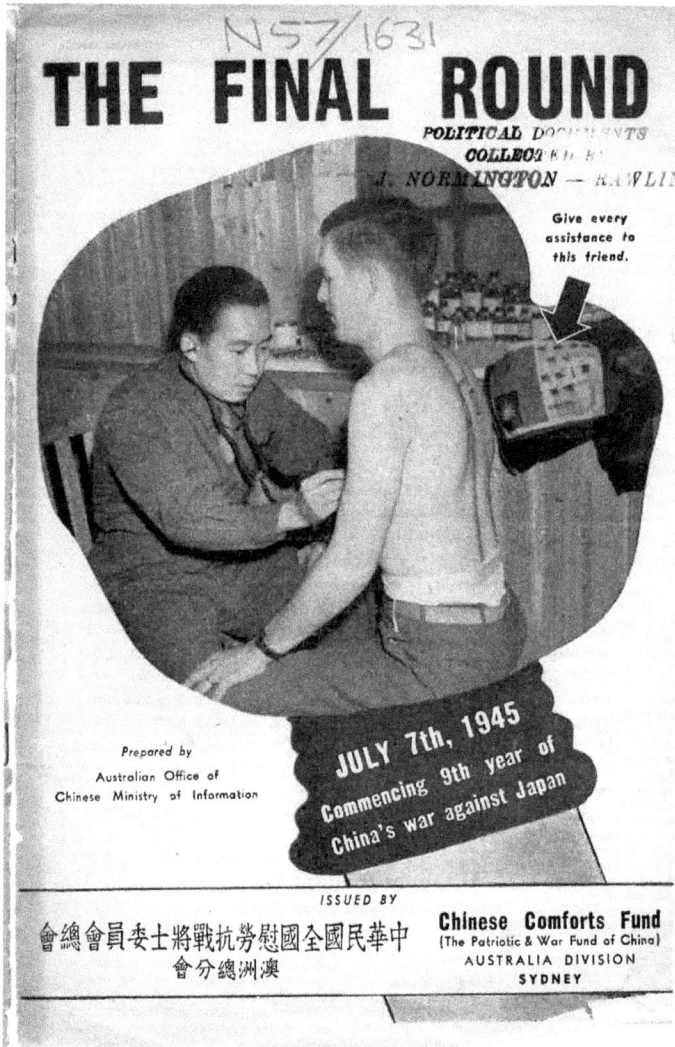

Figure 7.1 Cover of pamphlet, "The final round," Chinese Ministry of Information (1945d).

wartime situations, provide leadership and organise resistance while successfully controlling rural areas.[93] In contrast, many Australians perceived the Kuomintang as mired in internal power struggles, while the communists appeared resolutely committed to fighting the Japanese.[94] Australian leftists in particular displayed a pronounced enthusiasm for their Chinese comrades,[95] going so far as to translate Mao Tse-tung's (毛澤東) *China's New Democracy* into English and publish it in 1945.[96] They also collaborated with their Chinese Australian counterparts to promote communism within the Chinese community.[97] This apparent affinity for Chinese communists set alarm bells ringing among Chinese propagandists. Hollington Tong complained that Chinese communism was "innocuous . . . in the mind of the free world" and nurtured an escalating unfavourable sentiment against Chungking.[98] Chinese propaganda therefore came to grips with this tendency by reiterating the status of the communist party that was "virtually a separate regime" with a nature distinct from that of Australian political parties.[99]

Propaganda operated not only through language but also through the visual field, where photography functioned as a strategic medium of persuasion. War photography has often been perceived as a neutral and truthful form of documentation,[100] thereby frequently mobilised to serve as "unflinching witness" to what are in fact selective truths produced by multiple stakeholders.[101] Illustrations other than photographs can also heighten propaganda efficacy when published alongside the recorded events they depict.[102] Compared with efforts

93  Gatu 2008, 30–31; Lary 2010, 150.
94  Macdonald 1944, 50; Frank Stuckey, interviewed by Paul Macgregor, Australia-China Oral History Project (Kew, 18 April and 1 July, 1994), NLA.
95  League Against Imperialism 1934; *Maryborough Chronicle, Wide Bay and Burnett Advertiser*, "Chinese situation," 26 July 1935, 4.
96  Mao Tse-tung 1945.
97  Martínez 2021, 225–7.
98  Tong 2005, 143.
99  Chinese Ministry of Information 1945a, 6; 1945c, 12; "Prof. Chau Clarify KMT-CCP Controversy", *Pix* 16, no. 9 (1945): 4.
100  Foster 2016, 254.
101  Brothers 1997, 2, 17, 24, 28; Couchman 2011, 82; E. Edwards 1994, 7–8; Lemagny and Rouillé 1987, 9; Sontag 2003, 46; V. Williams 1994, 9, 13.

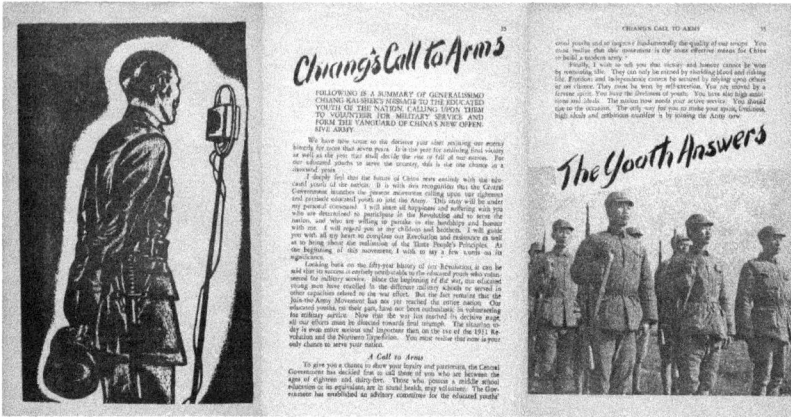

Figure 7.2 Chinese Ministry of Information (1945a).

prior to 1941, visual imagery became crucial in Chinese propaganda in Australia to convey the narratives to the public imagination of Australians. The overarching visual themes reflected the shifting priorities of wartime propaganda. Photographs no longer focused solely on Japanese atrocities but emphasised Chinese resilience, modernity and solidarity. Images portrayed industrious civilians and composed soldiers, serene domestic scenes unmarked by conflict, and a diverse citizenry unified across class, age and gender. These visuals performed ideological work: they rearticulated China not as a passive victim but as a stable, mobilised and modernising nation-state under Kuomintang leadership. Symbols of party legitimacy, portraits of Chiang Kai-shek and Sun Yat-sen and Kuomintang flags were prominently featured, while photos of Chinese aiding Allied soldiers or appearing alongside Westerners projected racial parity and geopolitical legitimacy.[103] Thus, the visual rhetoric contested racial hierarchies and asserted China's claim to modernity and equal standing among nations. After the war,

---

102 Lewinski 1978, 11.
103 Chinese Comforts Fund 1945, cover, 5–6; Chinese Ministry of Information 1945a, 32–37; 1945b, cover; Taylor 1944, 22; Chao 1944, cover, 22.

similar imagery persisted, now stripped of combat motifs but repurposed to gain Western support for the Kuomintang in its emerging civil conflict with the Chinese Communist Party.[104] In this sense, wartime visual propaganda partly laid the ideological groundwork for the Kuomintang's postwar diplomatic ambitions.

The Chinese propaganda campaign in the 1940s appeared to be influential in Australia, including among the Americans stationed in the country. The publications circulated by the Sydney office were well received by the Allied Land Forces Headquarters in Victoria who later distributed them to their education branches, library service and research section.[105] The University of Melbourne, encouraged by Chau, planned to establish an institute of Chinese studies. The perception of China by Australian-born Chinese and white Australians was reportedly positively enhanced.[106] Chau Kun-lin's office also received thousands of queries in relation to Chinese affairs and culture, including politics and cooking recipes, from people of diverse backgrounds.[107] Some Australian authorities and intellectuals began to re-evaluate China's values and integrate reflections in favour of China into their education courses. Criticism of Australian racism and China's commercial significance were recognised in the teaching programs of the Australian Army Education Service.[108] Much of the content was supplied by Chinese propagandists.[109] In the opinion of Frederic Eggleston, Chau's mission was so "successful".[110]

104 Chinese Ministry of Information 1945c, 35–9; 1946a, 16–17; 1946b, 10; Australia's importance to China by now located in sponsoring postwar reconstruction. See Albinski 1965, 6; Andrews 1985, 127; Strahan 1996, 51; Siam 2015, 63.
105 Correspondence between Colonel Wilcher and Chau Kun-lin, 1944–1945, MP742/1, 89/4/282, 4938572, NAA.
106 巢坤霖工作報告, November 1943–December 1944, 718(4)-323, SHAC.
107 "He Informs Australians about China," Pix 16, no. 9 (1945), 3; 巢坤霖工作報告, 1943–1944, 718(4)-323, SHAC.
108 Pratt 1942, Parts 1–4; Australian Army Education Service 1946; R.A.A.F. Rehabilitation Section 1942.
109 Margery Puisford to H.V. Dunphy, 17 January 1945, 3051769; Wang Chi-kuang to R.B. Madgwick, 24 August 1944, MP742/1, 89/4/282, 4938572, NAA. For attendance rate, see Pratt 1942, Part 3; Anonymous Correspondent 1941.

The Chinese in this war has shown the world that, for endurance, courage, and tenacity of purpose, he has no better: given modern equipment and training in its use he has proven more than a match for the Japanese aggressor.

One hundred thousand strong, well-equipped, and trained by Allied instructors, these Chinese youths shall form the vanguard of China's New Offensive Army.

Figure 7.3 Chinese Ministry of Information (1945a).

Despite his success, Chau Kun-lin's work was far from untroubled. Ironically, one of the most formidable challenges came not from abroad but from the very government he represented. As the Pacific War tilted in favour of the Allies, Australia's geopolitical importance to China waned, and Chau's office slipped into financial inertia. Despite receiving an annual allocation of 15,600 yuan, higher than those for the Canadian and Mexican branches, funding remained static in 1944, even as the British and Indian offices saw their budgets swell to 36,000 yuan.[111] Chungking's frugality, masked as fiscal prudence, proved another impediment to improving the efficiency of overseas propaganda work.[112]

---

110 Diary of Eggleston, 1, Papers of Frederic William Eggleston, NLA.
111 中宣部國宣處特別經常費支出計算書, 1942–1944, 718(5)-9, SHAC.

The material limitations were no less discouraging. The office, initially staffed by just Chau and one assistant, never exceeded five personnel.[113] Unlike other branches, it was not even furnished with propaganda films, leaving Hsu Mo to petition for them on Chau's behalf.[114] Structural shortcomings aside, the content itself was fraught with contradictions. Narratives celebrating gender equality were often undercut by portrayals of Chinese women in traditionally submissive roles, while cultural promotion veered into re-Orientalising tropes, neatly packaged under exoticist labels like "Chinese Oddities".[115]

To compound matters, the guidance sent from Chungking was often vaguer than visionary, sometimes even comically careless, such as misidentifying Sydney or Melbourne as the capital of Australia.[116] The symbolic and material neglect signalled an unmistakable reality: the Australian office, once central to China's wartime messaging, was quietly slipping from Chungking's radar.

The entrenched political fault lines within the Chinese Australian community, as Chapter 5 has shown, complicated Chau Kun-lin's propaganda enterprise. The animosity from Kuomintang opponents proved inextinguishable. In 1941, when Loh Kai-tze was dispatched by Chungking to Australia to oversee the local Kuomintang party's affairs and further Chinese fundraising campaigns, his entry was nearly derailed by an anonymous denunciation accusing him of smuggling large quantities of goods. Although Loh weathered the initial storm, local critic William C. Kwan escalated the controversy by writing protest letters to Wu Tieh-cheng (吳鐵城) and Chiang Kai-shek, condemning Loh for a litany of alleged improprieties, ranging from financial malfeasance involving Kuomintang funds to a libertine private life and self-aggrandising claims of being Chiang's personal envoy.

---

112 軍事委員會致國宣處, 28 June 1944, 718(5)-11, SHAC; Memorandum, J.D.O. Sullivan, 22 February 1946, A1067, IC46/4/7/5, 191715, NAA.

113 "Prof. Chau's Mission: Cultivating Friendship with China," *Pix* 13, no. 11 (1944): 16–17.

114 中澳關系及澳大利亞政情, 020-011502-0001, AH.

115 Chinese Ministry of Information 1945a, 31; 1945c, 74–75.

116 國宣處工作進度報告, 1943, 718(5)-10; 國宣處工作報告, 1942, 718(5)-44; 設置駐外重要使領館宣傳特派員, 1939–1944, 718(5)-12, SHAC.

Figure 7.4 Chinese Ministry of Information (1945b).

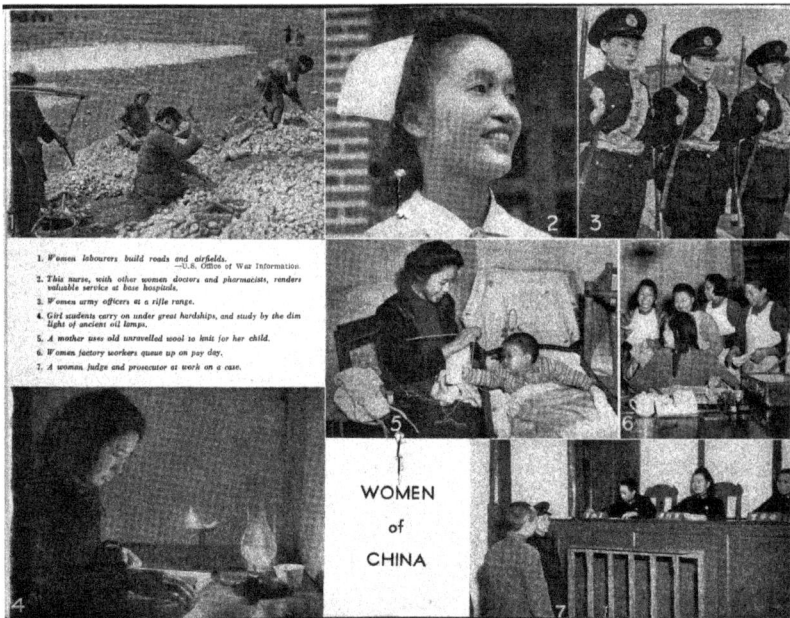

Figure 7.5 Chinese Ministry of Information (1945b).

Kwan framed Loh's arrival as "not only an insult to all Chinese but also very discourteous to friendly nations".[117] The accusations did not abate. Loh was later reported, again anonymously, for disseminating films depicting communist guerrilla warfare. Ironically, the footage in question documented Kuomintang-led guerrilla resistance in North China. Despite Loh's defence and the Australian Kuomintang's clarifications, the orchestrated campaign succeeded: Loh was dismissed and sent back to China.[118]

A similar political vendetta unfolded against Tsao Wen-yen in 1941, though with a different script. John Zhao (趙孫), manager of the Sino-Australian Trading Company (中澳商行), accused Tsao of

117 William C. Kwan to Woo To-Chan, 1941, 173582, NAA.
118 海外部處長駱介子宣慰僑胞, 31 July 1943, 020-011507-0012, AH.

illicitly overcharging remittances and colluding financially with the enemy (Japan). Nor was Zhao's bitterness confined to Tsao alone; he cast aspersions on Tsao's colleagues as well, claiming they were more adept at exploiting Chinese Australians than protecting them.[119] In 1942, Chen Li (陳利) lodged a similar complaint with the Overseas Chinese Affairs Commission, accusing Tsao of misappropriating funds subscribed for war bonds.[120] In both cases, internal factionalism within the diaspora became a potent force, capable of derailing official efforts and undermining the very propaganda infrastructure Chungking sought to consolidate abroad.

Challenges to Chau Kun-lin's enterprise also came, somewhat paradoxically, from within the official Chinese ranks in Australia. Although Chau was formally tasked with leading China's propaganda efforts in the country, local Chinese officials operated with a notable degree of autonomy, and, at times, ideological divergence. Some were markedly more nationalist than Chau, whose messaging was measured and conciliatory. Their more strident tone, while ostensibly patriotic, risked alarming Canberra and inadvertently undermining Chau's work. Tsao Wen-yen provides a revealing case in point. His public engagements embodied what Mark Finnane has termed "cultural diplomacy", portraying China as both an ancient civilisation and rapidly modernising, often through lectures and carefully crafted publications.[121] Yet Tsao's brand of diplomacy came wrapped in a robust nationalism that eventually proved untenable. His consistent disapproval of British imperialism and colonial governance unsettled Australian authorities, who came to regard him as "intensively nationalistic, non-cooperative and even obstructionist". Under increased surveillance, Tsao's activities were closely monitored, and Hsu Mo ultimately pressed Chungking to recall him in 1943, less for policy failure than for fear that his next speech might irreparably compromise Sino-Australian goodwill.[122]

---

119 億中公司駐墨爾本經理趙約翰案, 18 January 1941, 020-011507-0022, AH.
120 侨委会公函, 10 April 1942, 3(6)-1293, SHAC.
121 Finnane 2012, 223–44.

## Pro-China Australian lobbies

The Pacific War marked the institutionalisation of interracial collaboration between ethnic Chinese and Anglophone Australians, catalysing a surge of pro-China organisations across nearly every Australian state and elevating China's presence with unprecedented visibility. These wartime alliances stood in stark contrast to the more ad hoc, humanitarian impulses and opportunistic endeavours of the 1930s. From Melbourne's Australia–China Co-operation Association in 1939 to Brisbane's China Society of Australia in 1941, Perth's Australia–China Association in 1942 and Sydney's Australia–China Association in 1944, these groups reflected a strategic and sustained engagement with China's wartime struggle. Their memberships boasted figures with both public renown and political clout, such as Ian Clunies Ross.

While most of these associations were nominally headed by white Australians, they enjoyed robust backing from Chinese authorities and considerable support from local Chinese communities. The China Society of Australia, for instance, was fronted by W.G. Goddard but operated under the patronage of prominent Chinese diplomats such as Pao Chun-jien and Foreign Minister Wang Chung-hui (王寵惠). Leadership roles were shared by influential Chinese Australians from diverse ideological backgrounds such as Frank Yow, who had communist leanings, and Arthur King Koi, a linchpin of multiple Chinese organisations.[123] The Sydney Australia–China Association cultivated an even more intimate relationship with Chungking: headquartered in the same Trust Building on 155 King Street as Chau Kun-lin's office, it received direct cables from the Chinese Ministry of Information. These associations, though interracial in composition, became nodes in a transnational network of diplomacy, ideology and

---

122 Cablegram, 29 September 1943, A989, 1943/195/1/9/2, 183637; Press Reports, 1942–1943, PP227/7, 1942/C1412, 1545920, NAA; 澳大利亞政情, 1943, 020-011501-0001, AH.
123 China Society of Australia, 12 February 1941, A981, CHIN 95 PART 1, 173577, NAA.

information, each revealing the calculated choreography behind wartime solidarity.[124]

The heterogeneous political terrain within Chinese Australian communities significantly shaped the composition and character of wartime pro-China associations. In Perth, the Australia–China Association bore a strong resemblance to Kuomintang fundraising operations, drawing its strength from long-standing clan-affiliated networks centred on the Chung Wah Association. Leading figures such as Alex and Harold Shem – vice-president and treasurer respectively – partly embedded the association into these traditional networks.[125] The Australia–China Association in Sydney, by contrast, operated through broader social channels, incorporating prominent men and women from both China-born and Australian-born backgrounds. Familiar names such as T.Y. Lin, Rose Chuey, Alice Lim Kee and William Liu signalled its more expansive social footprint.[126] A striking outlier was Melbourne's Australia–China Co-operation Association, whose leadership consisted largely of non-Chinese and appeared notably disconnected from the already established Chinese Citizens Society.[127]

Though formally unaffiliated, these pro-China groups formed a dense web of collaboration, amplifying Chinese wartime propaganda and embedding it within Australian civic discourse. They shared overlapping objectives and rhetorical strategies, frequently exchanged personnel, and even drew support from segments of Australia's left-wing communities.[128] At their core lay a unified commitment to the modernisation of China under Kuomintang leadership, the projection of Chinese unity and wartime contributions, the strengthening of Sino-Australian ties across cultural and economic domains, and a pointed repudiation of Australian racial discrimination. By branding China as the "Russia of the East" and a potential saviour of Australia, these associations pushed back against entrenched Orientalist tropes

---

124  Cable No. 47, 1 February 1945, A659, 1945/1/807, 81137, NAA.
125  Australia–China Association, 1 March 1944, 1609496, NAA.
126  Australia–China Association 1944; 1945a.
127  Burchett 1941.
128  *Argus*, "China Society formed," 16 April 1943, 2; Australia–China Association, 1 March 1944, 1609496, NAA.

and reframed China as both partner and protector in the Pacific War effort.[129]

This ideological rebranding was realised through a medley of public campaigns: booklets, lectures, language classes, photo exhibitions and fundraising drives. The Australia–China Co-operation Association alone distributed over 15,000 publications in Melbourne; Perth's Australia–China Association claimed to have raised approximately £7,367 between 1942 and 1945, funnelling the proceeds via the Premier's Office to Chungking.[130] National networks of pro-China activism were also entangled with international ones: the Australia–China Co-operation Association, for instance, played a crucial role in supporting Rewi Alley's Industrial Cooperative movement, raising both funds and recruits for China's wartime industrial revival.[131]

The shared missions of wartime pro-China organisations did not flatten the ideological diversity within them. Among these groups, the Australia–China Co-operation Association stood out as the most radical. Though founded in 1939, it gained significant momentum under Aldred Barker's leadership in 1941 and soon claimed to wield considerable influence over Australian public opinion.[132] Within its purported 300-strong membership, comprising Chinese and white Australians from varied social strata, several members exhibited what officials termed "extreme political views", notably a sympathy for Chinese communism.[133] They aimed to demonstrate "there was a strong body of opinion in Australia that was loyal to China".[134]

---

129  Australia–China Association 1945b; Australia-China Co-operation Movement 1940; Australian Institute of International Affairs 1941, *China Today* (4): 9, 25; Barker 1944; Burchett 1941; 1944b; Burchett and Burchett 1943; Galbraith 1943.
130  Australia–China Association 1945a; Burchett 1944b, 15–16; *West Australian*, "China's Future," 22 October 1945, 4.
131  Mavis Ming to Rewi Alley, 19 February 1945, 3051769, NAA.
132  *Age*, "Co-operative Movement: aid for China," 17 October 1939, 10; Appendix C to Security Summary No. 63, 23 December 1943, BP242/1, Q30600, 1031901, NAA.
133  Appendix C to Security Summary No. 63, 23 December 1943, BP242/1, Q30600, 1031901; W.B. Simpson to the Secretary of the Department of External Affairs, 16 December 1944, A989, 1944/650/21, 184787, NAA.

For example, Roy Geechoun, a Chinese fruiterer and member of the Australian Communist Party, conducted educational classes on China. The Burchetts, George and his three sons – Wilfred, Winston and Clive – were also prominent figures, widely known for their staunch pro-communist stance. Despite their ideological leanings, the Australia–China Co-operation Association's leadership maintained cordial relations with Chinese consular officials, attending social functions and promoting shared ideals.[135] Their collaboration was anchored in a mutual investment in a strong China and an egalitarian Chinese–Australian relationship, though the paths they envisioned to achieve these goals diverged sharply.

Of all pro-China groups, the Australia–China Co-operation Association was the most forthright in its challenge to Australian racism, albeit within certain ideological limits. George Burchett in particular attacked the White Australia policy as a "subterfuge" masking racial exclusion beneath a veneer of national interest. He denounced it as "unscientific" and out of sync with "a changing world", calling for its replacement by a quota-based system.[136] In essence, he advocated not for the dismantling of White Australia, but for its preservation through more selective inclusion, an argument that ironically reproduced the very logic of racialised nationalism it claimed to oppose. This paradox was not unique. Even Ambrose Pratt, an outspoken critic of racial exclusion, demonstrated similar contradictions, lauding Chinese Australians for displaying "an agreeable anxiety to please us".[137] Such discursive entanglements echoed broader wartime patterns in the United States, where advocacy for racial liberalisation often remained tethered to strategic preferences and paternalistic tones.[138]

The association's blunt rhetoric, however, occasionally outpaced the cautious diplomacy favoured by the Chinese state. While the group's efforts aligned with China's interest in loosening immigration barriers,

---

134  Burchett 1941, 1–2, 5; Society of Friends, 1939, 1609496, NAA.
135  Martínez 2021, 227.
136  Burchett 1944a, 4, 16, 23–4.
137  Pratt 1942, 1.
138  Wu 2005, 119–84.

their assaults on the White Australia policy exceeded what officials such as Hsu Mo deemed prudent. Hsu advised that any appeal for relaxation should be carefully framed in order to "avoid unnecessary troubles", emphasising the political neutrality of Chinese Australians and their eagerness to collaborate with white Australians.[139] Chinese authorities hoped to minimise official Chinese involvement in sensitive racial matters and believed that leaving such provocations to sympathetic white Australians was a wise move. Yet the proximity between consular officers and the association blurred this tactic. The group's outspoken campaigns raised eyebrows in Canberra, fuelling suspicions that such pro-China activism might be orchestrated more centrally than it appeared.[140] For Chinese diplomats already walking a tightrope, the association's enthusiasm proved a double-edged sword.

Conversely, the Australia–China Associations in Perth and Sydney adopted a more subdued approach in their activism that largely sided in line with Chungking. The Perth association reported approximately 260 members, including 60 Chinese Australians, while the Sydney chapter boasted a membership of about 400.[141] Both associations also encouraged Australian women to participate in China's war effort.[142] Rather than lobbying for changes to Australia's immigration regime, the Australia–China Associations concentrated on laying the groundwork for future Chinese migration and cultivating public goodwill through familiar, palatable themes – trade cooperation, cultural exchange and a rhetoric of mutual respect.[143] Their strategy aimed less at confrontation than at constructing a framework of parity between China and Australia. Despite their proximity to the more assertive Australia–China Co-operation Association, they made clear that "their

---

139  改善旅澳華僑待遇 (二), 1938, 020-011507-0002, AH.
140  W.B. Simpson to Deputy Director of Security in Queensland, 12 November 1943, BP242/1, Q30600, 1031901, NAA.
141  W.B. Simpson to the Secretary of the Department of External Affairs, 16 December 1944, A989, 1944/650/21, 184787, NAA.
142  Australia–China Association 1944; *West Australian*, "Woman's Realm," 30 October 1944, 3.
143  *West Australian*, "Help China," 12 January 1943, 5; W.B. Simpson to the Secretary of the Department of External Affairs, 16 December 1944, A989, 1944/650/21, 184787; Chinese organisations, 1 February 1945, 3051769, NAA.

ideals were not the same" and that the former had "gone further".[144] Their tempered approach won favour in Chungking, yet even these measured efforts were not immune to Australian suspicion,[145] underscoring the persistent anxieties that trailed Chinese diplomacy, radical or restrained.

Interestingly, not all pro-China lobbies were embraced by the very communities they sought to serve. Racial dynamics often proved as formidable as political ones. This was particularly evident in the case of the China Society of Australia in Brisbane, which paralleled the aforementioned organisations in its contributions to the pro-China movement.[146] Its founder, W.G. Goddard, gained prominence as a radio commentator on 4BC, attracting Chinese officialdom with his zealous support for Republican China and strident denunciations of the White Australia policy. By the 1940s, Goddard was widely regarded as an authority on Asia.[147] A core ambition of the society was to bridge racial divides by fostering inclusive membership. Yet many Chinese nationalists refused to join an organisation chaired by a European, viewing it as yet another intrusion into Chinese affairs. In response, they established the Chinese Citizens Association, whose membership remained resolutely Chinese.[148] The society consequently became something of a one-man platform for Goddard, whose lectures, though attended by Chinese residents, reportedly provoked discontent, especially for his glorification of Sun Yat-sen.[149]

As the war neared its end, the influence of pro-China organisations only expanded. The Australia–China Co-operation Association alone claimed hundreds of affiliated members. Their growing prominence

---

144 *Sun*, "Quotas of Chinese migrants advocated," 10 December 1944, 8.
145 Australian Friends of China, 1940, PAM 951.042 A938L, Sir Louis Matheson Library, University of Monash, Melbourne; W.B. Simpson to the Secretary of the Department of External Affairs, 16 December 1944, A989, 1944/650/21, 184787, NAA.
146 *Courier-Mail*, "Brisbane to launch first China Society," 12 February 1941, 5; "China Society," 8 March 1941, 4; "Sees 'D' Day for China," 21 June 1944, 3; Goddard 1945.
147 Taylor 2007, 130–1; 2009, 212.
148 Chinese Societies in Queensland, 25 October 1941, 314820, NAA.
149 R.F. Lincoln's Correspondence, 9 August 1943, 1609496, NAA.

unsettled Australian security agencies, who warned that these organisations – buoyed by elite Chinese Australian figures, official Chinese backing and respected public supporters – should not be underestimated.[150] Their concerns were further sharpened by the vocal resistance of Chinese Australians to racial prejudice. When Brisbane's Chinese population increased in the 1940s, Justice Brennan, a white Brisbaner, recycled classic racist tropes to frame Chinese migrants as a social threat. His remarks were sharply rebuked by Chinese Australians such as Mar Leong Wah and C. Lai, who criticised British colonial hypocrisy, the discriminatory practices of Australian customs, and the prevailing "Super-White-Man" attitude. In their eyes, Chinese migrants who had contributed to the war effort deserved not suspicion, but respect, and at least a modicum of goodwill.[151]

Pro-China propaganda conducted by both ethnic Chinese and white Australians helped cultivate a shifting social milieu increasingly sympathetic to China, contributing to what historians have identified as one of the Pacific War's most striking legacies: the disruption of entrenched white supremacist ideologies among Australians.[152] This period witnessed a wave of political and intellectual re-engagement with China, as commentators began to reassess its cultural value, economic potential and political future in national, transnational and international contexts.[153] Some acknowledged the historical imbalance in Sino-Australian relations, recognising that Chinese Australians could make a "most valuable contribution" to society if granted "equal opportunities with whites".[154] Public interest in China surged. For instance, the Expeditionary Film Unit in Sydney proposed producing a documentary for the Chinese Ministry of Information, focusing on

---

150  W.B. Simpson to the Secretary of the Department of External Affairs, 16 December 1944, A989, 1944/650/21, 184787; Australia-China Co-operation Association, 4 February 1944, 1609496, NAA.
151  *Daily Telegraph*, "Letters to the editor," 4 January 1945, 10; "Letters to the editor," 8 January 1945, 8.
152  Lake and Reynolds 2008, 339–41; Thorne 1978, 7; Walker 2012, 299.
153  R.A.A.F. Education Service 1946; Blumer and Rowland 1944; Goldin 2011; Martin 1948; 1944; 1943; Pratt 1942; Ross 1945; Appeal for Hostel for Chinese Seamen, 24 May 1942, 31534643, NAA.
154  Blumer and Rowland 1944, 74.

postwar reconstruction, tourism, commerce and cultural heritage, designed to present China to the world through a "judicious interpretation".[155] Chinese culture and language gained visibility in both religious, print and educational institutions, with proposals to include Chinese as a subject in Intermediate and Leaving Certificate examinations in New South Wales.[156] Contemporary observers noted a perceptible softening in Australian attitudes towards Chinese migrants.[157] This moment, as David Walker has argued, reflects Australia's cyclical rediscovery of its proximity to Asia.[158]

Yet for all its momentum, Chinese propaganda failed to embed this new vision of China into Australian social memory or to translate goodwill into durable policy shifts in Canberra. The Australian Army Education Service, for example, resisted any fundamental change to the White Australia policy, clinging to the racial orthodoxy that Asian immigration posed an existential threat.[159] Orientalist and racist tropes remained embedded in popular publications for both adults and children, where China was still portrayed as stagnant and immutable.[160] Despite heightened diplomatic engagement, Canberra ultimately delayed, and then failed, to formalise any treaty with China.[161]

A key impediment to the success of Chinese propaganda was the difference between its idealised portrayals and the lived realities encountered by Australians who travelled to or resided in wartime China. Journalists, soldiers and diplomats complained loudly about public insecurity, political corruption and military frustrations.[162] As Eggleston said, the portrayal of China in the propaganda was often

---

155 Proposed Production of Documentary Films in China, 2 November 1945, A4144, 92/1945, 1713662, NAA.
156 Blumer and Arrowsmith 1943; Chiang Kai-shek 1942; Church Missionary Society 1944; Embery 1945; Fenwick 1945, 22; Kuhn, Hatton and Cooke 1944; Martin 1946a; 1946b; Matthew 1942; Sadler 1942; 1944; Soong 1942.
157 Loh 1989, 74.
158 Walker 2012, 1.
159 McBride 1944, 2–13.
160 Bushells Tea Company 1932; Castleton 1944; Mackie 1944; O'Harris 1946; Pirani 1945; Sisters of the Cross 1948–49, 9–10; Welsh 1945.
161 Williams 2021a, 145.

"quite false" in that strict Chinese censorship lead to the exclusion of Chinese hardship and exaggerated accounts of victories.[163] While censorship suppressed many unfavourable accounts, glimpses of wartime China nevertheless reached Australia through published travel writings and diplomatic correspondence. For example, China's propaganda aimed to dispel concerns that it wanted Australia to repeal the White Australia policy. In reality, Chungking was making moves to encourage emigration and export labourers while raising concerns about discriminatory treatments imposed on Chinese Australians.[164] Australian diplomats in China saw this and efficiently warned Canberra to dispel these efforts.[165] Thus, Chinese propaganda contended with contested views and lingering doubts about Chinese modernisation and its war effort.[166]

Despite their alliance, Australian authorities neither trusted China nor Chinese Australians. Downplaying racial thinking was Canberra's wartime strategy to undercut Japanese propaganda and not estrange Asian allies.[167] Close surveillance was imposed on Chinese officials, censoring their correspondence with Chungking and suspecting some of them of sabotage in collaboration with Japan.[168] Chinese Australians, believed by Canberra to be of importance to China as "a source of remittances" and as "potential source for political influence", were

---

162  Begley 1995, 19–52; Johnston 1948, 188–9; Noonan 1945, 77–184; "China", Papers of Keith Officer, 1911–1969, MS 2629, Box 7, 4–5, 12; Gordon King, Papers of Bill Harman, 1938–1965, MS 7724, 5, NLA.

163  Eggleston to Minister of External Affairs, 8 February 1944, A989, 1944/554/7/1, 184465, NAA.

164  改善旅澳華僑待遇 (二), 1938, 020-011507-0002; 1944–1948, 020-011507-0003; 澳洲華僑狀況, April 1945, 008-010602-00019-001, AH.

165  Chinese Migration and Overseas Chinese, 1943–1944, A989, 1944/554/7/1, 184465; Keith Officer's Report, 1945, 551440; Overseas Chinese Affairs, 1943, A4144, 181/1943, 237569, NAA; 澳大利亞政情, 1943, 020-011501-0001, AH.

166  Hasluck 1980, 101; 中澳關系及澳大利亞政情, 08 February 1944, 020-011502-0001, AH.

167  Hodge 1992, 95.

168  Complaint by Mrs Trixeena Hudson, 6 January 1942, C320, C21, 1495515; Chinese Legation Complaint, 22 July 1943, A989, 1943/235/1/2/8, 183714; B. Bundykin to Anstey Wynes, 15 November 1942, A981, CHIN 195, 173701; Colonel Wang, 2 April 1943, 466983, NAA.

likewise under surveillance, watched closely for their activities and opinions "antagonistic" towards White Australia.[169] They were considered aliens by the *National Security Regulations Act* 1939 and even requested identification badges to avoid being profiled as Japanese by white Australians, who collectively racialised people of Asian descent.[170] Despite visible political fragmentations among Chinese Australians, and between them and Chungking, Canberra still saw them as affiliated with their homeland and expected them to transmit any valuable information to China.[171] Ironically, it was White Australia that constantly declined many of the Chinese Australians who proactively registered for its war effort and it was China that encouraged diasporic Chinese to contribute to the Australian war effort.[172] Soong Mei-ling and Pao Chun-jien, for example, urged the Chinese in Warwick to contribute to Australia's war effort "in recognition for what the Australian people had done for China."[173] Canberra itself noticed that the Chinese government mobilised those who had previously refused to support the war effort due to Australian racism.[174]

For the Australian public, Chinese propaganda in the 1940s largely failed to capture their attention. With few Australian troops involved, China's War of Resistance remained a distant concern. As Selwyn Speight pointed out, media coverage of China was squeezed by the escalating battles in Europe. The general public, therefore, likely underestimated the scale of China's suffering – how thoroughly it was bombarded by the Japanese, the countless lives at risk and the everyday hardships endured by the Chinese population.[175] Much of the

---

169 Colonel Wang, 3 March 1943, 466983; Note on the Chinese Overseas Affairs Commission, 20 October 1947, A433, 1947/2/5303, 3095371, NAA.

170 Memorandum, 14 March 1942, A981, CHIN 6, 173454; Interview with Chinese Consul General, 21 March 1942, C320, C27, 1495527, NAA; Tan 2006, 70–3.

171 Kodo, 4 September 1944, 1609496, NAA.

172 For Australian racism stopping Chinese Australians from devoting themselves to Australia's cause, see Ling 2001, 35, 42, 49, 71.

173 *Warwick Daily News*, "Chinese flags," 17 June 1941, 2.

174 The problem of post-war overseas affairs, October 1943, A433, 1947/8/5303, 3095371, NAA.

propaganda also seemed foreign and unfamiliar to Australians, further intensifying the sense of a distant and somewhat abstract war.[176]

While some Australian press highlighted the China front, and certain white Australians expressed solidarity with China's calls for racial equality, occasionally sparking debates with advocates of the White Australia policy,[177] most Australians remained fixated on racial purity. They resisted any change to the White Australia policy, despite a preference for Chinese over non-English European immigrants.[178] Even a few members who delivered staunch support in alignment with China's agenda sustained their Orientalised views of the country.[179] The racialised narrative of the Pacific War, both during and after the conflict, made little room for the inconveniently stark contrast between China's long-term resistance against Japan and Australia's panic at the mere prospect of a small portion of the enemy sweeping through South-East Asia.

## Conclusion

Official participation from Chungking was a constant presence in the Chinese propaganda efforts in Australia. Following the centralisation of Chinese international propaganda apparatus in 1937, Chungking adeptly mobilised a web of transnational resources, ranging from Australian sojourners in China to non-governmental networks bringing the two nations together to counter Japanese misinformation and cultivate Australian sympathy. With the outbreak of the Pacific War, Australia's strategic importance grew in Chinese eyes, prompting a notable expansion and institutionalisation of propaganda activities on

---

175  Letters to Jo, 1 July 1943; Letters to Perry, 16 October 1944, 2, 6, Papers of Selwyn Speight, NLA.

176  曾虛白 1981, 311.

177  Borrie 1947; Coatney 2021, 97; Dixon 1945, 15; Report, 6 July 1944, A989, 1944/150/5/1/10, 183523, NAA; *Age*, "Letters to the editor," 11 March 1944, 2; Immigration Reform Group 1962, 25.

178  Huck 1968, 66–7; McCallum 1947; Saunders 1994.

179  Wilfred Burchett to Parents, 3 June 1944, Papers of Wilfred Burchett, 1944–1977, MS 10254, Box3, State Library of Victoria, Melbourne.

Australian soil. These efforts culminated in the establishment of formal propaganda nodes staffed by Chinese officials and Anglo-Australians, and the rise of pro-China Australian lobbies, sponsored by Chinese authorities, which effectively amplified Kuomintang China's voice. Yet despite this well-coordinated campaign, the broader goal of reshaping Australian public opinion remained elusive. Calls for racial and national equality were routinely deflected, revealing the limited success of Chinese propaganda in a settler society still clinging to its own hierarchies of whiteness and geopolitical anxieties.

# Conclusion

The period between 1931 and 1945 saw the relationship between China and Australia being shaped more by the Chinese and broader Asian diasporas than by the diplomatic or economic connections that have traditionally been the main focus of historians.[1] This relationship was primarily realised through proactive Chinese propaganda efforts in Australia, in which the Chinese Australian community and their diasporic experiences and identities played indispensable roles. These efforts not only reorganised the social and political landscapes within Chinese Australian communities but also reshaped interracial networks and racial boundaries between Chinese and non-Chinese Australians. Through this process, the China–Australia relationship evolved into something more complex and intertwined, effectively challenging the conventional notion of a distant and dispassionate alliance between the two nations.

The propaganda efforts directed towards the Australian public were characterised by a collaboration between diasporic Chinese elites and Australia-based Chinese officials. Their dedicated efforts were deeply embedded within the social and political networks of the Chinese Australian community, which extended into non-Chinese circles as

---

1   For examples emphasising diplomatic and economic connections, see Andrew 1985; Gibson and Ville 2019; Goldsworthy 2002.

241

well. This concerted work effectively addressed the gap left by the limited presence of the Kuomintang in Australia prior to 1941. In an environment marked by pervasive indifference to Chinese suffering and the appeasement of Japanese aggression, these Chinese propagandists sought to generate sympathy and support from the Australian public by highlighting the atrocities committed by Japan against the Chinese people and its broader ambition to subjugate China. They also aimed to present China's perspective, which had been misrepresented by Japanese propaganda and Western journalists who had been misled by Tokyo's deceptive narratives. Consequently, Chinese Australian elites and officials found themselves engaged in a fierce battle of propaganda with Japan, competing to win the favour of the Australian public.

Both sides in this propaganda contest shared several key strategies. Both invested considerable resources in integrating their respective diasporas into their national agendas and both leveraged interracial collaborations with white Australians to amplify their messages. In contrast to the fragmented Chinese propaganda apparatus in Australia, Japan's efforts were centralised and received robust support from Tokyo, which allowed it to gain an upper hand over its Chinese competitors throughout much of the 1930s. Much of Japan's propaganda was based on distorted narratives that portrayed Chinese inferiority and Japanese superiority, not only to justify Tokyo's unjust war against China but also to cultivate goodwill with Australia. Despite these formidable challenges, Chinese propagandists persisted, striving to advance their message through diasporic networks and diplomatic channels to reach non-Chinese audiences. Their campaigns primarily featured photographs and news reports highlighting Japanese atrocities against the Chinese people, as well as efforts to improve China–Australia trade relations to ease China's financial difficulties and reduce the commerce-oriented Japan–Australia connections.

The period that favoured Japan persisted until 1937, when China's international propaganda apparatus was reorganised to centralise its publicity efforts abroad. A pivotal moment came with the collaboration between Chinese propagandists and their Australian counterparts, which significantly disrupted the dominant narrative constructed by Japanese propaganda. By exposing the staggering atrocities committed by Japan in China – most notably the Rape of Nanking – Chinese propagandists effectively undermined Japan's misleading portrayal. This strategic effort, combined with growing Australian sympathy for China, culminated in widespread boycotts of Japanese goods and public protests against the Australian government's stance. Many of these movements were the result of close cooperation between Chinese propagandists and Australian sympathisers, who used transnational channels and the networks established by diasporic Chinese communities to circulate China's narrative. As the propaganda contest unfolded, the momentum shifted in favour of the Chinese side, and the campaign ended abruptly with the outbreak of the Pacific War.

As the war progressed, Chinese propaganda in Australia underwent increasing professionalisation and institutionalisation. The strategic importance of Australia – an essential player in the Pacific War with MacArthur-led American forces stationed there – became more evident to those shaping Chinese propaganda policy in Chungking. Efforts to influence the Australian public were increasingly centralised, with a Chinese propaganda centre first established in Melbourne and later moved to Sydney. This institutional shift was accompanied by the formation of pro-China lobbies, sponsored by Chinese authorities, in collaboration with diasporic Chinese leaders in Australia. Amid a changing wartime context, with China's international prestige rising, there was a noticeable shift in Chinese propaganda policy. The focus shifted from eliciting Western sympathy to asserting China's position as a leading and dependable member of the Allied powers. In Australia, Chinese propagandists directly pressured the Australian government to ease immigration restrictions, advocated for racial equality for Chinese Australians and demanded national parity for Kuomintang China.

However, the growing presence of China in Australia did not lead to the official monopolisation or centralisation of Chinese propaganda efforts. This outcome can largely be attributed to the significant reliance on the Chinese diaspora community for executing official publicity, with the sociopolitical dynamics of this community heavily influencing Chungking's efforts to establish leadership. Additionally, the agency of diasporic Chinese leaders, local Chinese officials and white elites in pro-China lobbies hindered the professionalisation of these efforts. The propaganda delivered by these leaders and Chinese diplomats were coloured by their own agency, operating partly independently of Kuomintang China's directives. Long before Chungking's shift in propaganda policy, diasporic Chinese leaders and Australia-based Chinese officials had already pursued similar goals in a more euphemistic manner, aimed at improving the China–Australia relationship and enhancing the racial status of Chinese Australians. The disparity between the official Chinese propaganda agenda and that advanced by the alliance of Chinese Australian elites and diplomats underscores the complexities inherent in understanding the mechanisms and practices of Chinese international propaganda in a context where Chinese authorities had limited direct presence.

This complexity highlights the significant role the Chinese diaspora played in shaping the course of Chinese propaganda in Australia. Their diasporic experiences and identities formed a critical intersection between China and Australia, while simultaneously defying the national agendas of both. When Kuomintang China attempted to integrate the Chinese Australian community into its political framework – using party-driven patriotism to support anti-Japanese propaganda and secure political and financial backing – it faced intense resistance from Chinese Australians. Their patriotism, grounded in a contested vision that merged Chinese heritage with Australian values, prioritised national interests over party allegiance. China's attempt to unite the diaspora under Kuomintang leadership to bolster the war effort against Japan backfired, deepening divisions not only within the Chinese Australian community but also between them and China. These conflicts, although less vibrant in the 1940s, continued and became more complex as factions emerged from diverse social, political, gender and generational backgrounds, further fragmenting China's efforts for Kuomintang-led solidarity and challenging attempts to consolidate propaganda efforts. Despite their synchronous engagement with major events in China, the diasporic Chinese community in Australia did not align with China's national agenda.

For Chinese Australians, the delivery of anti-Japanese propaganda, whether directed towards the Australian public or their own compatriots, was not merely a national mission to restore China's sovereignty, it also intersected with a broader process of negotiating their complex and often contradictory identities. Encouraging patriotism for China served as a stabilising force for the fluid, hybrid identities of Chinese Australians – particularly in the context of White Australia – while re-Sinicisation provided a similar framework for younger generations. Fundraising campaigns organised by diasporic Chinese elites, aimed at alleviating China's hardship and raising its profile, also became opportunities to practice and publicly showcase Chinese heritage to the Australian public. These initiatives often emphasised the Chineseness of the diaspora, sometimes at the expense of their Australianness, revealing the tension between these dual identities. The fabric of diasporic identities was further shaped by varying gender, class and generational experiences, as well as by Australia's involvement in the wars in Europe and the Pacific. While these elements forged a social resilience that helped mitigate political divisions within the Chinese diaspora, the fragmentation of identities posed a risk: Chinese Australians found themselves at odds with the Kuomintang's party-centric vision, which cast doubt on their loyalty to the party state, while simultaneously reinforcing the racialised, orientalised framework imposed by White Australia, which perpetuated longstanding perceptions of the Chinese diaspora as "un-Australian".

Australia's engagement with Chinese propaganda, both within the Chinese diaspora and the non-Chinese public, was complex, fragmented and heterogeneous. Traditional assumptions about Australia's indifference towards China often prioritise the role of geopolitics and its influence on Australian perceptions of China. However, these assumptions largely overlook the significant humanitarian sentiments embedded within Australian society and among its officials. While initially confined to left-wing groups and unionists, China's vigorous resistance to Japanese aggression found an expanding base of Australian sympathisers in the 1930s. These individuals were exposed to a steady flow of evidence of Japan's war crimes through Chinese propaganda efforts. Many of them participated in protests against both Japan and Canberra, while others contributed to Chinese fundraising and propaganda campaigns, which were largely rooted in humanitarianism, labourism and sisterhood. For some Australians who had previously visited China, their involvement in Chinese propaganda efforts was partly shaped by their position as manipulated conduits of Chinese messages, though this was not politically driven.

It was not until the 1940s that this sympathy for China became much more politicised, largely as a result of China's efforts to institutionalise and professionalise its propaganda initiatives. This shift contributed to Chinese propaganda efforts advocating for the relaxation of the White Australia policy. However, despite amplifying China's appeals, pro-China lobbies in Australia did not necessarily align themselves with Kuomintang China's political agenda. Their support for China remained selective and restrictive, largely framed within the confines of the entrenched white supremacy within Australian society, despite many Australians admiring Chinese people for their generosity, bravery and empathy.[2] As Michael Williams argues, the pervasive social exclusion of non-white individuals in Australia renders the term "White Australia policy" less accurate than the more fitting "White Australia project".[3] This racial mindset found little alignment with China's growing prominence in international affairs, particularly during the increasingly racialised Pacific War, leading white Australians to resist the narratives and pressures that Chinese propagandists sought to publicise.

Significantly detached from the rising public sympathy for China, the Australian government, as many historians have noted, adhered to a policy of appeasement towards Japan due to geopolitical concerns leading up to the Pacific War and tended to marginalise China in international postwar politics.[4] However, focusing solely on Canberra's diplomatic stance risks oversimplifying the complexity of its interactions during the Sino-Japanese war. In fact, Canberra walked a delicate tightrope between Kuomintang China, Imperial Japan, and the Chinese and Japanese diasporas, carefully managing these relationships without overtly offending any party. Although this approach indirectly

---

2   Gratitude to Chinese people was particularly intense from white Australian veterans who had been imprisoned in Japan's occupied places, see Ross-Webster, Edward R., NX26552, Australian Red Cross Society, 1945, Missing, Wounded and Prisoner of War Enquiry Cards, 15579, University of Melbourne Library, Melbourne.
3   Williams 2021a, 3.
4   Lowe 1996, 172–3.

favoured Japan, it contingently allowed Chinese propaganda to survive and ultimately gain the upper hand later. While Australian authorities censored war films depicting Japanese atrocities in China, they allowed the free circulation of books documenting similar themes. This approach also allowed for the appeasement of Japanese aggression without halting Chinese propaganda efforts or hindering the humanitarian support Australians offered to China. Similarly, while Canberra censured anti-Kuomintang Chinese for undermining China's authority, it did not pursue this with vigour. The Australian government, though geographically situated in the South Pacific, seemed aware that it was becoming increasingly involved in the politics of North-East Asia, even if its policies were still firmly grounded in a Europe-centric worldview.

The story of Chinese propaganda in Australia during the 1930s and 1940s is one of resilience, complexity and transformation. Amid racial divisions and geopolitical tensions, the Chinese diaspora emerged as an unlikely yet powerful force, reshaping not only the Australian public's perception of China but also their own sense of identity and agency. The collective efforts of Chinese Australians to influence public opinion and challenge racialised ideologies left a lasting imprint that resonated in the postwar period – and continues to reverberate today. Their legacy serves as a reminder of the enduring power of diasporic communities in shaping national narratives and international relations.

# Bibliography

Primary sources

*Archives*

**National Archives of Australia**

Aid Our Chinese Allies, MT395/1, 148, 31647699.
Andrew Melville Pooley, A1336, 30454, 3547142.
Appeal for Hostel for Chinese Seamen, MT359/1, 192, 31534643.
Association of Far Eastern Affairs, C320, J194, 3047904.
Australia-China Co-operation Association, A989, 1944/650/21, 184787.
Australia-China Co-operation Association, BP242/1, Q30600, 1031901.
Australian Born Chinese Limit of Time for Education in China, A1, 1932/10538, 45450.
Author John Harvey Crothers Sleeman, A1336, 23441, 3506297.
Black List, C320, C16, 1495444.
Censorship in Overseas Countries, SP109/3, 343/08, 266558.
Censorship of Chinese Liaison Mail, A989, 1943/235/1/2/8, 183714.
China – Australia National Herald, A981, CHIN 195, 173701.
China Overseas Chinese, A1838, 494/33 PART 1 A, 551440.
Chinese and Japanese Newspapers and Periodicals Ordered, A981, PUB 76, 180484.
Chinese Australian Association, A433, 1941/2/1444, 3091095.

Film Production, A4144, 92/1945, 1713662.

General Anti-Chinese Propaganda, A981, CHIN 41, 173502.

Hugh Millington, A373, 1652, 65352.

Identification Badges for Chinese Residents in Australia, A981, CHIN 6, 173454.

Indecent Chinese Fireworks, A425, 1937/3924, 66114.

Interview with Chinese Consul General, C320, C27, 1495527.

Japan - Australia, A981, JAP 131, 177551.

Japanese Activities Amongst Chinese Residents in Australia and Netherlands East Indies, A981, JAP 22, 177402.

Japanese Consular Mail, MP729/6, 10/401/345, 391203.

Japanese Espionage, A8911, 5, 821337.

Japanese Organisations in Sydney, C320, J208, 3047929.

L.K. Wang and Family, SP42/1, C1937/4628, 31103385.

Liability of Ministry of Information for Income Tax, A1067, IC46/4/7/5, 191715.

Map of Chinese War Front by Chinese Ministry of Information, A989, 1943/540/3, 184430.

National Security (Aliens Control) Regulations, Chinese – Registrations of Chinese in Australia, A373, 8774, 65573.

New China Citizens Association, A9108, ROLL 4/8, 1609509.

Newspapers in Foreign Languages, A367, C1822, 428437.

NSW Security Service File, C320, C21, 1495515.

Opening of Chinese Consulate in Melbourne. A1067, IC/15/11/5, 191828.

Overseas Chinese Affairs, A4144, 181/1943, 237569.

Overseas Chinese, A4144, 288/1947, 237615.

Pao Chun Chien, SP42/1, C1936/7875, 31102871.

Personal Papers of Prime Minister Lyons, CP103/19, 20, 362177.

Provision of Medical Relief in China, MP508/1, 282/704/56, 3362894.

Queck Papers, A989, 1943/150/5/3, 183527.

Remittance to China, F320, 1943/264, 339677.

Representations by Chinese Consul General, A981, CONS 314, 174499.

Representations from Chinese Consul General, A981, CONS 312, 174497.

Statements by Chinese Ministry of Information, MP742/1, 89/4/282, 4938572.

Talk Script, MT395/1, 97, 31647648.

Tsao Wen Yen, SP42/1, C1936/7734, 31102850.

*Tung Wah Times*, A433, 1945/2/3557, 3093972.

Visit of General Tsai Ting-kai, A981, CHIN 102, 173584.

Visit of K.T. Lok, A981, CHIN 100, 173582.

## National Library of China (*中國國家圖書館*)

全國慰勞抗戰將士委員會總會編(1947). 全國慰勞抗戰將士委員會總會慰勞
工作總報告. 重慶: 全國慰勞抗戰將士委員會總會出版.

## State Library of New South Wales

New South Wales Chinese Women's Relief Fund Records (1937–41), MLMSS
10277/Box 1X, 1JkPRroY, 9639983.

## New South Wales State Archives and Records

Chinese Masonic Society (1922–49), 12951, 8177.
Chinese Press Pty Ltd (1943), 12951, 21745.
Chinese Republic Newspaper & Trading Co. Ltd. (1938), 12951, 9834.
Chinese Times Ltd (1922–49), 12951, 7978.
Chinese World's News Ltd (1922–38), 12951, 8021.

## Academia Historica (*國史館*)

澳大利亞供我軍火 (1943). 020-011503-0004.
澳大利亞政情 (1943). 020-011501-0001.
澳洲華僑狀況 (1945). 008-010602-00019-001.
澳洲華僑狀況 (1945). 008-010602-00019-001.
澳洲僑務 (1946). 020-990600-2638.
陳立夫函吳鐵城轉蔣中正中國國民黨澳洲支部常委盧華岳發明電砲可抵禦
　　飛機請准匯旅費助其回國投效並附盧華岳函 (1933).
　　002-080102-00079-004.
改善旅澳華僑待遇 (二) (1944–1948). 020-011507-0003.
改善旅澳華僑待遇 (一) (1938). 020-011507-0002.
國民政府文官處函中國國民黨中央執行委員會秘書處為五全大會陳志明等
　　提議於澳大利亞墨爾本設領事館一案據行政院呈復已交外交部酌辦函
　　達查照轉陳 (1936). 001-061100-00001-022.
海外部處長駱介子宣慰僑胞 (1943). 020-011507-0012.
美麗濱中華公會電國民政府為保領負國殃民僑等誓不承認今復誣陷李副領
　　懇飭外交部依法查辦 (1932). 001-067101-00002-016.

# Bibliography

美利濱中華公會執行委員會常務委員雷宜爵呈國民政府主席蔣中正為呈報
　　歷次匯繳救國捐款情形恭祈鑒核准予分飭各收款機關速給歷次正式收
　　據 (1932). 001-067140-00007-020.

紐澳移民條例與華僑待遇 (1939). 020-070900-0035.

外人捐贈藥品醫具書籍 (1941). 020-011903-0001.

億中公司駐墨爾本經理趙約翰案 (1941–1943). 020-011507-0022.

駐各地領事館巡視轄區 (1940). 020-019999-0018.

中國國民黨五全大會設立駐外使館決議案 (1935). 001-061100-00001-018.

中澳貿易 (1944). 020-991100-0182.

中澳關系及澳大利亞政情 (1944). 020-011502-0001.


## Second Historical Archives of China (*中國第二歷史檔案館*)

中宣部國際宣傳處招待外國新聞記者及有關宣傳之外籍人士辦法等,
　　718(4)-231.

中宣部國際宣傳處工作概況等, 718(4)-239.

中宣部國際宣傳處關於英國記者田伯烈所著《外人目睹中之日軍暴行》和
　　各部門往來函件, 718(4)-250.

中宣部國際宣傳處《我國在美宣傳工作概況》等, 718(4)-262.

中宣部發給國際宣傳處的工作計劃等, 718(4)-311.

中宣部工作計劃等, 718(4)-319.

中宣部國際宣傳處工作報告等, 718(4)-321.

中宣部國際宣傳處駐澳辦事處主任巢坤霖之工作報告等, 718(4)-323.

中法會社成立經過之報告等, 718(4)-334.

國民黨中央宣傳部國際宣傳處與戴笠等的來往庶務函件, 718(4)-343.

日寇軍事情報等, 718(4)-346.

外交報告等, 718(4)-367.

國際反侵略運動工作報告半月刊等, 718(4)-368.

國際反侵略運動大會中國分會工作報告等, 718(4)-371.

國際廣播電臺每日節目時間總表等, 718(4)-419.

中宣部國際宣傳處各項工作計劃等, 718(5)-10.

中宣部國際宣傳處關於加強國際宣傳與新聞管製等的文書, 718(5)-11.

中宣部國際宣傳處加強海外宣傳工作等, 718(5)-12.

中宣部國際宣傳處出版外文小冊子統計工作報告等, 718(5)-44.

關於加強聯系外賓計劃等, 718(5)-63.

中宣部國際宣傳處關於統製外國新聞記者電報等的文書, 718(5)-88.

中宣部國際宣傳處一九四一年十二月和一九四二至一九四四年度特別費支
出計算書等, 718(5)-9.

## Newspapers and magazines

*Advertiser* (Adelaide)
*Age* (Melbourne)
*Argus* (Melbourne)
*Maryborough Chronicle, Wide Bay and Burnett Advertiser* (Maryborough)
*Australian Women's Weekly* (Sydney)
*Australian Worker* (Sydney)
*Barrier Daily Truth* (Broken Hill)
*Barrier Miner* (Broken Hill)
*Brisbane Courier* (Brisbane)
*Canberra Times* (Canberra)
*Catholic Freeman's Journal* (Sydney)
*Catholic Weekly* (Sydney)
*Cairns Post* (Cairns)
*Chinese Republic News* (Sydney)
*Courier-Mail* (Brisbane)
*Daily Mercury* (Mackay)
*Daily News* (Perth)
*Daily Standard* (Brisbane)
*Daily Telegraph* (Sydney)
*Dun's Gazette for New South Wales* (Sydney)
*Examiner* (Launceston)
*Glen Innes Examiner* (Glen Innes)
*Goulburn Evening Penny Post* (Goulburn)
*Government Gazette of the State of New South Wales* (Sydney)
*Herald* (Melbourne)
*Horsham Times* (Horsham)
*Illawarra Mercury* (Wollongong)
*Inverell Times* (Inverell)
*Labor Call* (Melbourne)
*Labor Daily* (Sydney)
*Macleay Argus* (Kempsey)
*Mail* (Adelaide)
*Maitland Mercury* (Maitland)
*Mercury* (Hobart)
*Methodist* (Sydney)

# Bibliography

*Mirror* (Sydney)
*Morning Bulletin* (Rockhampton)
*Newcastle Morning Herald and Miners' Advocate* (Newcastle)
*Newcastle Sun* (Newcastle)
*News* (Hobart)
*Northern Territory Times* (Darwin)
*Northern Standard* (Darwin)
*Pix* (Sydney)
*Queensland Times* (Ipswich)
*Shepparton Advertiser* (Shepparton)
*Smith's Weekly* (Sydney)
*Sun* (Sydney)
*Sun News-Pictorial* (Melbourne)
*Sunshine Advocate* (Melbourne)
*Sydney Morning Herald* (Sydney)
*Telegraph* (Brisbane)
*Townsville Daily Bulletin* (Townsville)
*Tribune* (Sydney)
*Truth* (Sydney)
*Tung Wah Times* (Sydney)
*Warwick Daily News* (Warwick)
*Wellington Times* (Wellington)
*West Australian* (Perth)
*Western Champion* (Parkes)
*Wiluna Miner* (Wiluna)
*Workers Star* (Perth)
*Workers' Weekly* (Sydney)
*大公報* (香港)
*福建日報* (泉州)
*革命日報* (貴陽)
*南寧民國日報* (南寧)
*新疆日報* (迪化, now 烏魯木齊)
*西京日報* (西安)
*西北文化日報* (西安)
*西安晚報* (西安)
*西康民國日報* (康定)
*陣中日報* (太原)

## Publications

### *National Library of Australia*

Anonymous Correspondent (1941). The Army Education Service. *A.I.I.A. Newsletter* 2: 1–3.

Association of Far Eastern Affairs (1938a). *Dawn of A New Era in China*. Sydney: Author.

Association of Far Eastern Affairs (1938b). *Red Activities in China and Japan's Mission in East Asia*. Sydney: Author.

Association of Far Eastern Affairs (1938c). *The Fall of Suchow and the Fate of the Kuomintang*. Sydney: Author.

Association of Far Eastern Affairs (1938d). *The Financial and Economic Position in Japan*. Sydney: Author.

Association of Far Eastern Affairs, ed. (1939a). *British-American Opinions on Japan in War and Trade*. Sydney: Author.

Association of Far Eastern Affairs, ed. (1939b). *Japanese-Australian Amity: A Japanese Appeal*. Sydney: Author.

Australia-China Co-operation Movement (1940). *China Marches On*. Melbourne: Author.

Australian Army Education Service (1946). *Our Pacific Neighbours*. Sydney: Government Printer.

Australian Institute of Anatomy (1932–1941). *The George Ernest Morrison Lecture in Ethnology* (1st–10th). Canberra: Institute.

Australian Institute of International Affairs (1937–1946). *Austral-Asiatic Bulletin*. Melbourne: Austral-Asiatic Section.

Australian Institute of International Affairs (1941a). *A.I.I.A. Newsletter*. Melbourne: Research Section.

Australian Institute of International Affairs (1941b). *China Today* 4. Melbourne: Research Section.

Ball, William Macmahon (1938). "The Australian Press and World Affairs," in *Press, Radio and World Affairs*, ed. William Macmahon Ball. Carlton: Melbourne University Press.

Ball, William Macmahon, ed. (1938). *Press, Radio and World Affairs*. Carlton: Melbourne University Press.

Barker, Aldred F. (1944). *China and the Chinese*. Melbourne: Robertson and Mullens.

Blumer, R.C. and E.C. Rowland (1944). *The Pacific and You: Our Duty to Our Neighbours*. Sydney: Australian Board of Missions.

Blumer, R.C. and H.M. Arrowsmith (1943). *Australia and the Pacific*. Sydney: Church Missionary Society.

Borrie, W.D. and A.P. Elkin (1947). *A White Australia: Australia's Population Problem.* Sydney: Australasian Publishing.

Burchett, G.H. (1941). *China's Co-operative Societies: Their Genesis and Development.* Melbourne: Australia-China Co-operation Association.

Burchett, G.H. (1944a). *China and the White Australia Policy.* Melbourne: Australia-China Co-operation Association.

Burchett, G.H. (1944b). *China, The Senior Partner.* Melbourne: Australia-China Co-operation Association.

Burchett, G.H. and W.H. Burchett (1943). *Building China's Republic.* Melbourne: Australia-China Co-operation Association.

Burton, Wilbur (1937). China fights to the last coolie. *Austral-Asiatic Bulletin* 1(6).

Bushells Tea Company (1932). *How to Read Tea Cups.* Melbourne: Bushells Ltd.

Castleton, A. (1944) *Rough, Tough and Far Away.* Melbourne: The Book Depot.

Chao, Samuel (1944). *Sky-Riding Over China.* Sydney: Australian Office of Chinese Ministry of Information.

Chau, K.L. (1945). China's Literary Revolution, *ABC Weekly* 7(22).

Chen, Pin-Ho (1938). A Chinese comment. *Austral-Asiatic Bulletin* 1(6).

Chen, Wei-ping (1934). *Manchuria or Manchukuo: The Effect of Three Years of Japanese Aggression.* Sydney: Author.

Chiang, Kai-shek (1942). *Why Believe in Jesus.* Melbourne: The Book Depot.

China Society in Australia (1939). *China To-Day.* Sydney: Author.

Chinese Citizens Society (1932). *Japanese Invasion of Shanghai: A Record of Facts.* Melbourne: Author.

Chinese Ministry of Information (1945a). *China Tomorrow.* Sydney: Australian Office of Chinese Ministry of Information.

Chinese Ministry of Information (1945b). *Interpreting China.* Sydney: Australian Office of Chinese Ministry of Information.

Chinese Ministry of Information (1945c). *Presenting China.* Sydney: Australian Office of Chinese Ministry of Information.

Chinese Ministry of Information (1946a). *A China Pictorial.* Sydney: Australian Office of Chinese Ministry of Information.

Chinese Ministry of Information (1946b). *China at Peace.* Sydney: Australian Office of Chinese Ministry of Information.

Church Missionary Society (1944). *Focus on China: Towards the Understanding of One of Australia's Pacific Neighbours.* Sydney: National Library of Australia.

Clune, Frank (1939). *Sky High to Shanghai.* Sydney: Angus and Robertson.

Clune, Frank (1941). *Chinese Morrison.* Melbourne: Bread and Cheese Club.

Cutlack, F.M. (1934). *The Manchurian Arena: An Australian View of the Far Eastern Conflict.* Sydney: Angus & Robertson.

Daugherty, William (1942). China's Official Publicity in the United States. *Public Opinion Quarterly* 6(1): 70–86.

Eggleston, F.W. (1936). The British Empire, Australia and the Pacific. *Australian Quarterly* 8(31): 5–11.

Embery, Winifred (1945). *Those That Endure: A True Story*. Melbourne: China Inland Mission.

Fenwick, A.H.(1945). "Chinese Studies in Australia", in *A Book To Commemorate a Common Victory 1945*. Issued by Chinese Community in N.S.W. Sydney: Boyland & Co.

Foxall, Edward (1903). *Colorphobia: an exposure of the "White Australia" Fallacy*. Sydney: R.T. Kelly.

Galbraith, Winifred (1943). *The Chinese*. Melbourne: Penguin.

Geechoun, Roy (1948). *Cooking the Chinese Way*. Melbourne: W.D. Joynt & Company.

Goss, Noel (1941). Modern China's Changing Patterns. *China Today* 4.

Hobsbawm, Eric (2013). "Introduction: Inventing traditions", in *The Invention of Tradition*, eds Eric Hobsbawm and Terence Ranger. New York: Cambridge University Press.

Japanese Chamber of Commerce Sydney and Melbourne (1937a). *An Endeavour to Throw Light on the Present Trouble in North China*. Sydney: Author.

Japanese Chamber of Commerce Sydney and Melbourne (1937b). *Misunderstanding is Dangerous: An Eye-Open to the Truth*. Sydney: Author.

Johnston, George (1948). *Journey Through Tomorrow*. Melbourne: Cheshire.

Kanamaru, Hideo (1939). "Let us understand one another: a plea for Japanese-Australian goodwill", in *Japanese-Australian Amity*. Sydney: New Century Press.

Kuhn, Kathryn, Betty Hatton and Joseph Cooke (1944). *From Internment to Freedom*. Melbourne: China Inland Mission.

Labour Supporter (1937). *Japan and China: Australia's necessity to look to her trade*. Sydney: Langlea Printery.

Lautenschlager, S. (1932). The Sino-Japanese Controversy. *Australian Quarterly* 4(15): 101–12.

League Against Imperialism (1934). *The Canton Commune and Soviet China*. n.p.: Author.

Liu, William (1931). *China and the Trouble in Manchuria: What It Means to China, Japan, Russia and the World*. Sydney: Society of Chinese Residents in Australia.

Liu, William (1932). *Chinese-Australian Trading Relationship*. Sydney: Society of Chinese Residents in Australia.

Liu, William, ed. (1942). *Wang Pao Chuan*. Sydney: Chinese Youth Club.

# Bibliography

Lockwood, Rupert (1938–39). Not cricket *Austral-Asiatic Bulletin* 3(3).

Lowenthal, Rudolf (1937). *Chinese Press in Australia*. s.l.: s.n..

Macdonald, Roderick (1944). *Dawn Like Thunder*. London: Hodder and Stoughton.

Mackie, E.F. (1944). *Chinese Adventure*. Sydney: Clarendon Publishing.

Martin, R. Ormsby (1943). *Tradition and Transition in Chinese Politics*. Sydney: Australian Institute of International Affairs.

Martin, R. Ormsby (1944). Modern Chinese Political Thought. *Australian Quarterly* 16(1): 18–28.

Martin, R. Ormsby (1946a). *A Tail in the Mud*. Canberra: Steran Press.

Martin, R. Ormsby (1946b). *Shan Shui: Translations of Chinese Landscape Poems*. Melbourne: Meanjin Press.

Martin, R. Ormsby (1948). Chinese Poetry: Its Philosophy and General Characteristics. *Australian Quarterly* 20(1): 61–70.

Mathews, Basil (1942). *Wings over China*. Melbourne: The Book Depot.

McBride, Patricia (1944). Immigration and Australia's Population Problem. Sydney: R.A.A.F. Educational Service.

McCallum, J.A. (1947). The Asian Relations Conference. *Australian Quarterly* 19(2): 13–17.

McPhee, E.T. (1936). *Official Year Book of the Commonwealth of Australia* 28: 1935. Canberra: Government Printer.

Melbourne, A.C.V. (1932). *Report on Australian Intercourse with Japan and China*. Brisbane: Government Printer.

Melbourne, A.C.V. (1935). Trade Commissioners and Their Work. *Australian Quarterly* 7(27): 26–29.

Millington, Hugh (1938). *Japan's Right, or We're Wrong*. Perth: Paterson.

Millington, Hugh (1939). *Japanese Democracy versus Chinese Dictatorship*. Sydney: New Century Press.

Mitchell, Janet (1939). *Spoils of Opportunity: An Autobiography*. New York: E.P. Dutton.

Miyake, Kijiro (1939). "Japan's Economic Expansion: With Special Reference to Its Relation to Australia," in *Japanese-Australian Amity*.

Moore, William Harrison (1932). The Institute of Pacific Relations. *Australian Quarterly* 4(13): 32–41.

N.S.W. Chinese Residents' Refugees' Relief Fund Committee (1938). *Chinese Pageant and Fireworks Display: Official Souvenir Programme*. Sydney: Holland and Stephenson.

New South Wales State (1933). *Government Gazette of the State of New South Wales* 15. Canberra: National Library of Australia.

Noonan, William (1945). *The Surprising Battalion: Australian Commandos in China*. Sydney: N.S.W. Bookstall.

O'Harris, Pixie (1946). *Princess of China*. Sydney: Currawong Publishing.

Pao, Chun-jien (1938). *A Century of Sino-Australian Relations*. Sydney: John Sands.

Pearson, A.G. (1938). "The Australian press and Japan," in *Press, Radio and World Affairs*.

Philips, P.D. (1933). The Far Eastern Situation: Some Aspects. *Australian Quarterly* 5(20): 28–40.

Phillips, A.L. (1941). Economic Problems. *China Today* 4.

Pirani, Leila (1945). *Lazy the Pig and His Chinese Adventures*. Melbourne: Ramsay Ware.

Pratt, Ambrose (1942). *Some Other Nations*. Melbourne: R.A.A.F. Rehabilitation Section.

R.A.A.F. Education Service (1946). *Our Pacific Neighbours*. Sydney: Government Printer.

R.A.A.F. Rehabilitation Section (1942). *So What*. Melbourne: R.A.A.F. Rehabilitation Section.

R.G. Dun & Co. (1925). *Dun's Gazette for New South Wales* 34(15).

Reginald, Dixson (1945). *Immigration and the White Australia Policy*. Sydney: Current Book Distributors.

Ross, I. Clunies (1933). Australia's Trade and Diplomatic Relations with Japan: The Need for Research. *Australian Quarterly* 5(17): 79–92.

Ross, I. Clunies (1934). Australian Representation in Japan. *Australian Quarterly* 6(22): 61–68.

Ross, I. Clunies, ed. (1936). *Australia and the Far East: Diplomatic and Trade Relations*. Sydney: Angus and Robertson.

Ross, I. Clunies (1945). The Dependence of the Wool Industry on External Trade. *Australian Quarterly* 17(3): 39–45.

Sadler, A.L. (1942). *Selections from The Confucian Texts*. Sydney: Australasian Medical Publishing.

Sadler, A.L. (1944). *Three Military Classics of China*. Sydney: Australian Medical Publishing.

Sale, G.S. (1939). *Impressions of A Visit to the Far East*. Sydney: Reprinted by the Association of Far Eastern Affairs.

Sisters of the Cross (1948–1949). *China, Old and New*. Summer Hill: Author.

Sleeman, John (1933). *White China: An Austral-Asia Sensation*. Sydney: Author.

Society of Chinese Residents in Australia (1933a). *An Appreciation Addressed to J.H.C. Sleeman*. Sydney: Society of Chinese Residents in Australia.

Society of Chinese Residents in Australia (1933b). *The Sino-Japanese Question Relating to China's Three Eastern Provinces (Manchuria)*. Sydney: Author.

Taronga (1937). Letters to the editor: a protest from Shanghai, *Austral-Asiatic Bulletin* 1(3).

Taylor, Lloyd (1944). *The City of Bamboo and Mud and Courage*. Sydney: Australian Office of Chinese Ministry of Information.

Timperley, H J. (1942). *Japan: A World Problem*. New York: John Day.

Timperley, H.J. (1942). *Australia and the Australians*. New York: Oxford University Press.

Timperley, H.J., ed. (1938). *What War Means: The Japanese Terror in China*. London: Victor Gollancz.

Tsao, Wen-yen (1940). *Historical Development of Chinese Philosophy*. Melbourne: China Cultural Society in Victoria.

Tsao, Wen-yen (1941). *Two Pacific Democracies: China and Australia*. Melbourne: F.W. Cheshire.

Uranus (1938–39). Commentary, *Austral-Asiatic Bulletin* 3(3).

Ward, E.E. (1937). Sidelights at Home and Abroad, *Austral-Asiatic Bulletin* 1(5).

Watt, Raymond R. (1933). "The League of Nations": Has It Failed? What of Its Future?. *The Australian Quarterly* 5(20): 99–107.

Welsh, Lionel (1945). *Gim Shan*. Ballarat: Author.

Wilkie, D. (1941). The People and the Parties, *China Today* 4.

William, Edward (1903). *Colorphobia: An Exposure of the "White Australia" Fallacy*. Sydney: R. T. Kelly.

Wilson, Hardy (1937). Grecian and Chinese Architecture. Melbourne: Hardy Wilson.

Wilson, Hardy (1937). Letters to the editor: China's creative role, *Austral-Asiatic Bulletin* 1(4).

Yuan, C.M., ed. (1945). *A Book to Commemorate a Common Victory*. Sydney: Chinese Community in NSW.

澳洲總支部執行委員會秘書處 (1931). *中國國民黨澳洲總支部四全大會紀念冊*, 雪梨: 中國國民黨澳總支部.

陳誌明 (1935). *中國國民黨澳洲黨務發展實況*. 雪梨: 國民黨澳大拉西亞支部.

袁中明 (1945). *勝利專冊*, 雪梨: 中國駐澳總領館.

## State Library of New South Wales

Australia–China Association (1944). *Progress Report*. Sydney: Author.

Australia–China Association (1945a). *Second Report*. Sydney: Author.

Australia–China Association (1945b). *Third Report*. Sydney: Author.

Chinese Ministry of Information (1944a). *Introducing China*. Sydney: Australian Office of Chinese Ministry of Information.

Goddard, W.G. (1945). *Truth About China*. Sydney: NSW Chinese National Association.

Mao, Tse-tung (1945). *China's New Democracy*. Sydney: Current Book Distributors.

NSW Chinese Women's Relief Fund Photograph and Badge, P1/2426, R2414, 1JkOywxY, 9676001.

Soong, Mei-ling (1942). *Practical Christianity in China*. Melbourne: Book Depot.

## Sir Louis Matheson Library, University of Monash

Australian Friends of China (1940). *Letters of Thanks from Chinese Ministry of Foreign Affairs of the Republic of China*, PAM 951.042 A938L.

## University of Melbourne Library

Ross-Webster, Edward R, NX26552, Australian Red Cross Society, 1945, Missing, Wounded and Prisoner of War Enquiry Cards, 15579.

## State Library of Victoria

Japanese Chamber of Commerce Sydney and Melbourne (1937c). *Shanghai Incident*. Sydney: Author.

Papers of Wilfred Burchett, 1944–1977, MS 10254, Box 3.

## Other primary sources

## National Library of Australia

Chin, Ray and Diana Giese (1996). *Ray Chin interviewed by Diana Giese, Post-War Chinese Australians Oral History Project*. Darwin: National Library of Australia.

Fong, William and Diana Giese (1992). *William Fong interviewed by Diana Giese, Post-War Chinese Australians Oral History Project*. Darwin: National Library of Australia.

Leong, Maurice and Diana Giese (2000). *Maurice Leong interviewed by Diana Giese, Chinese Australian Oral History Partnership Collection*. East Malvern: National Library of Australia.

Papers of Bill Harman, 1938–1965, MS 7724.

Papers of Frederic William Eggleston, 1911–1954, MS 423.

Papers of Marina Mar, 1918–1992, MS 10707.

Papers of Selwyn Speight, 1940–1979, MS 6633.

Papers of Sir Keith Officer, 1911–1969, MS 2629.

Stuckey, Frank and Paul Macgregor (1994). *Frank Stucky interviewed by Paul Macgregor, Australia-China Oral History Project*. Kew: National Library of Australia.

Tsang, Charles See-Kee and Diana Giese (1993). *Charles Tsang See-Kee interviewed by Diana Giese, Post-War Chinese Australians Oral History Project*. Darwin: National Library of Australia.

## Noel Butlin Archives Centre, Australian National University

Chinese Chamber of Commerce of New South Wales (05/1923). Minute Book. AU NBAC 111-1-1.

Chinese Chamber of Commerce of New South Wales (1932–1937). Committee for the Collection of Donations to Help the Struggle Against Japanese Invasion Minute Book. AU NBAC 111-6-1.

Chinese Chamber of Commerce of New South Wales (1913–1926). AU NBAC 111-2-3.

Chinese Consulate General (1931). Correspondence from Chinese Consul General in Melbourne and Overseas Chinese Affairs Council in China. AU NBAC 111-9-4.

Chinese Debating Society (1921–1922). Minute Book. AU NBAC 111-5A.

Chinese Ministry of Information (1945d). *The Final Round*. AU NBAC N57-1631.

### Private collection

雪梨中國銀行, Sam He Private Collection.

## Secondary sources

Akio, Tsuchida (2010). China's "Public Diplomacy" toward the United States before Pearl Harbor. *Journal of American-East Asian Relations* 17: 35–55.

Albinski, Henry (1965). *Australian Policies and Attitudes Toward China*. Princeton, NJ: Princeton University Press.

Alford, Williams (1995). *To Steal a Book Is an Elegant Offense: Intellectual Property Law in Chinese Civilization*. Stanford: Stanford University Press.

Anderson, Benedict (2006). *Imagined Communities: Reflections on the Origin and Spread of Nationalism*. London: Verso.

Andrews, E.M. (1981). The Australian Government and the Manchurian Crisis, 1931–1934. *Australian Journal of International Affairs* 35(3): 307–16.

Andrews, E.M. (1985). *Australia and China: The Ambiguous Relationship*. Carlton: Melbourne University Press.

Ashplant, T.G., Graham Dawson, and Michael Roper, eds (2000). *The Politics of War Memory and Commemoration*. New York: Routledge.

Austin, Denise A. (2020). Women and Guangdong Native-Place Charity in Chinese Australian Pentecostalism: "The Miracle of Grace". In John Fitzgerald and Hon-ming Yip, eds. *Chinese Diaspora Charity and the Cantonese Pacific, 1850–1949*, 173–192. Hong Kong: Hong Kong University Press.

Bagnall, Kate (2011). Rewriting the History of Chinese Families in Nineteenth-Century Australia. *Australian Historical Studies* 42(1): 62–77.

Bagnall, Kate (2015a). Early Chinese Newspapers: Trove Presents A New Perspective on Australian History.

Bagnall, Kate (2015b). *The Chungking legation: Australia's Diplomatic Mission in Wartime China*. Melbourne: Museum of Chinese Australian History.

Bagnall, Kate and Julia Martínez, eds (2021). *Locating Chinese Women: Historical Mobility between China and Australia*. Hong Kong: Hong Kong University Press.

Baldwin, Jennifer Joan (2019). *Languages Other than English in Australian High Education: Policies, Provision and the National Interest*. Cham: Springer.

Ball, Desmond J. (1978). Allied Intelligence Cooperation Involving Australia during World War II. *Australian Journal of International Affairs* 32(3): 299–309.

Baumler, Alan (2020). Masculinity, Feminity, Sacrifice, and Celebrity during China's War of Resistance: Telling the Lives of the Aviators Yan Haiwen (1916–37) and Lee Ya-Ching (1912–98). *Nan Nü* 22(1): 70–115.

Beaumont, Joan (1988). *Gull Force: Survival and Leadership in Captivity, 1941–1945*. Sydney: Allen and Unwin.

Beaumont, Joan, ed. (1996). *Australia's War, 1939–1945*. Sydney: Allen and Unwin.

Begley, Neil (1995). *An Australian's childhood in China under the Japanese*. Sydney: Kangaroo Press.

Bell, Catherine (2009). *Ritual Theory, Ritual Practice*. New York: Oxford University Press.

# Bibliography

Benton, Gregor (2007). *Chinese Migrants and Internationalism: Forgotten History, 1917-1945*. London: Routledge.

Benton, Gregor and Hong Liu, *Dear China: Emigrant Letters and Remittances, 1820-1980* (Oakland: University of California Press, 2018).

Berkhoff, Karel (2012). *Motherland in Danger Soviet Propaganda during World War II*. Cambridge: Harvard University Press.

Bodnar, John (1992). *Remaking America: Public Memory, Commemoration, and Patriotism in the Twentieth Century*. Princeton: Princeton University Press.

Boileau, Joanna (2017). *Chinese Market Gardening in Australia and New Zealand: Gardens of Prosperity*. Cham: Palgrave Macmillan.

Boyle, John (1972). *China and Japan at War 1937-1945: The Politics of Collaboration*. Stanford: Stanford University Press.

Brettell, Caroline and Deborah Reed-Danahay (2014). *Civic Engagements: The Citizenship Practices of Indian and Vietnamese Immigrants*. Stanford: Stanford University Press.

Brooks, Tim (2007). *British Propaganda to France, 1940-1944: Machinery, Method and Message*. Edinburgh: Edinburgh University Press.

Brothers, Caroline (1997). *War and Photography: A Cultural History*. New York: Routledge.

Byrne, Denis, Ien Ang and Phillip Mar, eds. (2023). *The China–Australia Migration Corridor: Heritage and History*. Melbourne: Hong Kong University Press.

Campbell, Malcolm (2008). *Ireland's New Worlds: Immigrants, Politics, and Society in the United States and Australia, 1815-1922*. Madison: University of Wisconsin Press.

Carr, Edward Hallett (1939). *Propaganda in International Politics*. Oxford: Clarendon Press.

Catherwood, Christopher (2003). *The Balkans in World War Two: Britain's Balkan Dilemma*. Basingstoke: Palgrave Macmillan).

Chan, Shelly (2015). The Case for Diaspora: A Temporal Approach to the Chinese Experience. *Journal of Asian Studies* 74(1): 107–128.

Chan, Shelly (2018). *Diaspora's Homeland: Modern China in the Age of Global Migration*. Durham: Duke University Press.

Chen, Yong (2006). Understanding Chinese American Transnationalism During the Early Twentieth Century: An Economic Perspective. In Sucheng Chan, ed., *Chinese American Transnationalism: The Flow of People, Resources, and Ideas between China and America during the Exclusion Era*, 156–173. Philadelphia: Temple University Press.

Cheng, Christopher (2022). Australian Migrant Heritage in South China: The Legacy of Diaspora-Funded Schools in Twentieth Century Zhongshan. PhD thesis, Western Sydney University, Sydney.

Choi, C.Y. (1975). *Chinese Migration and Settlement in Australia*. Sydney: Sydney University Press.

Coatney, Caryn (2021). Recovering an Optimist Era: Chinese-Australian Journalism from the 1920s to the 1940s. In Catherine Dewhirst and Richard Scully, eds. *Voices of Challenge in Australia's Migrant and Minority Press*, 83–106. London: Palgrave Macmillan.

Coble, Parks (2015). *China's War Reporters: The Legacy of Resistance against Japan*. Cambridge: Harvard University Press.

Cohen, Paul (1987). *Between Tradition and Modernity: Wang T'ao and Reform in Late Ch'ing China*. Cambridge: Council on East Asian Studies, Harvard University.

Cole, Robert (1990). *Britain and the War of Words in Neutral Europe, 1939–1945: The Art of the Possible*. New York: Palgrave Macmillan.

Connerton, Paul (1989). *How Societies Remember*. Cambridge: Cambridge University Press.

Cottle, Drew (2003). Forgotten Foreign Militants: The Chinese Seamen's Union in Australia, 1942–1946. In Hal Alexander and Phil Griffiths, eds. *A Few Rough Reds: Stories of Rank and File Organizing*, 135–51. Canberra: Australian Society for the Study of Labor History.

Couchman, Sophie (2011). Making the "Last Chinaman": Photography and Chinese as a "Vanishing" People in Australia's Rural Local Histories. *Australian Historical Studies* 42(1): 78–91.

Couchman, Sophie and Kate Bagnall, eds. (2015). *Chinese Australians: Politics, Engagement and Resistance*. Leiden: Brill.

Cresciani, Gianfranco (1980). *Fascism, Anti-Fascism and Italians in Australia*. Canberra: Australian National University Press.

Cronin, Kathryn (1982). *Colonial Casualties: Chinese in Early Victoria*. Carlton: Melbourne University Press.

Cull, Nicholas (1995). *Selling War: British Propaganda Campaign against American "Neutrality" in the World War II*. New York: Oxford University Press.

Cushman, Jennifer (1984). A "Colonial Casualty": The Chinese Community in Australian Historiography. *Asian Studies Association of Australia* 7(3): 100–13.

Daniels, Roger (1988). *Asian America: Chinese and Japanese in the United States since 1850*. Seattle: University of Washington Press.

Darian-Smith, Kate (2023). Australian-Japanese Cultural Connections. In Kate Darien-Smith and David Lowe, eds. *The Australian Embassy in Tokyo and Australia-Japan Relationship*, 183–208. Canberra: ANU Press.

Davidson, Andrew P. (2008). The Play of Identity, Memory and Belonging: Chinese Migrants in Sydney. In Kuah-Pearce Khun Eng and Andrew P.

Davison, eds *At Home in the Chinese Diaspora: Memories, Identities and Belongings*, 12–32. New York: Palgrave Macmillan.

Day, David. (1992). *Reluctant Nation: Australia and the Allied Defeat of Japan 1942–1945*. New York: Oxford University Press.

Denton, Kirk A. (2007). Horror and Atrocity: Memory of Japanese Imperialism in Chinese Museums. In Ching Kwan Lee and Guobin Yang, eds. *Re-envisioning the Chinese Revolution: The Politics and Poetics of Collective Memory in Reform China*, 245–86. Stanford: Stanford University Press.

Dryburgh, Marjorie (2001). Regional Office and the National Interest: Song Zheyuan in North China, 1933–1937. In David P. Barret and Larry N. Shyu, eds. *Chinese Collaboration with Japan, 1932–1945*, 38–55. Stanford: Stanford University Press.

Drysdale, Peter (1987). The Relationship with Japan: Despite the Vicissitudes. In L.T. Evans and J.D.B. Miller, eds. *Policy and Practice: Essays in Honour of Sir John Crawford*, 66–71. Canberra: Australian National University Press.

Du, Yue (2019). Sun Yat-sen as Guofu: Competition over Nationalist Party Orthodoxy in the Second Sino-Japanese War. *Modern China* 45(2): 201–35.

Edkins, Jenny (2003). *Trauma and the Memory of Politics*. Cambridge: Cambridge University Press.

Edwards, Elizabeth, ed. (1994). *Anthropology & Photography 1860–1920*. London: Yale University Press.

Edwards, Grace (2013). Dancing Dragons: Reflections on Creating a Cultural History of the Chinese Australian Community. *Chinese Southern Diaspora Studies* 6: 102–11.

Elliott, Andrew (2019). "Oriental Calls": Anglophone Travel Writing and Tourism as Propaganda during the Second Sino-Japanese War, 1937–1941. *Japan Review* (33): 117–42.

Eng, Kuah-Pearce Khun and Andrew P. Davidson, eds (2008). *At Home in the Chinese Diaspora: Memories, Identities, and Belongings*. New York: Palgrave Macmillan.

Fairbank, John and Denis Crispin Twitchett, eds (2002). *The Cambridge History of China, Vol. 13*. Cambridge: Cambridge University Press.

Finnane, Mark (2012). In the Same Bed but Dreaming Different. In David Walker and Agnieszka Sobocinska, eds. *Australia's Asia: from Yellow Peril to Asian Century*, 223–244. Crawley: UWA Publishing.

Fitzgerald, John (2006). Transnational Networks and National Identities in the Australian Commonwealth: The Chinese-Australasian Kuomintang, 1923–1937. *Australian Historical Studies* 37(127): 95–116.

Fitzgerald, John (2007). *Big White Lie: Chinese Australians in White Australia*. Sydney: University of New South Wales Press.

Fitzgerald, John (2010). Revolution and Respectability: Chinese Masons in Australian History. In Ann Curthoys and Marilyn Lake, eds., *Connected Worlds: History in Transnational Perspective*, 89–110. Canberra: ANU Press.

Fitzgerald, John and Mei-fen Kuo (2017). Diaspora Charity and Welfare Sovereignty in the Chinese Republic: Shanghai Charity Innovator William Yinson Lee (Li Yuanxin, 1884–1965). *Twentieth Century China* 42(1): 72–96.

Fitzgerald, Shirley (1997). *Red Tape, Gold Scissors: The Story of Sydney's Chinese*. Sydney: State Library of New South Wales Press.

Fitzgerald, Shirley (2001). The Chinese of Sydney with Particular Focus on the 1930s. In Henry Chan, Ann Curthoys, and Nora Chiang, eds. *The Overseas Chinese in Australasia History, Settlement and Interactions*, 140–51. Canberra: Australian National University.

Forchtner, Bernhard (2016). *Lessons from the Past? Memory, Narrativity and Subjectivity*. London: Palgrave Macmillan.

Foster, Kevin (2016). Regimes of Truth: Australian Combat Photography in the Second World War. *Journal of Australian Studies* 40(3): 253–75.

Frei, Henry (1991). *Japan's Southward Advance and Australia: From the Sixteenth Century to World War II*. Carlton, Melbourne University Press.

Gabaccia, Donna R. and Dirk Hoerder, eds. (2011). *Connecting Seas and Connected Ocean Rims: Indian, Atlantic, and Pacific Oceans and China Seas Migrations from the 1830s to the 1930s*. Leiden: Brill.

Gao, Mobo (2017) Early Chinese Migrants to Australia: A Critique of the Sojourner Narrative on Nineteenth-century Chinese Migration to British Colonies. *Asian Studies Review* 41(3): 389–404.

Gardener, Tess (2024). "Our Friends the Chinese": Australian Advisers and Images of China in the World Wars. *History Australia* 21(1): 54–71.

Gassin, Grace (2021). All Eyes on You: Debutantes' Explorations of Chinese Australian Womanhood at the Dragon Festival Ball. *Australian Historical Studies* 52(4): 533–48.

Gatu, Dagfinn (2008). *Village China at War*. Vancouver: UBC Press.

Gibson, Peter (2020). The Market Gardens of Dark Dragon Ridge, New South Wales, Australia, 1876–1930. *Australian Economic History Review* 60(3): 1–22.

Gibson, Peter (2022). *Made in Chinatown: Chinese Australian Furniture Factories, 1880–1930*. Sydney: Sydney University Press.

Gibson, Peter and Simon Ville (2019). Australian Wool and Chinese Industrialization, 1901–41. *Twentieth Century China* 44(3): 265–87.

Giese, Diana (1997). *Astronauts, Lost Souls and Dragons: Voices of Today's Chinese Australians in Conversation with Diana Giese*. St Lucia: University of Queensland Press.

# Bibliography

Giese, Diana (1999). *Courage and Service: Chinese Australians and World War II.* Sydney: Courage and Service Project.

Gilson, Miriam (1962). *Bibliography of the Migrant Press in Australia 1847–1962.* Canberra: Department of Demography and Australian National University.

Godley, Michael (1981). *The Mandarin-Capitalists from Nanyang: Overseas Chinese Enterprise in the Modernization of China, 1893–1911.* Cambridge: Cambridge University Press.

Goldin, Paul R. (2011). *Confucianism.* Berkeley: University of California Press.

Goldsworthy, David, ed. (2002). *Facing North: A Century of Australian Engagement with Asia.* Melbourne: Melbourne University Press.

Govor, Elena (2005). *Russian Anzacs in Australian History.* Sydney: UNSW Press.

Greene, Charlotte (2005). Fantastic Dreams: William Liu, and the Origins and Influence of the Protest against the White Australia Policy in the 20th Century. PhD thesis, University of Sydney, Sydney. https://ses.library.usyd.edu.au/handle/2123/4028.

Gutiérrez, Ramón A. and Geneviève Fabre, eds (1995). *Feasts and Celebrations in North American Ethnic Communities.* Albuquerque: University of New Mexico Press.

Hall, Robert A. (1990). "An Invitation to National Disunity": Chinese Support for Australia's War Effort in the Second World War and the White Australian Response. *War and Society* 8(2): 104–19.

Hasluck, Paul (1980). *Diplomatic Witness: Australian Foreign Affairs 1941–1947.* Carlton: Melbourne University Press.

Hazareesingh, Sudhir (2004). *The Saint-Napoleon: Celebrations of Sovereignty in Nineteenth-Century France.* Cambridge: Harvard University Press.

Hench, John (2010). *Books As Weapons: Propaganda, Publishing, and the Battle for Global Markets in the Era of World War II.* Ithaca: Cornell University Press.

Herf, Jeffrey (2006). *The Jewish Enemy: Nazi Propaganda during World War II and the Holocaust.* Cambridge: Harvard University Press.

Hilliker, J.F. (1984). Distant Ally: Canadian Relations with Australia during the Second World War. *Journal of Imperial and Commonwealth History* 13(1): 46–67.

Hobsbawm, Eric and Terence Ranger, eds (2013). *The Invention of Tradition.* New York: Cambridge University Press.

Hodge, Errol (1992). Radio Australia in the Second World War. *Australian Journal of International Affairs* 46(1): 93–108.

Hornadge, Bill (1976). *The Yellow Peril: A Squint at Some Australian Attitudes towards Orientals.* Dubbo: Review Publications.

Hu, Bolin (2021). Reporting China: Chinese-Language Newspapers and Diasporic Chinese Identity in Australia, 1931–37. *Journal of Chinese Overseas* 17(1): 84–116.

Hu, Bolin (2023). Diasporic Rituals and Identity: Chinese Commemorations of War in Australia in the Early Second Sino-Japanese War, 1931–1933. *Australian Historical Studies* 54(1): 44–60.

Hu, Bolin (2024). Fractured Patriotism: General Tsai Ting-kai and the Divided Allegiances of Chinese Australians in the Early 1930s. *Australian Historical Studies* 55(4): 688–704.

Huang, Zhong and Wenche Ommundsen (2015). Towards a Multilingual National Literature: The *Tung Wah Times* and the Origins of Chinese Australian Writing. *Journal of the Association for the Study of Australian Literature* 15(3): 1–11.

Huck, Arthur (1968). *The Chinese in Australia*. Croydon: Longmans.

Immigration Reform Group (1962). *Immigration: Control or Colour Bar?* Melbourne: Melbourne University Press.

Jacobson, Matthew (1995). *Special Sorrow: The Diasporic Imagination of Irish, Polish, and Jewish Immigrants in the United States*. Cambridge: Harvard University Press.

Johnson, Mathew (2011). Propaganda and Sovereignty in Wartime China: Morale Operations and Psychological Warfare under the Office of War Information. *Modern Asian Studies* 45(2): 303–44.

Jones, Paul (2001). Trading in a "Fool's Paradise"? White Australia and Trade Diversion Dispute of 1936. In Vera Mackie and Paul Jones, eds. *Relationships: Japan and Australia, 1870s–1950s*, 133–62. Parkville: University of Melbourne.

Jones, Paul (2005). The View from the Edge: Chinese Australians and China, 1890 to 1949. In Charles Ferrall, Paul Millar, and Keren Smith, eds. *East by South: China in the Australasian Imagination*, 46–69. Wellington: Victoria University Press.

Jowett, Garth S. and Victoria O'Donnell (2015). *Propaganda and Persuasion*. Los Angeles: Sage.

Kallis, Aristotle A. (2005). *Nazi Propaganda and the Second World War*. New York: Palgrave Macmillan.

Kamp, Alanna (2022). *Intersectional Lives: Chinese Australian Women in White Australia*. London: Routledge.

Kennedy, Alastair (2015). *Chinese ANZACS: Australians of Chinese Descent in the Defence Forces 1885–1919*. Wellington: New Zealand Chinese Association.

Khoo, Tseen and Rodney Noonan (2011). Wartime Fundraising by Chinese Australian Communities. *Australian Historical Studies* 42(1): 92–110.

Kildea, Jeff (2007). *Anzacs and Ireland*. Sydney: University of New South Wales Press.

Knightley, Phillip (1986). Cracking the Jap: Burchett on World War Two. In Ben Kiernan, ed. *Burchett Reporting the Other Side of the World 1939–1983*, 3–12. Melbourne: Quartet Books.

Knorr, Daniel (2015). Debating China's Destiny: Writing the Nation's Past and Future in Wartime China. In Joseph W. Esheric and Matthew T. Combs, eds. *1943: China at the Crossroads*. Ithaca: Cornell University Press.

Koh, Ernest (2013). *Diaspora at War: The Chinese of Singapore between Empire and Nation, 1937–1945*. Leiden: Brill.

Kuhn, Philip A. (2008). *Chinese among Others: Emigration in Modern Times*. Laham: Rowman and Littlefield Publishers.

Kuo, Mei-fen (2009). The Making of a Diasporic Identity: The Case of the Sydney Chinese Commercial Elite, 1890s–1900s. *Journal of Chinese Overseas* 5: 336–63.

Kuo, Mei-fen (2013). *Making Chinese Australia: Urban Elites, Newspapers and the Formation of Chinese-Australian Identity, 1892–1912*. Clayton: Monash University Publishing.

Kuo, Mei-fen (2018). Jinxin: The Remittance Trade and Enterprising Chinese Australians, 1850–1916. In Gregor Benton, Hong Liu, and Huimei Zhang, eds., *The Qiaopi Trade and Transnational Networks in the Chinese Diaspora*. London: Routledge.

Kuo, Mei-fen (2020). The "Invisible Work" of Women: Gender and Philanthropic Sociability in the Evolution of Early Chinese Australian Voluntary Organizations. In John Fitzgerald and Hon-ming Yip, eds. *Chinese Diaspora Charity and the Cantonese Pacific, 1850–1949*, 154–172. Hong Kong: Hong Kong University Press.

Kuo, Mei-fen (2024a). Chinese Entrepreneurs Connecting Rural Australia to Asia: Harry Fay of Hong Yuen Pty Ltd. In Julia T. Martínez, Claire Lowrie, and Gregor Benton, eds., *Chinese Colonial Entanglements: Commodities and Traders in the Southern Asia Pacific, 1880–1950*, 132–52. Honolulu: University of Hawaii Press.

Kuo, Mei-fen (2024b). "Girls Doing A Big Job" in Diaspora: Cosmopolitan Minority and Making Modern Chinese Women Associations in White Australia. *Ethnic and Racial Studies* 47(16): 3602–24.

Kuo, Mei-fen and Judith Brett (2013). *Unlocking the History of the Australasian Kuo Min Tang*. Melbourne: Australian Scholarly Publishing.

Kushner, Barak (2006). *The Thought War: Japanese Imperial Propaganda*. Honolulu: University of Hawaii Press.

Lake, Marilyn and Henry Reynolds (2008). *Drawing the Global Colour Line: White Men's Countries and the International Challenge of Racial Equality.* Cambridge: Cambridge University Press.

Lary, Diana (2010).*The Chinese People at War: Human Suffering and Social Transformation, 1937-1945.* Cambridge: Cambridge University Press.

Lee, Ching Kwan and Guobin Yang (2007). Introduction: Memory, Power and Culture. In Ching Kwan Lee and Guobin Yang, eds. *Re-envisioning the Chinese Revolution: The Politics and Poetics of Collective Memory in Reform China*, 1-20. Stanford: Stanford University Press.

Lee, David and David Lowe (2023). In Kate Darien-Smith and David Lowe, eds. *The Australian Embassy in Tokyo and Australia-Japan Relationship*, 41-76. Canberra: ANU Press.

Lemagny, Jean-Claude and André Rouillé (1987). *A History of Photography: Social and Cultural Perspectives, trans. Janet Lloyd.* Cambridge: Cambridge University Press.

Lewinski, Jorge (1978). *The Camera at War: A History of War Photography from 1848 to the Present Day.* London: W.H. Allen.

Light, Rowan (2018). Unknown Anzacs: The Politics and Performance of Bodily Repatriation in Postcolonial State Formation. *Australian Historical Studies* 49(2): 237–54.

Lim, Shirley Jennifer (2012). Glamorising Racial Modernity. In David Walker and Agnieszka Sobocinska, eds. *Australia's Asia: from Yellow Peril to Asian Century*, 145–169. Crawley: UWA Publishing.

Ling, Chek (2001). *Plantings in a New Land: Stories of Survival, Endurance and Emancipation.* Brisbane: Society of Chinese Australian Academics of Queensland.

Ling, Huping (1998). *Surviving on the Gold Mountain: A History of Chinese American Women and Their Lives.* Albany: State University of New York.

Liu, Hailong (2020). *Propaganda: Ideas, Discourses and Its Legitimization.* Abingdon: Routledge.

Llewelyn, James (2019). Pre-Pacific War Japanese Espionage and Propaganda Activities in Australia: A Case of Too Little Too Late. *Journal of Intelligence History* 18(1): 18–37.

Loh, Morag (1989). *Dinky-Di: The Contributions of Chinese Immigrants and Australians of Chinese Descent to Australia's Defence Forces and War Efforts 1899-1988.* Canberra: Australian Government Publishing Service.

Lowe, David (1996). Australia in the World. In Joan Beaumont ed. *Australia's War, 1939–45*, 232–259. St Leonards: Allen and Unwin.

Loy-Wilson, Sophie (2009). Peanuts and Publicists: "Letting Australian Friends Know the Chinese Side of the Story" in Interwar Sydney. *History Australia* 6(1): 1–20.

Loy-Wilson, Sophie (2011). Liberating Asia: Strikes and Protest in Sydney and Shanghai, 1920-39. *History Workshop Journal* 72(1): 75–102.

Loy-Wilson, Sophie (2014). Rural Geographies and Chinese Empires: Chinese Shopkeepers and Shop-Life in Australia. *Australian Historical Studies* 45(3): 407–24.

Loy-Wilson, Sophie (2017). *Australians in Shanghai: Race, Rights and Nation in Treaty Port China*. Abingdon: Routledge.

Lydon, Jane (1999). *Many Inventions: The Chinese in the Rocks 1890-1930*. Clayton: Monash Publications in History.

Macgregor, Paul (2021). Alice Lim Kee: Journalist, Actor, Broadcaster, and Goodwill Ambassador. In Kate Bagnall and Julia T. Martínez, eds. *Locating Chinese Women: Historical Mobility between China and Australia*, 175–203. Hong Kong: Hong Kong University Press.

Mackie, Vera and Paul Jones, eds (2001). *Relationships: Japan and Australia, 1870s-1950s*. Parkville: University of Melbourne.

Markus, Andrew (1994). *Australia Race Relations 1788-1993*. St Leonards: Allen and Unwin.

Martínez, Julia T. (2015). Chinese Politics in Darwin: Interconnections between the Wah On Society and the Kuo Min Tang. In Sophie Couchman and Kate Bagnall, eds., *Chinese Australians: Politics, Engagement and Resistance*, 240–66. Leiden: Brill.

Martínez, Julia T. (2021). Mary Chong and Gwen Fong: University-Educated Chinese Australian Women. In Kate Bagnall and Julia T. Martínez, eds. *Locating Chinese Women: Historical Mobility between China and Australia*, 204–29. Hong Kong: Hong Kong University Press.

Mayo, James (1988). War Memorials as Political Memory. *Geographical Review* 78(1): 62–75.

McDonald, Matt (2010). "Lest We Forget": The Politics of Memory and Australian Military Intervention. *International Political Sociology* 4(3): 287–302.

McKeown, Adam (1999). Conceptualizing Chinese Diasporas, 1842 to 1949. *Journal of Asian Studies* 58(2): 306–37.

Meo, Lucy (1968). *Japan's Radio War on Australia, 1941-1945*. Carlton: Melbourne University Press.

Mitter, Rana (2013). *Forgotten Ally: China's World War II, 1937-1945*. Boston: Houghton Mifflin Harcourt.

Mittler, Barbara (2004). *A Newspaper for China? Power, Identity, and Change in Shanghai's News Media, 1872-1912*. London: Harvard University Asia Center.

Murray, Jacqui (2004). *Watching the Sun Rise: Australian Reporting of Japan, 1931 to the Fall of Singapore*. Lanham: Lexington Books.

Ngan, Lucille (2008). Generational Identities through Time: Identities and Homelands of the ABCs. In Kuah-Pearce Khun Eng and Andrew P. Davidson, eds. *At Home in the Chinese Diaspora: Memories, Identities, and Belongings*, 74–93. New York: Palgrave Macmillan.

O'Connor, Peter (2010). *The English-Language Press Networks of East Asia, 1918–1945*. Folkstone: Global Oriental.

Oliver, Pam (2012). World Wars and the Anticipation of Conflict: The Impact on Long-Established Australian-Japanese Relations, 1905–43. In Peter Dean and Kim Beazley, eds. *Australia 1942: In the Shadow of War*, 33–52. Cambridge: Cambridge University Press.

Oliver, Pam, (2010). *Raids on Australia: 1942 and Japan's Plans for Australia*. Melbourne: Australian Scholarly Publishing.

Ozouf, Mona (1991). *Festivals and the French Revolution*. Alan Sheridan, trans. Cambridge: Harvard University Press.

Papalia, Gerado (2020). The Italian "Fifth Column" in Australia: Fascist Propaganda, Italian-Australians and Internment. *Australian Journal of Politics and History* 66(2): 214–31.

Pratkanis, Anthony R. and Elliot Aronson (2001). *Age of Propaganda: The Everyday Use and Abuse of Persuasion*. New York: Henry Holt.

Price, Charles (1984). *The Great White Walls Are Built: Restrictive Immigration to North America and Australasia, 1836–1888*. Canberra: Australian Institute of International Affairs.

Purcell, William (1981). The Development of Japan's Trading Company Network in Australia, 1890–1941. *Australian Economic History Review* 21(2): 114–32.

Putnis, Peter (2012). International News Agencies, News-Flow, and the USA-Australia Relationship from the 1920s till the End of the Second World War. *Media History* 18(3–4): 423–41.

Rankine, Wendy (1995). Australia's Chinese Army Corps. In Jan Ryan, ed. *Chinese in Australia and New Zealand: A Multidisciplinary Approach*, 67–74. New Delhi: New Age International Publishers.

Rasmussen, Amanda (2004). Networks and Negotiations: Bendigo's Chinese and the Easter Fair. *Journal of Australian Colonial History* 6: 79–92.

Reis, João José (2003). *Death Is a Festival: Funeral Rites and Rebellion in Nineteenth-Century Brazil*. Chapel Hill: University of North Carolina Press.

Roper, Michael (1985). Inventing Tradition in Colonial Society: Bendigo's Easter Fair, 1871–1885. *Journal of Australian Studies* 9(17): 31–40.

Ryan, Jane (1995). *Ancestors: Chinese in Colonial Australia*. South Fremantle: Fremantle Arts Centre Press.

# Bibliography

Ryō, Namikawa (1983). Japanese Overseas Broadcasting: A Personal Review. In K.R.M. Short, ed. *Film and Radio Propaganda in World War II*, 319–33. Beckenham: Croom Helm.

Saunders, Kay (1997). "An Instrument of Strategy": Propaganda, Public Policy and the Media in Australia during the Second World War. *War and Society* 15(2): 75–90.

Saunders, Kay (1994). The Dark Shadow of White Australia: Racial Anxieties in Australia in World War II. *Ethnic and Racial Studies* 17(2): 325–41.

Schedvin, Boris (2008). *Emissaries of Trade: A History of the Australian Trade Commissioner Service.* Canberra: Department of Foreign Affairs and Trade.

Seraphim, Franziska (2006). *War Memory and Social Politics in Japan, 1945–2005.* Cambridge: Harvard University Asia Center.

Shen, Yuanfang (2001). *Dragon Seed in the Antipodes: Chinese-Australian Autobiographies.* Carlton: Melbourne University Press.

Shu, Sheng-chi (2015). Managing International News-Agency Relations under the Kuomintang: China's Central News Agency, Zhao Minheng, and Reuters, 1931–1945. *Frontiers of History in China* 10(4): 594–644.

Siam, William (2015). *China and ANU: Diplomats, Adventurers, Scholars.* Canberra: ANU Press.

Sinn, Elizabeth and Wai-Ling Wong (2005). Place, Identity and Immigrant Communities: The Organisation of the Yulan Festival in Post-War Hong Kong. *Asia Pacific Viewpoint* 46(3): 295–306.

So, Wai Chor (2002). The Making of Guomindang's Japan Policy, 1932–1937: The Roles of Chiang Kai-shek and Wang Jingwei. *Modern China* 28(2): 213–52.

Sobocinska, Agnieszka (2014). *Visiting the Neighbours: Australians in Asia.* Sydney: University of New South Wales Press.

Sontag, Susan (2003). *Regarding the Pain of Others.* New York: Penguin.

Stevens, Keith (2005). A Token Operation: 204 Military Mission to China, 1941–1945. *Asian Affairs* 36(1): 66–74.

Stoler, Mark (2000). *Allies and Adversaries: The Joint Chiefs of Staff, the Grand Alliance, and U.S. Strategy in World War II.* Chapel Hill: University of North Carolina Press.

Strahan, Lachlan (1996). *Australia's China: Changing Perceptions from the 1930s to the 1990s.* Cambridge: Cambridge University Press.

T.G. Ashplant, Graham Dawson and Michael Roper. (2000). The Politics of War Memory and Commemoration: Contexts, Structures and Dynamics. In T. G. Ashplant, Graham Dawson, and Michael Roper, eds. *The Politics of War Memory and Commemoration*, 3–85. New York: Routledge.

Tan, Carole (2006). "The Tyranny of Appearance": Chinese Australian Identities and the Politics of Difference. *Journal of Intercultural Studies* 27(1–2): 65–82.

Tavan, Gwenda (2005). *The Long, Slow Death of White Australia*. Melbourne: Scribe Publications.

Taylor, Jay (2009). *The Generalissimo: Chiang Kai-shek and the Struggle for Modern China*. Cambridge: Harvard University Press.

Taylor, Jeremy (2007). Taipei's "Britisher": W. Goddard and the Promotion of Nationalist China in the Cold-War Commonwealth. *New Zealand Journal of Asian Studies* 9(2): 126–146.

Taylor, Jeremy (2009). Being a "Friend of Free China": W.G. Goddard in Nationalist Taiwan. *Chinese Historical Review* 16(2): 208–227.

Thorne, Christopher (1978). *Allies of a Kind: The United States, Britain and the War against Japan, 1941–1945*. London: Hamish Hamilton.

Todman, Daniel (2020). *Britain's War: A New World, 1942–1947*. Oxford: Oxford University Press.

Tong, Hollington (1950). *Dateline: China; The Beginning of China's Press Relations with the World*. New York: Rockport Press.

Tong, Hollington and Mih Walter, ed. (2005). *Chiang Kai-shek's Teacher and Ambassador*. Bloomington: Author House.

Tsai, Tsan-Huang (2016). From Cantonese Religious Procession to Australian Cultural Heritage: The Changing Chinese Face of Bendigo's Easter Parade. *Ethnomusicology Forum* 25(1): 86–106.

Tsai, Weiping (2010). *Reading Shenbao: Nationalism, Consumerism and Individuality in China 1917-37*. New York: Palgrave Macmillan.

Tsokhas, Kosmas (1989). The Wool Industry and the 1936 Trade Diversion Dispute between Australia and Japan. *Australian Historical Studies* 23(93): 442–61.

Turner, Victor, ed. (1982). *Celebration: Studies in Festivity and Ritual*. Washington: Smithsonian Institution Press.

Twomey, Christina (2007). *Australia's Forgotten Prisoners: Civilians Interned by the Japanese in World War Two*. Cambridge: Cambridge University Press.

Vanelli, Ron (2015). *The Evolution of Human Sociability*. Cambridge: Cambridge University Press.

Vehviläinen, Olli (2002). *Finland in the Second World War between Germany and Russia*. Basingstoke: Palgrave Macmillan.

Volkan, Vamik (2001). Transgenerational Transmissions and Chosen Traumas: An Aspect of Large-Group Identity. *Group Analysis* 34(1): 79–97.

Volkan, Vamik (2005). 'Large Group Identity and Chosen Trauma,' *Psychoanalysis Downunder* 6(2005): 1–11.

Walker, David (2012). *Anxious Nation: Australia and the Rise of Asia 1850–1939*. Crawley: UWA Publishing.

# Bibliography

Walker, David (2019). *Stranded Nation: White Australia in an Asian Region*. Crawley: UWA Publishing.

Waller, Keith (1990). *A Diplomatic Life: Some Memories*. Nathan: Griffith University.

Wang, Gungwu (1991). *China and the Chinese Overseas*. Singapore: Times Academic Press.

Wang, Zheng (2012). *Never Forget National Humiliation: Historical Memory in Chinese Politics and Foreign Relations*. New York: Columbia University Press.

Waters, Christopher (2001). Australia, the British Empire and the Second World War. *War and Society* 19(1): 93–107.

Watt, Alan (1967). *The Evolution of Australian Foreign Policy*. Cambridge: Cambridge University Press.

Wei, Shuge (2017). *News Under Fire: China's Propaganda against Japan in the English-Language Press, 1928–1941*. Hong Kong: Hong Kong University Press.

Wellington, Jennifer (2017). *Exhibiting War: The Great War, Museums and Memory in Britain, Canada and Australia*. Cambridge: Cambridge University Press.

Willcox, David (2005). *Propaganda, the Press and Conflict: The Gulf War and Kosovo*. Abingdon: Routledge.

Williams, Michael (1998). Brief Sojourn in Your Native Land: Sydney's *Huaqiao* and Their Links with South China during the First Half of the Twentieth Century. Master's thesis, University of New England, Armidale. https://chinozhistory.org/wp-content/uploads/2021/04/Sojourn.pdf

Williams, Michael (2018). *Returning Home with Glory: Chinese Villagers around the Pacific, 1849 to 1949*. Hong Kong: Hong Kong University Press.

Williams, Michael (2021a). *Australia's Dictation Test: The Test It Was a Crime to Fail*. Leiden: Brill.

Williams, Michael (2021b). Smoking Opium, Puffing Cigars, and Drinking Gingerbeer: Chinese Opera in Australia. In Jane W. Davidson, Michael Halliwell, and Stephanie Rocke, eds. *Opera, Emotion and the Antipodes Volume I Historical Perspectives: Creating the Metropolis; Delineating the Other*, 166–208. London: Routledge.

Williams, Val (1994). *Warworks: Women, Photography and the Iconography of War*. London: Virago Press.

Winter, Jay (1995). *Sites of Memory, Sites of Mourning: The Great War in European Cultural History*. Cambridge: Cambridge University Press.

Winter, Jay (2006). *Remembering War: The Great War between Memory and History in the Twentieth Century*. London: Yale University Press.

Winter, Jay and Emmanuel Sivan (1999). Setting the Framework. In Jay Winter and Emmanuel Sivan, eds. *War and Remembrance in the Twentieth Century*, 6–39. Cambridge: Cambridge University Press.

Winter, Jay and Emmanuel Sivan, eds (1999). *War and Remembrance in the Twentieth Century*. Cambridge: Cambridge University Press.

Wong, K. Scott (2005). *Americans First: Chinese Americans and the Second World War*. Cambridge: Harvard University Press.

Wu, Judy Tzu-Chun (2005). *Doctor Mom Chung of the Fair-Haired Bastards: The Life of a Wartime Celebrity*. Berkeley: University of California Press.

Yao, Steven G. (2010). *Foreign Accents: Chinese American Verse from Exclusion to Postethnicity*. New York: Oxford University Press.

Yarwood, A.T. (2008). The "White Australia" policy: A Re-Interpretation of Its Development in the Late Colonial Period. *Australian Historical Studies* 10(39): 257–269.

Yen, Ching-huang (1976). *The Overseas Chinese and the 1911 Revolution, with Special Reference to Singapore and Malaya*. Kuala Lumpur: Oxford University Press.

Yen, Ching-Hwang (2008). *The Chinese in Southeast Asia and Beyond: Socio-economic and Political Dimensions*. Singapore: World Scientific Publishing.

Yin, Xiao-huang (2000). *Chinese American Literature since the 1850s*. Urbana: University of Illinois Press.

Yong, C.F. (1977). *The New Gold Mountain: The Chinese in Australia, 1901–1921*. Richmond: Raphael Arts.

Yong, C.F. and R.B. McKenna (1990). *The Kuomintang Movement in British Malaya 1912–1949*. Singapore: National University of Singapore.

Yoshida, Takashi (2006). *The Making of the "Rape of Nanking" History and Memory in Japan, China, and the United States*. New York: Oxford University Press.

Yu, Henry and Stephanie Chan (2017). The Cantonese Pacific: Migration Networks and Mobility Across Space and Times. In Lloyd Wong, ed. *Trans-Pacific Mobilities: The Chinese in Canada*, 25–48. Vancouver: UBC Press.

Zarrow, Peter (2005). *China in War and Revolution, 1895–1949*. New York: Routledge.

Zhao, Xiaojian (2002). *Remaking Chinese America: Immigration, Family, and Community, 1940–1965*. New Brunswick: Rutgers University Press.

麥禮謙 (1992). *從華僑到華人: 二十世紀美國華人社會發展史*. 香港: 三聯書店.

劉建軍 (2012). 論五四時期的信仰危機與信仰求索. *中國人民大學學報* (3): 111–118.

柳存仁 (2002). *外國的月亮*. 上海: 上海古籍出版社.

# Bibliography

郭美芬 (2011). 二十世紀初澳洲都市化下華裔社群的「華僑」敘事與政治結社. *近代史研究所集刊* (71): 157–202.

郭美芬 (2019). 近代移民慶典與女性交誼: 以澳洲"舞龍"慶典爲例 (1870–1938). *全球史評論* (16): 88–105.

郭輝 (2019). *國家紀念日與現代中國 1912–1949*. 北京: 社會科學文獻出版社.

黃紹竑 (1990). *五十回憶*. 臺北: 龍文出版社.

趙靜蓉 (2015). *文化記憶與身份認同*. 北京: 三聯書店.

陳建新 (2006). 大公報與抗戰宣傳. 博士論文, 浙江大學, 杭州.

張克明與沈嵐選編 (2000). 曾虛白工作日記(二). *民國檔案* (3): 20–32.

張克明與沈嵐選編 (2001). 曾虛白工作日記(四). *民國檔案* (1): 34–46.

張克明與沈嵐選編 (2001a). 曾虛白工作日记(五). *民國檔案* (2): 25–35.

沈劍虹 (1989). *半生憂患: 沈劍虹回憶錄*. 台北: 聯經出版社.

程美寶 (2006). *地域文化與國家認同: 晚清以來"廣東文化"觀的形成*. 北京: 三聯書店.

曾虛白 (1981). *曾虛白自選集*. 臺北: 黎明文化事業股份有限公司.

曾虛白 (1988). *曾虛白自傳*. 臺北: 聯經出版社.

王光輝 (2018). 澳洲中文報刊中的華僑捐獻與愛國主義 (1894–1937). 碩士論文, 國立臺灣師範大學, 臺北. ProQuest (27716137).

王建朗與黃克武主編 (2016). *兩岸新編中國近代史 (晚清卷)*. 北京: 社會科學文獻出版社.

# Index

Index

Wai, Stanley 149, 155
Wong Chih-hwa 14, 16, 104
Wang Ching-wei 16, 23, 54, 197

Young Chinese Relief Movement 118,
    139, 142, 146

Yu Shun 101
Young Suey Chong 22
Yee Ben 60, 162, 169
Yuan Chung-Ming 14, 65

Zeng Xubai 218